WORLD HERITAGE SITES
(see back of book for insert map and key to sites)

MASTERWORKS *of*
Man *&* Nature

Facts On File®

AN INFOBASE HOLDINGS COMPANY

MASTERWORKS *of*
Man *&* Nature

Facts On File®

AN INFOBASE HOLDINGS COMPANY

First published 1992
2nd edition 1994
Harper-MacRae Publishing Pty. Limited (ACN 003 376 583)
6-8 Patonga Drive
Patonga 2256 Australia
Facsimile 61-(0)2-660 4188
Telephone 61-(0)2-660 4400
© Harper-MacRae Publishing Pty. Limited 1994

Facts On File, Inc
460 Park Avenue South
New York, NY 10016
Publisher: Robert S. Osborne
Managing Editor: Mark Swadling
Design and Art Production: BPD Graphic Associates
Assistant Editor: Tim Baker
Project Co-ordination: Kay Osborne, Robert Osborne,
Tony Duffy, John Burke (IUCN)
Editorial Consultants: World Heritage Center, UNESCO; IUCN -
The World Conservation Union: Jim Thorsell, Senior Advisor
Natural Heritage, Jeffrey McNeely, Chief Conservation Officer;
World Conservation Monitoring Center (WCMC)
Writing: Mark Swadling and Tim Baker
Research: Linda Newton, Jinki Trevillian, Kim Brelsford,
Lydie Martin, George Shelvey, Robert Mahoud, Kelvin McQueen,
Keith Shelvey, Robert Osborne
Concept: Robert Osborne and Mark Swadling
Pre-press Production: Fancy Graphic Pty Limited
National Library of Australia Cataloguing-in-Publication data:
Harper-MacRae Publishing Pty. Limited
Masterworks of Man & Nature
Includes Index
ISBN 0-8160-3177-0
Printed in Australia by Boswell Printing Pty Ltd, Quality Endorsed
Company AS3902 Lic 4001 Standards Australia
for Harper-MacRae Publishing Pty. Limited
Special Note: Facts On File Books are available at special discounts
when purchased in bulk quantities for business, associations,
institutions, or sales promotions. Please call our Special Sales
Department in New York at 212/683-2244 or 800/322-8755
Printed on acid free paper produced from new growth, plantation
forests.

Photographs

*Page 1 Machu Picchu, Peru; Page 2 Venice, Italy; This page Grand Canyon,
USA; Page 6 Geysers at Yellowstone National Park, USA; Puma and her cub,
Yosemite National Park, USA; Page 7 Angkor, Cambodia.*

CONTENTS

PREFACE

It is no co-incidence that in 1972, when the World Heritage Convention was first adopted, it was also the centenary of the founding of the world's first national park at Yellowstone. In fact the establishment of this most important convention was largely a direct result of an American initiative, one that was led by the distinguished American conservationist, Mr. Russell Train, who refers in his essay on page 372 to the words he helped draft for the late President Nixon in 1971:

Yellowstone is the first national park to have been created in the modern world, and the national park concept has represented a major contribution to world culture... It would be fitting by 1972 for the nations of the world to agree to the principle that there are certain areas of such unique worldwide value that they should be treated as part of the heritage of all mankind and accorded special recognition...

The next year the USA became the first state party to the World Heritage Convention, and Yellowstone National Park was listed as the first World Heritage site. It is therefore appropriate that this book should begin by honoring that place. In the words of Mr. Gilbert Grosvenor, Chairman and President of the National Geographic Society (page 366):

Visionary, idealistic, and democratic, preservation has often been called the best idea America ever had.

FOREWORD

Here is a book which leads us into a world of beauty in all its glorious diversity. This homage to the splendors of nature and to the genius of mankind presents beauty wrought by nature and beauty wrought by human hands. To read it is to travel through the high canopies of age-old forests, to alight upon the spires of great cathedrals, to wander the wide savanna or the mountain gorge alongside magnificent animals, and to drink in the poetry of ancient sites.

All of these wonders have been and are a source of inspiration for the whole of humanity. They recount the histories of civilizations that have enriched us all; they tell the story of the planet Earth. They must be preserved.

The adoption of the Convention Concerning the Protection of the World Cultural and Natural Heritage by the General Conference of UNESCO in 1972 was the earliest effective expression and first formal recognition of the urgent need to protect the heritage of humanity. In 1975, there were twenty state parties to the convention. Today there are more than 130.

This convention, innovative in many other ways, introduced for the first time a notion of a shared responsibility for the cultural and natural heritage. It was not the country in which the cultural or natural site was located which was alone responsible for its safeguarding, but the international community as a whole. In other words, the whole of humanity was to be involved in protecting our cultural and natural heritage.

In order to apply the principles of the 1972 convention, UNESCO set up a committee of 21 state parties to the convention. This is the World Heritage Committee, which, acting on proposals from all the state parties, is responsible for establishing the list of natural and cultural sites of exceptional and universal value. The 412 properties currently inscribed on the list represent the natural and spiritual treasures of 96 countries.

The committee meets once a year not only to extend and enrich the World Heritage List, but also to decide on financial and technical help to state parties for the preservation of the sites on their territory. The committee also guarantees the integrity and authenticity of any conservation or restoration work.

Sadly, the demands made on the committee increase in proportion with the increasing number of dangers which

threaten our natural and cultural heritage. Turn away for a moment from these enchanting sites and consider their fragility. Time and the elements have already taken their toll on many, and to these natural dangers we must now add those of unconsidered industrial and urban development, pollution and the growth of international tourism. Today, thousands of feet are marching where once time stood still.

UNESCO will fulfil to the utmost of its ability its role as the official 'curator' of the international heritage. But UNESCO cannot accomplish this task alone. It is essential that each and every one of us should be conscious of the threats posed to our natural and cultural sites and should contribute in every way possible to their preservation.

UNESCO is proud to be associated with 'Masterworks of Man and Nature'. It is my sincere hope that, in giving great pleasure to all its readers, it may also serve to increase awareness of the urgent need to save the thousand and one natural and cultural beauties of our planet which we hold in trust for future generations.

FEDERICO MAYOR
Director General, UNESCO

INTRODUCTION

We live in a diverse, beautiful and continually changing world. Over the past three thousand million years, the movement and collision of the continents has crumpled the earth and thrown up great ranges of mountains. The oscillations of climate have brought alternate glaciations and periods of warmth to vast tracts of land. These processes, which continue today, have provided a constantly shifting stage on which evolution has generated the wonderful assemblage of plants and animals we see around us.

Over the past three million years, and more especially within the last ten thousand, our own species has increasingly set its mark on nature. People have altered the world in order to cater more efficiently for their own needs. They have replaced forests by crop lands and pastures, domesticated some species of plant and animal and eliminated others, and, as an unwelcome but all-pervasive by product of urban and industrial civilizations, have now polluted the planet on such a scale that the balance of the climate is in peril.

Wilderness and natural beauty have been in retreat before this onslaught. The retreat has accelerated within recent decades, and there is now no place on Earth that has wholly escaped the mark of humanity. Conservationists everywhere have become increasingly alarmed at these transformations and are concerned to save the best of the nature that remains to us.

There are a number of reasons why it is right to do this. First, the World Charter for Nature, adopted by the General Assembly of the United Nations in 1982, which asserts that species other than our own deserve respect regardless of their worth to us. Second, wild nature is our own life support system: green plants release the oxygen that makes the air breathable. Natural ecosystems recycle the elements essential for life, and control the flow of water from the hills to the sea. Third, we depend on nature for a vast range of products: food, fuel, fibre, medicines, and many other resources whose continual replenishment we take for granted. We have learned that we cannot just assume that nature will remain resilient in the face of human pressure. Conservation has become a global necessity, not just a minority concern.

UNESCO's World Heritage Convention was first discussed in the United States in 1965, and was given impetus at the 9th General Assembly of IUCN held in Lucerne, Switzerland, in 1966. It was proposed that there should be an international legal instrument under which the most outstanding samples of the world's natural and built heritage would be preserved, for the benefit of present and future generations. The criteria which have been chosen to guide the selection of natural sites are themselves interesting. Under the convention, the aim is to safeguard outstanding areas that demonstrate the evolutionary stages in the history of the earth, include the most outstanding examples of scenic beauty, provide habitats for rare and endangered species, demonstrate evolution in action, and provide outstanding examples of harmonious relationships between humanity and the world of nature. IUCN-the World Conservation Union, is proud of its central role as independent assessor of natural sites proposed for listing under the convention, and believes that the long-term protection of these sites is of immense importance.

This book illustrates the wonderful places that have been listed under the convention, and the ways in which they meet these various criteria. But nominating a site under the convention is not just a matter of identifying somewhere outstanding, and putting it on a list. It is a positive political act by the governments concerned. It demonstrates that these governments recognize that the areas thus designated are not just important within their own frontiers, but are in a real sense a heritage shared with the whole world community. Designation confirms that the governments accept a responsibility to care for these areas, on behalf of all humanity, now and in the future.

Such actions are both timely and difficult. They are timely because we have come to realize that we live in a world where all people, and all nature are interdependent. Through the collective actions of people in all nations, the world climate is at risk and the ozone layer is being eroded. Pollution knows no frontiers. Nature can no longer defend itself from these threats: we have to change our life-styles and put conservation high up on the agenda if we want our descendants to live in a world that is diverse and beautiful. We have to change our behaviour out of self-interest if not altruism. Our nations share many environmental resources, such as great rivers and marine fisheries. Biological diversity is the foundation of all peoples' futures, even though individual governments are responsible for caring for those parts of it that are located within their territories. World trade, economics and communications link us and make us depend more on one another than ever before. We all have to work together to create a sustainable society — a society in which people live in enduring harmony within the natural world. It is therefore timely that the world has joined together in action to choose and protect its most outstanding natural sites and cultural heritage.

But it is difficult. The 5.3 billion people already living in the world are pressing heavily upon its fragile resources. In less than a century from now those resources may have to sustain between eight and twelve billion human individuals—if they can. The pressure on most areas of land and sea is becoming heavier, and safeguarding even the most outstanding natural areas designated under this convention requires a continuous effort of management, going far beyond the initial commitment of listing. We see around the world many sites, some designated under this convention and others worthy of such designation, that are in danger. We in IUCN regularly bring these problems to the attention of the World Heritage Committee, but their powers and resources, like those of many governments, are severely limited. Mining, forest destruction, over-fishing, pollution, urban encroachment, and the sheer pressure of the desperately poor are all eroding sites which the governments concerned, and the wider world community, would like to safeguard.

We shall only safeguard these masterworks of man and nature if there is genuine international co-operation, to help the governments that are custodians of these places to carry out the commitments they have entered into under the convention. Many lower-income countries lack the resources for monitoring and safeguarding the sites that they have named. Some lack even the capability to survey the sites that they know they would like to designate. Even in developed countries, with much more abundant resources, the apportionment of national budgets has very often placed less emphasis on protecting the environment than it should.

Nonetheless, this book shows how much has already been done. The achievements are extraordinary when you consider that the World Heritage Convention was run in 1990 on the tiny sum of US$2. 5 million, with a relatively small full-time secretariat. There are immense gaps in coverage, and in monitoring the protection given to the sites on the list.

There is no World Heritage area designated in the whole of Antarctica, despite its immense scenic beauty and wonderful wildlife: largely because of the disputed sovereignty there. Within Africa, there are no sites in Namibia, Botswana, Kenya or the Republic of South Africa, although they have many areas that would fully merit designation. There are no natural sites in a broad swathe of northern South America, including much of the main basin of the Amazon. We have a long way to go before the World Heritage Convention lists the outstanding sites of our planet completely. We have yet longer to go before those sites are safeguarded for all time, as the convention intends that they should be.

The key to the future is in the commitment of human individuals. Those who read this book should not just treat it as a brochure for armchair travel. They should see it as a challenge. Only with their support, their commitment, their funding, their willingness to adopt life-styles that nature can sustain, their pressure on their governments and their demand for higher levels of international co-operation to safeguard their world's environment, can the objectives of the convention truly be fulfilled. We have a great deal more work to do, and I urge all those who buy or read this book to commit them selves to that end.

MARTIN W. HOLDGATE
Director General 1988–1994
IUCN—The World Conservation Union

AFRICA

A lioness cuffs her mate

Djemila

LOCATION

50km (31mi) east of Setif, in the Babors mountains.

DESCRIPTION

The ruins of this ancient Roman town are exceptionally well preserved. The street plan is rectangular with a broad, colonnaded street running centrally from the northern gate through to the southern gate. The forum, capitol, basilica and market are all centrally located. Other important buildings include a family temple and a sanctuary to Saturn.

SIGNIFICANCE

This town was founded in the 1st century AD under the reign of Nerva. The sanctuary later became an important focus to the town as the deity, known as Saturn or Frugifer, was one of the great African gods whose importance was centered around the function of granting good crops for the year.

Almost 2,000 years old, the Roman ruins at Djemila are beautifully preserved

Kasbah of Algiers

LOCATION

*City of Algiers, approximately
N 36° 45', E 02° 58'.*

DESCRIPTION

The site of the ancient city of Algiers plunges dramatically down a steep slope from the kasbah, or fortress, to the sea shore. The architecture of the kasbah is a unique blend of Turkish skills and a particularly prosperous Arab-Mediterranean style. The houses, arranged on steep and meandering streets, are based on the Arab-Mediterranean model with terraces arranged around an atrium. Interior decoration is ornate and extravagant, displaying the past glory of this city's wealth.

SIGNIFICANCE

The ancient city of Algiers started its rich and varied history as a Phoenician trading post in the 6th century BC. Numerous wars and invasions, prompted by the strategic location and consequent prosperity of the city, saw Algiers successively occupied by Carthaginians, Berbers, Romans, Byzantines, Arabs and Spaniards. When the city came under Turkish rule in 1516 the 'modern' city, referred to as the kasbah due to its fortifications and the military nature of its administration, was built. This historic Maghreb city incorporates an array of traditional buildings in which the ancestral Arab lifestyle and Moslem culture has been preserved.

M'zab Valley

LOCATION

*Laghouat Wilaya, 600km (373mi) south of Algiers,
N 33° 00' to 31°15', E 02° 30' to 05° 00'.*

DESCRIPTION

There are five main elements to this site: 1. the 5 ksour (plural of the Berber word ksar, meaning a fortified place), which are named: El Atteuf, Bou Noura, Melika, Beni Isguen and Ghardaia; 2. the palm groves of El Atteuf, Bou Noura, Beni Isguen, and Ghardaia; 3. the former sites of Arram n'tlasdit, Baba Hanni and Baba Saad; 4. 13 religious buildings outside the ksour; and 5. the natural site.

SIGNIFICANCE

Before the advent of Islam, this region was originally inhabited by nomadic Berber and Zanata tribes. The word 'M'zab' is thought to derive from the word for the first Berber Moslems - 'Beni Mesaab'. The first town, El Atteuf, was founded by Moslems in 1014AD. The 5 Mozabite towns are striking for their architectural planning which reflects the religious, social and political organization of the day. Typically, the mosque is built on a rocky knoll and forms the nucleus around which the town descends to the profane outer limits of its ramparts. The palm groves are situated outside the ksour; they provided an area for cultivation and relief from the intense summer heat. They are remarkable for their intricate water distribution systems.

*ABOVE Bou Noura, one of the five ksour in the M'Zab Valley
LEFT Atrium and terraces of a typical house, Kasbah of Algiers*

Timgad

LOCATION

38km (23.6mi) southeast of Batna.

DESCRIPTION

The ruins of a Roman city featuring a theater, a forum, a capitol southwest of the town, two temples, an imposing library, a basilica and two markets. Close to the markets is a large ornamental arch. The so called 'House of Sertius' was a private residence covering an area of 2,500sqm (27,750sqft) and is a fine example of a house of the nobility of the time.

SIGNIFICANCE

The Roman colony of 'Thamugad' was founded in 100AD under the reign of Trajan. It was originally fortified. The small town quickly expanded into a big city. During the 3rd century it became a center of Christian activity. Destroyed during the 5th century, Timgad was rebuilt and enjoyed prosperity again as a Christian town, until disappearing from history in the 7th century with the coming of the Arabs. These ruins are quite intact, some having been restored, and include some interesting items such as numerous inscriptions and a series of standard measures.

ABOVE The Arch of Trajan, Timgad
BELOW Fortifications at Al Qal'a of Beni Hammad

Al Qal'a of Beni Hammad

LOCATION

34km (21mi) southeast of M'sila, 7km (4mi) from the Hodna mountains.

DESCRIPTION

These are the ruins of an old fortified city. The city walls extend for 8km (5mi) and surround a multitude of palaces, government buildings and houses. An exceptionally large mosque stands in the center of the town.

SIGNIFICANCE

This was the capital city of the Hammadite Empire during the 11th century AD. It was destroyed in 1152 by the Almohals. The mosque is of considerable architectural significance, it is the second largest in Algeria. Its minaret is almost 25m (82ft) high and is distinctive in being decorated on only one side.

Tassili N'Ajjer National Park

LOCATION

South-eastern part of the Algerian Sahara near the frontiers with Niger and Libya,
N 23° 00' to 26° 50',
E 05° 20' to 12° 00'

DESCRIPTION

In the heart of the Sahara in southern Algeria, close to the frontiers of both Niger and Libya, lies the immense massif of Tassili N'Ajjer. This triangular-shaped National Park embraces a massif which runs 700km (440mi) from north-west to south-east, *averaging around 100km (66mi) in width. The formation of the massif is unusual in that there is an inner and outer "tassili", or plateau, made of sandstone, separated by a plunging canyon created when the original clay sandstone between the two plateaux eroded. The region is also famous for its "ergs", or shifting sand dunes, which are found particularly in the south-west of the park. Originally enormous lakes, the ergs' massive, silent forms lend themselves to the stark, arid beauty which encompasses all of Tassili N'Ajjer's 720,000sqkm (280,000sqmi).*

SIGNIFICANCE

Tassili N'Ajjer is home to the central Sahara's only permanent river, at Iherir, as well as to a rich cross section of desert fauna and flora, including some endangered species. Most threatened is the "Tarout" or Duprey cypress, of which it is estimated that there are fewer than 250 individual specimens in the world. Most of the park's animal life consists of reptiles, insects or spiders. There are over 20 species of large mammal, including cheetah, Barbary sheep, which was once believed to be extinct in the park, and dorcas gazelle. There is a small *chance that the park still shelters one of the rarest animals on earth, the magnificent scimitar-horned oryx, although it hasn't been sighted alive for many years now. Because of its guaranteed water supplies, the park is also an important stop for migratory birds, including the spotted crane, the golden eagle, the glossy ibis, and the purple heron. This region has been inhabited by humans for thousands of years: the most celebrated legacy of this presence are some remarkable prehistoric rock paintings dating as far back as 7,000-6,000BC.*

Tipasa

LOCATION

70km (43.5mi) west of Algiers, on the coast.

DESCRIPTION

Extensive Roman ruins are found on the western edge of the modern town of Tipasa. They include a 4,000 seat theater, a forum, two temples, a necropolis, a basilica, the 'Villa of the Frescoes' and the 'Gate of Caesarea'. On the eastern side of the town are some Byzantine ruins which include houses, churches and cemeteries.

SIGNIFICANCE

Originally a Phoenician town, Tipasa was made a Roman military colony by Claudius. It was an early seat of Christianity, becoming a bishop's see in the 3rd century AD. After a period of Arab domination in the 5th century, the town declined. The Great Basilica here is the largest Christian monument in Algeria.

TOP The Roman theater at Tipasa

BOTTOM Some of the remarkable prehistoric rock paintings at Tassili N'ajjer

BENIN

Royal Palaces of Abomey

LOCATION

Zou Province.

DESCRIPTION

The ruins of the 12 royal palaces of Abomey are to be found on this site which spreads over 40ha (96ac) right in the center of the present day town of Abomey. There are 2 zones, both surrounded by partially preserved walls; the zone which contains Akaba Palace and another to the south east which contains the balance of the palaces.

SIGNIFICANCE

The Kingdom of Abomey ruled for almost 300 years, from 1625 to 1900, with a succession of 12 kings. It was one of the most powerful kingdoms on the west coast of Africa, with high levels of economic and military power and consequently, quite remarkable political stability. These ruins provide an important record of this once great kingdom.

TOP Fortifications at Abomey
BOTTOM Fon artwork on display

CAMEROON

Dja Faunal Reserve

LOCATION

In the south of Cameroon,
N 02° 49' to 03° 23',
E 12° 25' to 13° 35'.

DESCRIPTION

This forest and fauna Reserve of
526,000ha (1,300,000ac) is
almost completely encircled by the
Dja River which acts as a natural
boundary, especially in the south
where steep cliffs shadow the course
of the Dja for over 60km (37 mi).
The reserve sits in the heart of the
South Cameroon Plateau, at a
general altitude of around 600m
(1,968ft), with a succession of hills
and river valleys breaking the
monotony of an outright uniform
relief. This 'sea of hills' is a charac-
teristic of most tropical rainforest
regions, but is particularly striking
in Dja.

SIGNIFICANCE

Dja Fauna Reserve is a magnificent
example of primary Congo
rainforest. The rainforest is
extremely dense and varied, with
over 40 different plant species
making up the canopy, which
reaches heights in some cases of up
to 60m (200ft). Within the reserve
is a modest population of pygmies,
who live in small communities and
still practice their traditional way
of life, with a special emphasis on
hunting using ancient methods and
weapons. There are several large
mammals found in the forest,
including forest elephant, buffalo,
mandrill and lowland gorillas.
Reptiles include python, lizard and
two species of crocodile (both of
which are threatened species).

ABOVE *Indigenous pygmies hunting in Dja Faunal Reserve*
LEFT *Portrait of a male mandrill*

CENTRAL AFRICAN REPUBLIC

Manovo-Gounda Saint Floris National Park

LOCATION

In the province of Bamingui - Bangoran, N 08° 05' to 09° 50', E 20° 28' to 22° 22'.

DESCRIPTION

This park is located in the north of the country. Bounded by the Bongo Massif in the south, it mainly comprises the foothills of the Massif and the sandy plateau to its north. It covers an area of 17,400sqkm (6,960sqmi) and may be divided into 3 vegetation zones: (i) a large grassy plain to the north, (ii) a savanna plain in the center, (iii) the plateau of the Massif, with a marked escarpment which cuts the park's several rivers.

SIGNIFICANCE

The importance of this park rests with its wealth of flora and fauna. Over 1,200 species of flora have so far been identified, two of them new. The population of large mammals is particularly notable, with over 55 species, including the elephant, rhinoceros, hippopotamus, topi and giraffe. There is also a healthy population of predators, including the panther and leopard. More than 320 species of birds have been identified, vultures, storks and ostriches among them. This wealth and diversity of species make this park an area vital to our world's heritage.

Combatants, ostrich (top) and topi (below) in Manovo-Gounda Saint Floris National Park

EGYPT

ABOVE *Part of the archeological site at Abu Mena, Egypt*

Abu Mena

LOCATION

Mariut Desert, District of Burgal-Arab
N 30° 51', E 29°40'.

DESCRIPTION

An archeological site 1sqkm (0.4sqmi) in area, it comprises two churches, a baptistery, several public buildings, baths and workshops.

SIGNIFICANCE

Abu Mena was an early center of pilgrimage for Christians as it was the burial place for Saint Menas, an Egyptian serving in the Roman army who was martyred for his faith. During the 5th and 6th centuries AD its importance increased. It was heavily patronised by several Byzantine emperors and bishops from Alexandria. Its importance declined after the advent of Islam, until being abandoned during the 9th century.

Safeguarding the Splendor of the Pyramids

Few groups of great monuments blend so well with their natural surroundings as the pyramids of Giza. At night beneath a canopy of stars, or in the blinding light of the desert in daytime, the pyramids rise, impressive and alone in a world of rock and sand. Those who built this royal necropolis long ago clearly intended it to be a haven of peace, isolation and silence.

The tranquility of the archeological site is today threatened by a rash of uncontrolled building development, and the plateau is being taken over by tourist coaches and amenities. Some promoters have even envisaged making golf courses and artificial lakes for pleasure boats. In short, there is a risk that one of the wonders of the world may lose its splendor owing to the anarchic growth of tourism.

To prevent this from happening and to restore serenity to the plateau, the Egyptian Minister of Culture, Farouk Hosny, has decided to take a number of measures:

- Access to the plateau, today open to all, will be strictly controlled, as is the case with almost all historic monuments elsewhere in the world;

- The modern buildings which have been constructed near the site over the years, contrary to the advice of architects, will be demolished. Also scheduled for demolition is the structure which houses the famous royal boat of Pharaoh Khufu and which disfigures one side of the Great Pyramid. The boat will of course not be removed until all necessary technical precautions have been taken to prevent damage to this fragile masterpiece;

- The tarmac roads, whose color clashes with that of the site, will be replaced by roads made of solidified sand;

- Motor traffic, a source of noise and pollution which damages the stone of the monuments, will be prohibited. Archeologists and service staff will use electric vehicles;

- Unsupervised animals such as dogs and goats which harm the monuments and discourage visitors will be prohibited;

- Bridle paths will be designed to provide spectacular views for visitors on camel and horse-back. They will also make it easier to keep the site free of litter;

Islamic Cairo

LOCATION

Cairo, N 30° 06', E 31° 26'.

DESCRIPTION

The historic part of Cairo is on the east bank of the Nile, surrounded by the modern city. It contains many notable buildings and monuments, including a large necropolis, several important mosques, Coptic churches, a citadel and extensive remnants of the city's fortifications, including the impressive 11th century city gates.

SIGNIFICANCE

Cairo became an Islamic city after the Moslem conquest of 641AD. Its importance in the Islamic world grew steadily, reaching its zenith after the fall of Baghdad in 1261, when it was the capital of a vast empire which embraced the Sudan, northern Mesopotamia, Palestine, Syria and the Hejaz, and which included the two Holy cities of Mecca and Medina. The historic center retains a remarkable degree of originality, a testimony, not just to its commercial importance but to the high regard in which Cairo has always been held in the Islamic world.

LEFT Muhammad Ali Mosque, part of Islamic Cairo

ABOVE *The necropolis, Islamic Cairo*

- Also in the interests of tourists and visitors, the area set aside beneath the Sphinx for son et lumiere (sound and light) shows will be extended. This area will be lowered so as to improve the view of the Sphinx and the pyramids from the eastern access road to the plateau;

- As is the case with other historic monuments, revenue from visitors will contribute to the conservation of the irreplaceable heritage left by the ancient Egyptians;

- The existing buffer zone will be defined more clearly and improved both aesthetically and functionally, so as to provide a better view of the monuments and to respect the dignity of the site. The cafeteria to the east of the pyramids will disappear.

It is clearly necessary that the plateau of Giza should be fenced off to channel the movement of visitors - at least in the part which is accessible to everyone. Inconspicuous light fencing would be quite suitable for this.

Anyone who has ever marvelled at the mysterious silhouette of the Sphinx and the majestic mass of the pyramids as they suddenly come into view from behind a sand dune will appreciate the importance of safeguarding their timeless splendor.

GERARD BOLLA, Swiss jurist and economist, is a former Assistant Director-General of UNESCO. From 1971 to 1981 he was in charge of UNESCO's program for the conservation of the cultural heritage, and was notably responsible for archeological safeguard and rescue operations at Philae (Egypt), Venice, Borobudur and Carthage. He has served as chairman of an international advisory committee of experts on the development projects for the plateau of the pyramids.

Memphis and its Necropolis with the Pyramid Fields

LOCATION

Giza Governorate, N 29° 45' to 30° 00', E 31°10' to 31°15'.

DESCRIPTION

There are two main elements to this site: 1. the ruins of the town of Memphis which is partly excavated and includes part of a temple, an embalming place, an alabaster sphinx and a statue of Ramesses II; 2. the royal tombs, or pyramids, of which there are 6 groups, probably the most well known being those of Cheops, Chephren and Mycerinus, all found at Giza.

SIGNIFICANCE

When the kingdoms of Upper and Lower Egypt were united at around 3000BC, Memphis was created as the center of the new State's administration. Remnants of this original Pharaonic civilization still exist in the ruins of the stone tombs, or mastabas, at the Archaic Pharaonic Cemetery at Saqqara where the 'Step Pyramid' is located. One of the 'Seven Wonders of the World', the pyramids are famous for their enormous scale and simple beauty. We of the modern world can only gaze in awe and wonder at these remarkable feats of ancient engineering.

TOP The Great Sphinx, with one of the pyramids in the background

RIGHT The temple complex of Philae on the island of Algilkia
INSET Facade of the Temple of Ramesses

Nubian Monuments from Abu Simbel to Philae

LOCATION

Aswan Governorate, N 22° 46' to 24° 05', E 31° 37' to 32° 54'.

DESCRIPTION

There are five groups of temples which were restored and re-erected in the most spectacular architectural rescues ever undertaken, when UNESCO mounted a successful operation to save them from being flooded by the waters of the newly created Lake Nassar, thus preserving this priceless ensemble: 1. the two rock temples of Ramesses II at Abu Simbel; 2. the temples of Amada and Derr at Amada; 3. the temples of Wadies Sebua, Dakka and Maharaqqa at Wadi Sebua; 4. the temple of Kalabsha and the rock temple of Beit et Wali, both near the High Dam; 5. the temple complex of Philae, which has been moved to the island of Agilkia. The second element to this listing comprises a group of monuments at Aswan, including the remains of stone quarries, tombs, a monastery and an Islamic cemetery.

SIGNIFICANCE

A border town built on the Nile between Egypt and Nubia, Aswan was important as a center for political and military control, finances and trade. The Nubian temples testify to the richness of Egyptian architecture and art. The temples of Ramesses II in particular are of outstanding value with their unique architectural features and timeless beauty. The largest temple has a 38m (125ft) facade with a sanctuary cut 63m (207ft) into the rock. Before being moved in 1968, this was positioned so that at sunrise on the two days of the yearly equinoxes, the statues inside the sanctuary were illuminated by the rays of the morning sun.

ABOVE Ancient Thebes - the giant columns of Karnak Temple,

Ancient Thebes with its Necropolis

LOCATION

*At the town of Luxor,
N 25° 43', E 32° 37'.*

DESCRIPTION

The ancient town of Thebes is situated underneath the modern town of Luxor on the east bank of the Nile River. There are two massive neighboring temple complexes, Karnak and Luxor, while on the west bank is the necropolis, with its many pharaonic mortuary temples, including the spectacular, multi-terraced temple of Hatshepsut. The necropolis also contains the famous tomb complexes known as 'The Valley of the Kings' and 'The Valley of the Queens'. Dozens of other funerary monuments include the Tomb-Chapels of the Nobles and the Workmen's Tombs.

SIGNIFICANCE

Thebes has a rich and important history. It was founded almost 5,000 years ago and became the capital of a united Egypt at around 2000BC. It was ruled by the Hyksos for a while until Egypt was liberated and became the center of a vast empire, stretching from North Sudan up to the Euphrates. During the 19th Dynasty, Thebes lost its role as capital, but not as the first city in the empire; later when it started to decline, it still remained an important religious center. It was an important city for the Greeks - Homer called it 'the city of the one hundred gates' - and a popular tourist destination for the Romans.

*OPPOSITE PAGE An aerial view of the Awash Lower valley
INSET The desolate Omo Lower Valley*

ETHIOPIA

Awash Lower Valley

LOCATION

Eastern Ethiopia, in the region of Harrar.

DESCRIPTION

This prehistoric archeological site has been under study since 1973, when excavations were commenced by an international team of experts.

SIGNIFICANCE

The site has uncovered a wealth of exceptionally well preserved fossils. Dating back four million years, the remains include one of the most complete hominid skeletons ever found. Remains of animals such as elephants, rhinoceros and monkeys have also been found.

Omo Lower Valley

LOCATION

Southern Ethiopia, in the Gemo Gofa region. N 04° 48', E 35° 58'.

DESCRIPTION

This prehistoric site is protected by the Administration of Antiquities and is very well preserved. The deposits of humanoid fossils uncovered here have been particularly rich, with numerous teeth, jaw bones and other bones. Many stone objects and tools have also been unearthed.

SIGNIFICANCE

The evidence from some of the stone objects on this site points to one of the oldest known campsites of prehistoric humanoids in existence. There is also evidence which further suggests some of the most ancient technical activity (use of tools). These factors, along with the wealth of humanoid fossils make this site crucial to a better understanding of our ancestors.

Aksum

LOCATION

Northern Ethiopia, in the Tigre region, N 14° 09', E 34° 42'.

DESCRIPTION

This archeological site consists of palace ruins, over 100 stelae (carved stone monoliths) and various other stone remains, such as thrones and walls.

SIGNIFICANCE

These ruins date back to the 1st century AD and were built by the powerful Aksumites. Testimony to their power was the size of their stelae, the tallest being a massive 33m (110ft) in height. Another important feature of this site are the ruins of St. Mary of Zion, thought to be the earliest Christian church built in Ethiopia, probably around 340AD.

Fasil Ghebbi and Gondar Monuments

LOCATION

Gondar Region, N 12° 34', E 37° 36'.

DESCRIPTION

There are numerous monuments and buildings in this listing. Some of the more important are: the monastery and church of Socinios, the palace of Guzara, the monastery and church of Debre Berhan Selassie and the bath of Fassilides.

SIGNIFICANCE

All of these buildings and monuments are considered to be of the same architectural style - that of the 'Gondar' period. This period is normally dated from the beginning of the 15th century through to the beginning of the 19th century. It is a style that is thought to have been created when Jesuit Priests brought the technique of lime burning from India. The Socinios monastery and church is believed to be the earliest construction. It is thought to have been designed and built by Pedro Paez, a Jesuit under King Socinios.

TOP Aksum, the tallest of the stelae
BOTTOM King Jassu II Castle
LEFT Fasil Ghebbi and Gondar Monuments - wall paintings

Lalibela Rock-Hewn Churches

LOCATION
Wollo region of the Lasta District, N 12° 02', E 38° 49'.

DESCRIPTION
There are 11 churches in two groups of five, with one, Biet Ghiorgis, isolated from the others. The others are, in the first group: Biet Modhani Alem, Biet Mariam, Biet Denagel, Biet Golgotha Mikael, Biet Mascal, and in the second group: Biet Amanuel, Biet Cheddus Morcoreos, Biet Abba Libanos, Biet Gabriel Raphael and Biet Lehem.

SIGNIFICANCE
These churches are all carved and chiselled out of solid rock, an amazing testimony to the faith and dedication of those involved in their construction. More astonishing still, there is an extensive system of trenches, passageways and drainage tunnels lying under each church. These buildings are laid out according to a secret religious pattern based on the topography of Palestine or of a new Jerusalem, with each church thought to represent a stage in the life of Christ.

Tiya

LOCATION
In the Soddo region, south of Addis Ababa, 38km (23.6mi) south of Awash.

DESCRIPTION
There are 36 monuments found within this site. Thirty two of these are 'stelae' - sculptured monoliths with unique carvings and a distinctive funerary character. These vary between 1 to 5m (3 to 17ft) in height.

SIGNIFICANCE
This is one of the most important of some 160 sites that have been discovered in the Soddo region. The stelae provide valuable and scarce information about ancient Ethiopian civilization .

*TOP One of the rock-hewn churches at Lalibela
LEFT Carved stela at Tiya*

Simen National Park

LOCATION

*In the western Simen Mountains, 120km (75mi)
north-east of Gondar in Begemder Province,
N 13° 11', E 38° 04'*

DESCRIPTION

*This 22,000ha (53,000ac) park occupies a broad,
undulating plateau of vast, grassy plains bordering the
northern edge of the Ethiopian Amhara plateau. The area
is part of the Simen Massif which includes the highest peak
in Ethiopia, Ras Dashan. These mountains are extremely
rugged and rocky. Numerous cliffs and precipices dot the
landscape, some with a sheer drops over 1,500m (4,950ft)
and extending over long distances (up to 35km - 22mi).
The vegetation is a mixture of Afro-Alpine woods, heath
forest, high montane vegetation, montane savanna and
montane moorland.*

SIGNIFICANCE

*The rugged and inaccessible terrain provides the perfect
environment for numerous animals, including two that are
endangered. The walia ibex which is found on the north
scarp of the massif is endemic to Simen Mountain, with
most of the population occurring in the park, and the
Simen fox is endemic to Ethiopia. Other mammals include
gelada baboon, hamadryas baboon, colobus monkey,
serval, leopard, caracal, wild cat, spotted hyena, jackal,
and several large herbivores including bushbuck, common
duiker and klipspringer. The 400 bird species include
lammergeier, Verreaux's eagle, kestrel, lanner falcon, and
augur buzzard. A total of 21 mammals have been
recorded, with three endemics and 63 bird species,
including seven endemics. The Simen region, being
surrounded by old cultural centers like Aksum, Lalibela
and Gonder, was inhabited by human settlers and culti-
vators for at least 2,000 years and was at the crossing of
old trade routes.*

ABOVE Simen National Park - the endemic Walia Ibex
INSET TOP RIGHT Gelada baboon
INSET BOTTOM RIGHT General mountain view

GHANA

Forts and Castles Of Ghana

LOCATION

In the provinces of Volta, Greater Accra, Central and Western Regions between the towns of Keta and Beyin, E 02° 36′ to 01° 02′, N 04° 58′ to 05° 09′.

DESCRIPTION

There are numerous forts and castles in varying states of disrepair up and down the coast of Ghana. Many have been renovated and converted for such uses as guesthouses, nurses residences, prisons, lighthouses and museums.

SIGNIFICANCE

These fortifications date from Portuguese times through to the 19th century. Many were originally forts of the numerous trading companies which plied the 'Gold Coast'. This trade, which began in gold, eventually turned to slaving in the 18th century. The forts are a record of the shifting balance of trading power throughout those turbulent times.

Ashante Traditional Buildings

LOCATION

In the Ashante Region, N 06° 30′ to 07° 30′, W 03° 30′ to 00° 00′.

DESCRIPTION

This listing comprises 13 villages, all similar in plan. Each village consists of an open-air rectangular court surrounded by four rectangular covered buildings. The thatched-roof houses are built with mud brick and the walls are decorated with traditional paintings related to popular culture.

SIGNIFICANCE

These traditional buildings of the Ashante people were constructed at the beginning of this century. Originally used as residences for the chiefs, they are now used as sanctuaries and mausoleums. The architecture is distinctive and unusual in its use of sloping thatched roofs. They now serve as a living museum of a valuable and threatened culture.

TOP Elmina Castle, built by the Portugese in 1482
MIDDLE Main courtyard of Cape Coast Castle
BOTTOM Shrine of an Ashante spirit medium

OPPOSITE PAGE Young bushbabies in Mount Nimba Reserve
INSET View of Mount Nimba

Mount Nimba Reserves

LOCATION

This is a joint listing between Guinea and Ivory Coast. The reserves are situated on the southern extremities of these countries, bordering with Liberia.

N 07°14′ to 07° 44′, W 08° 20′ to 10° 40′.

DESCRIPTION

The reserves cover a total area of over 22,000ha (52,800ac). The terrain is mountainous and heavily forested. The highest peak is Mount Richard Molard, at 1,752m (5,830ft) above sea level. Climatically, the area is classified as montane/sub-equatorial, differentiating it from the surrounding tropical plateau. The higher slopes are characterised by subalpine meadows.

SIGNIFICANCE

This spectacular, isolated area is home to more than 200 endemic species. The species diversity is exceptionally rich because of the variety of ecosystems created by the presence of grasslands laced with forest. Mammals include bushbuck, Maxwell's duiker, black duiker, bay duiker, forest buffalo, bush pig, warthog, scaly anteaters, pygmy hippopotamus, leopard, lion, golden cat, two-spotted palm civet, African civet, forest genet, servaline genet, Johnston's genet, cane rat, African clawless otter, lesser otter shrew (a new genus discovered on Mount Nimba), potto, western black and white colobus, red colobus, Diana monkey, chimpanzee, and lesser bushbaby. One of the most interesting species is the viviparous toad, which occurs in montane grasslands at 1,200-1,600m (4,000-5,300ft) and is one of few tailless amphibians in the world that are totally viviparous (bearing live young). There are also numerous species of rare and endemic birds.

Comoe National Park

LOCATION

Northeast Ivory Coast,
N 08° 05' to 09° 06',
W 03° 01' to 04° 04'.

DESCRIPTION

Mainly a plateau, Comoe covers
an area of 1,150,000ha
(2,770,000ac). The altitude is
generally between 250-300m
(820-984ft), although some rocky
outcrops rise to 650m (2,133ft).
The Comoe River flows through
the park, its banks covered with
forests.

SIGNIFICANCE

This park is rich in animal life,
with 11 species of apes, 17 species
of different hoofed mammals, three
different crocodiles, four out of the
six storks found in West Africa
and five out of the six species of
vultures. The great diversity of
landscapes and vegetation give this
park an ecological prominence in
West Africa.

Taï National Park

LOCATION

Southwest Ivory Coast,
N 06° 07' to 05° 15',
W 07° 25' to 07° 54'.

DESCRIPTION

This park covers 330,000ha (792,000ac) of dense tropical rainforest. There is also a peripheral buffer zone of a further 156,000ha (374,400ac) which was created in 1977 to protect the national park proper.

SIGNIFICANCE

The park represents the only surviving remnant of the vast primary forest that once stretched across present-day Ghana, Ivory Coast, Liberia and Sierra Leone, and is the largest island of forest remaining in West Africa. This humid tropical forest has a high level of endemism with over 150 species identified as endemic to the Taï region. The fauna is fairly typical of West African forests and the park contains 47 of the 54 species of large mammals known to occur in Guinean rainforest including five threatened species. Mammals include: mona monkey, white-nosed monkey and Diana monkey, black and white colobus, red colobus and green colobus, sooty mangabey, chimpanzee of which there are 2,000 to 2,800 in Taï, giant pangolin, tree pangolin and long-tailed pangolin, golden cat, leopard, elephant, bushpig, giant forest hog, pygmy hippopotamus, water chevrotain, bongo, buffalo and an exceptional variety of forest duikers including Jentink's duiker, banded duiker or zebra antelope, Ogilby's duiker, black duiker, bay duiker, yellow-backed duiker and the royal antelope. Over 230 bird species have been recorded, including white-breasted guineafowl, Nimba flycatcher, western wattled cuckoo-shrike, and yellow-throated olive greenbull.

TOP Taï National Park - banded duiker
LEFT chimpanzee

OPPOSITE PAGE Comoe National Park, needle-nosed crocodile, lioness carrying one month old cub

LIBYA

Cyrene

LOCATION

District of Gebel Akhdar, E 21° 51', N 32° 40'.

DESCRIPTION

Here are the remains of an ancient city and several large cemeteries which once surrounded it. Its most important features are; the Sanctuary of Apollo, the acropolis, the Greek agora and Roman forum. There are also various remains which have been excavated along Valley Street. To the northeast of the town is another excavation zone with the remains of a large temple to Zeus.

SIGNIFICANCE

The city was founded in 630BC by Greeks from Santorini who were in search of a reliable water supply. It was an important city of northeast Libya for the next 1,200 years, until the arrival of the Arabs, after which it declined and then fell into ruin. The Great Temple of Zeus is the largest Greek temple in North Africa.

ABOVE Ruins of the forum at Cyrene

Old Town of Ghadamès

LOCATION

Al Hamadah Al Hamra, E 09° 30', N 30° 08'.

DESCRIPTION

This city is unique in both its style and planning. It forms small irregular blocks in the southwest part of an oasis of palm trees and is protected by a system of walls and towers. The outer walls of the houses themselves form the surrounding wall with gates and a guard chamber on every gate. The surrounding wall has bastions which frequently project 6m (20ft) outwards and vary in thickness. The houses all have three levels and are linked by terraces.

SIGNIFICANCE

Ghadamès (ancient Cydamae), once referred to by the Arabs as 'the pearl of the desert' is situated on the three main lines of communication between the interior and the coast and played a key role in trans-Saharan trade. The architecture is considered to be the original ancient Libyan style, with massive walls and covered passageways. A special feature is the walled terraces that link the houses, allowing women freedom of movement without contravening the cultural tradition of separation of the sexes.

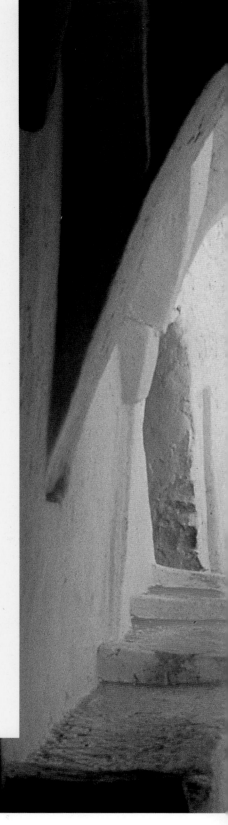

Leptis Magna

LOCATION

District of Khoms,
E 14° 18, N 32° 38'.

DESCRIPTION

There are traces of a Phoenician-Punic city, but the main component to this site is the collection of Roman ruins dating from the 1st century AD. Here we have remains from three periods including a theater, two forums, an amphitheater, a complex of thermal baths, several arches and two churches.

SIGNIFICANCE

During the whole of the 1st millennium BC Tripolitania was profoundly influenced by the Phoenicians and their successors the Carthagenians. Leptis Magna was a major market of the period. It was one of the largest olive oil producers, producing 1,067,000 litres (250,000 gal) for Julius Caesar. The town was finally conquered around 698AD, deserted by the inhabitants and left to the engulfing sands.

ABOVE *One of the walled terraces at Ghadames*
INSET *Statue of Crispina, wife of Emperor Commodus, Roman Theater, Leptis Magna*

Sabratha

LOCATION

District of Zawia, E 12° 29', N 32° 48'.

DESCRIPTION

There are several Roman and Byzantine monuments, including a forum, Temple of Antoninus Pius, Temple of Serapis, Temple of Isis, an amphitheater and a theater. Some Phoenician-Punic remains have also been uncovered including a Punic mausoleum.

SIGNIFICANCE

The Roman and Byzantine monuments of Sabratha constitute landmarks of classical architecture in Africa. The Phoenician-Punic ruins are crucial to the understanding of the early history of the area.

Rock-Art Sites of Tadrart Acacus

LOCATION

Southwest region, east of Ghat,
N 24° 30' to 27° 00', E 09° 00' to 11° 00'.

DESCRIPTION

This site covers an extensive area of the Tadrart Acacus mountain range. Scattered throughout the valleys of these mountains are the remains of many prehistoric communities. Most importantly, the artwork of these ancient peoples has been well preserved. Some 300 frescoes and thousands of rock paintings have been preserved at different sites such as Matkendush, Galghien and Tilizzagham.

SIGNIFICANCE

These paintings date back over 8,000 years and are unique in providing a continuous artistic record over a period of almost 6,000 years. Both the development of artistic styles and the evolution of subject matter provide a comprehensive record of cultural changes over this long period of time.

...man have no pre-eminence above a beast: for all is vanity. All go unto one place; all are dust, and all turn to dust again.

———

ECCLESIASTES

Top Left Amphitheater at Sabratha
Top Right Rock art, Tadrart Acacus

Tsingy de Bemaraha Strict Nature Reserve

LOCATION

Located almost in the center of the island of Madagascar, S 18° 17' to 19° 06', E 44° 36' to 44° 58'.

DESCRIPTION

This immense reserve sits on the western plateau of Madagascar. It is rich in flora and fauna including some rare and endangered species. Lush vegetation is typical of the reserve which also includes large areas of savanna. Many gorges and the rugged nature of the reserve offer spectacular views. Within the Manambolo gorges, ancient tombs reputedly housing the remains of the Island's first inhabitants (the 'Vazimbas') can be found.

SIGNIFICANCE

The reserve provides a sanctuary for several endangered species, including the island's famous lemurs. The geological formations of the ranges form impressive walls and gorges. In particular, the erosion of the lime-stone cliffs make them visually spectacular. The combination of cliffs, gorges and grottoes make the reserve unique. The dry arid forests provide an abundance of plant life including six species of Vangidae which are native to Madagascar. The reserve also is the home to a large number of endemic land birds, including the giant Coua and Madagascan Owl.

MADAGASCAR

TOP Tsingy de Bemaraha - karst formation
MIDDLE Black male lemur
BOTTOM Ringtail lemur

MALAWI

Lake Malawi National Park

LOCATION

On and around Nankumba Peninsula at the southern end of Lake Malawi, including Boadzulu, Maleri and other offshore islands, S 14° 02', E 34° 53'

DESCRIPTION

This 9,400ha (22,500ac) park is an area of great beauty with rugged, precipitous slopes falling directly down to the lake shore. It includes Cape Maclean Peninsula, which is the headland separating the south-east and south-west arms of the lake, two smaller headlands in the south-east and twelve islands. The protected area includes the headlands and islands themselves and an aquatic zone extending 100m (330ft) offshore. The lake is unique, it is estimated to be between one and two million years old and forms part of the Western Rift Valley. The lake water is remarkably clear. The islands are mainly of rock, separated from one another and from the mainland by sandy plains and deep water. Habitat types vary from rocky shorelines to sandy beaches and from wooded hillsides to swamps and lagoons. A range of underwater habitats are represented including sand zones, weed zones and reed beds.

SIGNIFICANCE

This is the only lacustrine park in Africa. Lake Malawi contains the largest number of fish species of any lake in the world, probably over 500 from ten families with perhaps half occurring in the park area. Endemism is thought to exceed 90% of the population. Particularly noteworthy are the cichlidae, of which all but five of over 400 species are endemic to Lake Malawi. The lake contains 30% of all known cichlid species. Of particular interest is the 'mbuna' rock fish. More than 70% of mbuna are undescribed. Other fish species include 28 endemic to the lake. Mammals include hippopotamus, leopard, greater kudu, bushbuck, zebra, klipspringer, impala, grey duiker, chacma baboon, vervet monkey, bush pig and occasional elephant. The varied birdlife includes fish eagle along the shoreline. The islands, especially Mumbo and Boadzulu, are important nesting areas for several thousand white-breasted cormorant. Reptiles include crocodile and an abundance of water monitor lizards on Boadzulu Island.

TOP *Female cichlid exhibiting characteristic mouth breeding*
INSET *The rock dwelling mbuna of Lake Malawi*

MALI

Cliff of Bandiagara (Land of the Dogons)

LOCATION
Region of Mopti, N 14° 00' to 14° 45', W 03° 00' to 03° 50'.

DESCRIPTION
The arid, rocky plateau land of the Bandiagara escarpment in eastern Mali is the remote homeland of the Dogon, the unique and renowned people of this area. They live primarily on the escarpment which extends about 200km (124mi) from Bandiagara to Docientza. The listing covers 400,000ha (964,400ac) and represents the authentic secular culture of the Dogon, its houses, granaries, altars, sanctuaries and garden complexes.

SIGNIFICANCE
The Dogons are well known for their sophisticated religious and cultural systems. Their entire demeanour reflects the Dogon concept of creation. In their dress, their colorful and distinctive face masks, their unique mud brick houses and their behaviour, the metaphysical world is ever present. Sirius, the dog star, plays an important part in their religion and some of their traditional beliefs have been traced back to the ancient Egyptians. It is unfortunate that a lot of insensitive tourism is ruining the area and affecting the culture - exemplified by many tourists' blatant disregard for the Dogon belief that cameras steal the soul.

LEFT Hooded vulture
INSET A Dogon village

The Dogon, Mali's People of the Cliffs

Within the loop of the Niger River in Mali, between the town of Mopti and the Burkina Faso border, there is a place where steep cliffs at the edge of an arid plateau dominate a sandy plain. Over 500m (1,665ft) high in places, the escarpment is fissured with deep ravines, where rain caught in the cracks of the grey rock supports the growth of dense and varied vegetation. This is the Land of the Dogon, whose natural features alone would justify exceptional measures of protection.

Against the rock face and on the scree slope below, the Dogon have built villages which are remarkable for their architecture and for the profoundly original culture of those who live in them described by the French ethnologist Marcei Griaule as a 'relic of a lost Africa'. In 1989, an area of some 400,000ha (960,000ac) along the Bandiagara cliffs, including almost 250 traditional villages, was placed on UNESCO's World Heritage List as a site of outstanding natural and cultural importance.

The Dogon, who today number about 300,000 are of Malinke (Mandingo) stock. Their ancestors are thought to have fled from the Keita empire in the 15th century and found refuge at the Bandiagara cliffs, where they displaced another people, the Tellem, who left behind abundant evidence of their own cultural traditions in tombs set in caves in the rock face.

Most of these caves can only be reached with the aid of ropes and crampons. Some have been explored in the past decade, and have revealed interesting evidence of the highly developed techniques, especially for weaving, which had been employed by the Tellem since the Iron Age.

On the cliffs themselves, aspects of Dogon ritual and cosmogony are illustrated by cryptic signs and paintings, the best-known of which adorn the famous 'Shelter of Masks', at the village of Songo (15km from Bandiagara) which forms part of the World Heritage site.

The Pale Fox, Bringer of Anarchy

According to Dogon cosmogony, from the union of the supreme deity Amma and his creation, the Earth, issued a being known as the Pale Fox. Unique and imperfect, the Fox introduced the principle of disorder into creation. It is associated with human weakness and the anarchy inherent in the universe. Amma also created Nommo, a hermaphroditic creature who represents celestial harmony and is linked symbolically to water and to fecundity. Then Amma modelled a human couple from clay. They gave birth to the eight ancestors of the Dogon, whom Nommo taught to speak.

Every aspect of Dogon domestic, social and economic life is linked to this cosmogony. Villages are designed in the image of the cosmos. Built on rock in order to preserve scarce arable land, they are laid out on a north-south axis in the form of a prone human body, supposedly that of Nommo, the great ancestor. The head is represented by the *togu na* (literally, 'big shelter'), a meeting-place reserved for men. This open-sided structure is always the first to be built in a new village. It consists of a platform on which stand several rows of rough-hewn timber pillars that support a roof of branches topped by a thick mat of millet straw. The number of pillars has significance. Decisions taken in the *togu na* are solemn and irrevocable.

In each settlement there is also a large family dwelling, or *ginna*, which is reserved for the spiritual leader. Corresponding to Nommo's breast, this building has a raised living area reached by a ladder carved from a tree trunk. The windowless facade is decorated with 80 niches, representing the eight original ancestors and their descendants. The two doors are often carved with rows of male and female figures which, like the niches, symbolize earlier generations.

Ordinary homes, which are smaller and are generally made of mud-brick, are grouped around the *ginna*. They are built to a rectangular design, with flat-roofed rooms opening onto an inner court-yard. They are flanked by granaries with distinctive conical thatched roofs. These structures are used for storing millet, seeds, rice, dried onions and various other foodstuffs. Their narrow entrances are protected by wooden doors, which are often carved and secured by ornate locks.

Many of the granaries are circular, like the houses at the edge of the village where menstruating women are sequestered. The forge, and the homes of members of various artisan castes - blacksmiths, wood and leather workers and griots - are also on the outskirts. Those who farm the land are the aristocrats of this patriarchal, agrarian society. Almost all the villages, and certainly the oldest ones, possess one or more shrines, whose walls are decorated with totems or chessboard patterns. The most venerated of these shrines, which are square chambers in the rock containing altars, are protected

by the *hogon*, a spiritual leader who serves several villages and who formerly dispensed justice and presided over the council of elders that directed public affairs. Today he still conducts major religious ceremonies and transmits to posterity the people's myths and beliefs.

A century and a half ago the influence of Islam began to reach the land of the Dogon from the neighboring Tukulor and Fulani (Peul) peoples, nomadic pastoralists of the plain, and many of the villages now have mosques. Whether modest or imposing, the mosque is often built next to the *togu na*, which even among the Islamized Dogon has kept the role of men's house and council chamber.

Statues and masks: a rich artistic heritage

Among the many different arts mastered by the Dogon, the most sacred is weaving, held to be the first art bestowed on humanity, at the same time as speech. In fact the Dogon have a single word for the two concepts, both of which are considered to have a question-and-answer structure. Griaule sees the act of weaving as a metaphor for culture itself: the warp represents uncultivated land; the weft, life-giving human activity.

But the aesthetic talents of the Dogon are probably best illustrated by their sculpture, whose primary purpose is ritualistic. Roughly carved or highly elaborate figures represent ancestors or mythical heroes. They are usually made by the village blacksmith, who also carves the wooden doors and shutters, while his wife is responsible for making pottery for ceremonial use.

Masks, associated with the spirits of the dead, are used only in funeral rites or to mark the end of a period of mourning, which may be celebrated either by public dances and ceremonies or by secret gatherings for initiates. The masks form part of a costume made of fabric or plant fibres, complete with trimmings and accessories. They may be fashioned from wood, bark or braided fibres decorated with cowrie shells and painted designs, or topped with high crests like the kanaga mask, whose upper portion is shaped like a cross of Lorraine. Its two branches represent the demiurge Amma gesturing towards his creations, Earth and sky.

CAROLINE HAARDT, French journalist, was a staff member of UNESCO's Division of Cultural Heritage from 1983 to 1987.

Timbuktu

LOCATION
Northern region, N 16° 45', W 03° 04'.

DESCRIPTION
Lying on the southern fringe of the Sahara Desert, Timbuktu is surrounded by sand dunes. The ruins of the ancient town sit to the west and to the north of the modern town. There are three mosques of significance - the Great Mosque, the Mosque of Sawkore and the Mosque of Sidi Yahia.

SIGNIFICANCE
Described as 'the meeting point of the camel and the canoe', Timbuktu's importance developed from its strategic proximity to the Niger River and the 'Sahelian Tracks' - a series of ancient tracks across the desert. The town possesses several notable Arabic texts - including the 'Tarik es-Sudan', an important 17th century historical treatise on the Sudan. It has been an intellectual and teaching center for Islam for many centuries and has been a principal meeting point for the various Saharan and Sudanese races.

TOP LEFT *Timbuktu - where the camel meets the canoe*
TOP RIGHT *The historic town of Djenne*

Old Towns of Djenné

LOCATION
In the Mopti province, N 13° 54', W 04° 25'.

DESCRIPTION
This site consists of the existing town of Djenné and the ruins of the ancient town. The modern town of Djenné was founded on several 'Toggere' (mounds) surrounded by a seven-gated rampart. The historic center spreads around the market place which is dominated by the mosque. There are many traditional buildings, mainly in ruins, and more than 50 two-level houses. The 'Nana Wangera', a sacred well erected in the residence of the heir prince, is a magnificent piece of art. The royal palaces northeast of the town were the residences of the Songhay Emperors. The tomb of Tepama is one of the oldest monuments of the city. The archeological site of the ancient city lies 3km (1.9mi) southeast of the modern town in the flood plain of Barii. It is composed of six 'Toggere' spread 5km (3.1mi) around the town. Most of them are entirely covered by ceramic pieces.

SIGNIFICANCE
Djenné was a very important African trading place and a center of Koranic studies. According to legend it was founded by the Nonos in 10th century AD who sacrificed a young girl, Tepama, to gain the favours of the gods and bring prosperity to the city. In 1240 the Emperor Koikombero, converted to Islam and turned his palace into a mosque. The city became part of the Mali Empire in 1325 and was conquered by Sonni Ali Ber in 1468. Its importance continued to grow after the 1591 Moroccan invasion when several new buildings were erected. It was not until 1870 and the Penth invasion with the subsequent closure of most mosques, that the city's decline began. However Djenné's earlier pre-eminence is clearly evident in these surviving buildings.

Banc d'Arguin National Park

LOCATION

On the Atlantic desert-coast of Mauritania, midway between Nouakchott in the south and Nouadhibou in the north, approximately 150km (93mi) south-south-east of Nouadhibou, N 19° 21' to 21° 51', W 16° 00' to 16° 45'

DESCRIPTION

The park is a unique example of a transition zone between the Sahara Desert and the Atlantic Ocean. It is a vast area of islands and coastline, largely composed of windblown sand of Saharan origin, together with a large expanse of mudflats, with well developed tidal flats around Tidra Island. Of the 15 named islands there are several up to 1km (0.6mi) wide and 5km (3mi) long; the largest, Isle of Tidra, is 8km (4.8mi) by 35km (23mi). The coastal waters between Cap Blanc and Cap Timiris are very shallow, and only reach 5m (15ft) deep at low tide even up to 60km (36mi) offshore. The arid inland is mainly composed of areas of sand hills and cliffs rising to 15m (45ft). There is an enormous mangrove swamp in the park which is a relict of a previous humid geological period when Banc d'Arguin was a vast estuary mouth for rivers flowing from the Sahara. A large marsh runs along the eastern shore of the Isle of Tidra and other expanses are found next to Cap Timirist and either side of the mouth of the bay of Saint-Jean.

SIGNIFICANCE

Of the estimated seven million wading birds which use the Atlantic flyway, approximately 30% spends the winter at Banc d'Arguin, which hosts the largest concentration of wintering waders in the world and one of the most diversified communities of nesting piscivorous (fish eating) birds in the world. In all, at least 108 bird species have been recorded. Wintering shorebirds number over three million and include hundreds of thousands of black tern and flamingo, ringed plover, grey plover, knot, redshank and bar-tailed godwit. The area is one of the most important wintering grounds for European spoonbill. Breeding birds include white pelican, reed cormorant, gull-billed tern, Caspian tern, royal tern and common tern, together with several species or subspecies with an African distribution, such as endemic heron, spoonbill and western reef heron. Mammals include Dorcas gazelle, jackal, fennec fox, sand fox, sand cat, ratel and striped hyena. Marine mammals regularly recorded include orca, Atlantic hump-backed dolphin, common dolphin, rough-toothed dolphin, bottle-nosed dolphin and Risso's dolphin. Fin whale or common rorqual and common porpoise have also been sighted. A small population of about 150 monk seals is found at Cap Blanc.

TOP Banc D'Arguin - American flamingoes
BOTTOM Sand hills

MOROCCO

The ruins at Aït Ben Haddou

*Lives of great men
all remind us
We can make our
lives sublime,
And, departing,
leave behind us
Footprints on the
sands of time.*

HENRY WADSWORTH LONGFELLOW

Aït-Ben-Haddou

LOCATION

In the province of Uuarzazate, sub-Saharan region.

DESCRIPTION

This collection of monuments at Aït-Ben-Haddou represents an ancient village site. There are six main kasbahs or fortified residential buildings, plus a structure which is situated up on the hill overlooking the village. All of these buildings are constructed of bricks made from pounded earth.

SIGNIFICANCE.

The unique geometric arrangement of the bricks at oblique angles and in zig zag patterns is distinctive of buildings in this region. These ruins at Aït-Ben-Haddou are the earliest surviving examples of this architectural style.

Medina Of Fez

LOCATION

Approximately 160km (100mi) inland from the Atlantic Coast, N 34° 06', W 04° 38'.

DESCRIPTION

This is a fortified medieval city spanning ten centuries of history through military, religious and civil buildings. It is situated in a deep valley. There are two main zones, Andalusian and Qarawiyin, which are separated by the river Fez.

SIGNIFICANCE

Founded in 809AD by Idriss II, the great Moorish king, the original settlement was divided into two zones - the Andalusian which was settled by Arab refugees from Spain and the Qarawiyin, settled by Arabs from Tunisia. The Qarawiyin zone houses the University Mosque, El Qarawiyin, the largest in Morocco. Its roof is supported by 366 pillars of stone. Fez flourished under the Merinid Dynasty and was the most important intellectual and religious center in Morocco. With the expulsion of the Moors from Spain, refugees flocked to Fez bringing with them knowledge of the arts, sciences and manufacturing, thus encouraging students to utilize its extensive libraries. The colleges of Fez and Jadid, built in the 13th century to house foreign students are the purest examples of Spanish-Moorish art in Morocco.

Medina of Marrakesh

LOCATION

In a plain surrounded by the high Atlas Mountains, N 31° 36', W 08° 00'.

DESCRIPTION

The city is surrounded by high walls with eight gates. The mosque of Koutoubia with its magnificent 7m (23ft) high minaret dominates the town. The Kasbah includes many splendid palaces, a Great Mosque, a large market, the gates of Bag Agnoou and Bab Rob, and the ruins of the Al Badi Palace. Marrakesh is a city of gardens and famous for its palm groves dating back to the Almoravid Empire.

SIGNIFICANCE

Marrakesh was founded in 1062AD by Yussef ibn Tashfin, ruler of the Almoravid Dynasty from 1062-1147AD. He was responsible for introducing the irrigation canals which still supply the city's gardens with water. The city was destroyed by the Almohads in 1147. It was rebuilt and became the capital of the empire until its collapse in 1262. It was restored to its position as capital after the defeat of the Meriniclo by the Saadians in 1520. Marrakesh was restored to some of its former Moroccan brilliance in the arts by Monlay Hassan in 1873. The numerous monuments and buildings that now stand are important records of the major dynasties which shaped this great city.

ABOVE Koutoubia Mosque, Medina of Marrakesh
LEFT Medina of Fez - the city's gateway
FAR LEFT Medina of Fez - earthen vats store vegetable dyes in a courtyard

MOZAMBIQUE

Island of Mozambique.

LOCATION

Province of Nampula. S 15° 02', E 40° 44'.

DESCRIPTION

The Island of Mozambique (Ihla de Mozambique) is a small urbanised island around 3km (1.9mi) long and averaging 300m (985ft) in width. It lies on a coral reef 4km (2.5mi) off the coast of the mainland. There are several monuments of importance: San Sebastian Fortress, San Paulo Palace and Chapel, San Domingos Convent, San Antonio Fortress, San Lourenco Fortress, the hospital church, the hospital and a mosque. Construction is mainly of ochre-colored limestone masonry with white detailing and flat roofs. A smaller island, St. Laurent is also included in the listing.

ABOVE *Ihla de Mozambique*

SIGNIFICANCE

Ihla de Mozambique was an Arab trading post from the early 10th century. The nature of society on the island changed dramatically after the arrival of the Portuguese explorer Vasco da Gama in 1498. It was established by the Portuguese as a station on the sea route to India and became the capital of Portuguese operations in Mozambique. The first fortress was built in 1508, construction of San Sebastian Fortress commenced 50 years later and was finished in 1620. San Paulo Palace, a Jesuit college, was established in 1610. Urban and commercial districts developed rapidly throughout the 17th and 18th centuries, resulting in the formation of a town council in 1761. At the beginning of the 19th century, a new quarter was laid out in a grid pattern with a central square. Expansion continued until 1898, when the capital was transferred to the mainland. Today, the town and fortifications on Ihla de Mozambique, and the smaller island of St. Laurent, are beautifully preserved examples of a distinctive architectural style which blends local traditions, Portuguese influences, and to a lesser extent, Indian and Arab influences.

Aïr and Ténéré Reserve

LOCATION

Department of Agades. N 17° 12' to 20° 30', E 08° 06' to 10° 57'.

DESCRIPTION

This 77,360sqkm (29,861sqmi) reserve includes the 12,805sqkm (4,943sqmi) Sanctuary of Addax. The entire area lies within the Saharan region of Niger. It is arid, with an average rainfall of only 50mm (2in) per annum. There are two distinct zones, the extensive flat plain of the Tenere desert, and the mountains of the Aïr which rise 2,000m (6,564ft) above it. Habitats are surprisingly diverse, including heavily wooded valleys and permanent rock pools in the mountains. Vegetation includes wild olives and figs, as well as the wild relatives of several important crops, such as millet and sorghum. There are significant populations of fauna, including 40 species of mammals, 165 birds, 18 reptiles and one amphibian. The mammals include several species of gazelles, Barbary sheep, monkeys, baboons, foxes and a small population of cheetah. Birds include the Nubian bustard and ostrich.

SIGNIFICANCE

This reserve protects several species which are threatened with extinction including three species of desert antelope - the addax, dama gazelle and slender-horned gazelle and the last viable population of the West African race of the ostrich. Several animal populations such as those of the olive baboon and patas monkey, have been isolated in the Aïr mountains for thousands of years and thus constitute a genetic heritage. The rare beauty of this environment is constantly undergoing change as the desert sands shift, endlessly eroding and modifying the many relict ecosystems that are of outstanding value to the world's heritage.

ABOVE *Aïr and Ténéré Reserves - rock paintings*
INSET *The endangered addax*

SENEGAL

Niokolo-Koba National Park

LOCATION

Lying across the border between the regions of Sénégal-Oriental and La Casamance, on the River Gambia, close to the Guinea border in south-eastern Senegal,
N 12° 30' to 13° 20', W 12° 20' to 13° 35'.

DESCRIPTION

This large 9,130sqkm (3,500sqmi) park is relatively flat, Mont Assirik being the highest point at 311m (1,000ft). Small 200m (660ft) high hills are separated by wide flood plains which become inundated during the rains. The area is rocky, with numerous sandstone outcrops dotting the landscape. The park is crossed by the River Gambia and its two tributaries, the Niokolo Koba and the Koulountou. Vegetation varies, with savanna predominating. There is more luxuriant vegetation along the course of the rivers and a varying cover of trees and bushes. The rainy season brings dramatic changes to the area, with grasslands being flooded and marshes rejuvenated. There are also areas of bamboo, gallery forests and dry forests.

SIGNIFICANCE

This is the largest protected area in western Africa. A significant feature of the park is the sizeable self-sustaining elephant population. There are about 80 species of mammal, 330 species of bird, 36 reptiles, 20 amphibians, and 60 species of fish recorded, as well as numerous invertebrates. Carnivores include leopard, lion, and hunting dog. There are also buffalo, roan, giant eland, Guinea baboon, green monkey, patas monkey, bay colobus, all three African crocodiles - Nile, slender-snouted and dwarf - four tortoise species, and hippopotamus, which is present in all three large watercourses in the park. The park is the last refuge in Senegal for giraffe and elephant. About 150 chimpanzee live in the gallery forest of the park and on Mont Assirik (the north-western limit of their distribution). Birds include Denham's bustard, ground hornbill, violet turaco, spur-winged goose, white-faced tree duck and martial eagle.

ABOVE Niokola-Koba - the Gambia River at Simenti
INSET Patas monkey

Djoudj Bird Sanctuary

LOCATION
In the delta area of the river Senegal, 60km (37mi) from St. Louis, N 16° 30', W 16° 10'.

DESCRIPTION
This park which spreads over more than 18,000ha (43,200ac), is mainly covered in water with three rivers crossing it, a quarter of it covered by lake, and a vast area which is largely swampland. Water birds travel here in the thousands, migrating each year from Europe and East Africa. Numerous animals have been reintroduced, most importantly the crocodile, which is now thriving.

SIGNIFICANCE
This bird sanctuary is the only natural environment for the thousands of water birds that migrate annually 2,000km (1,200mi) across the Sahara Desert. It has the largest concentration of herons in west Africa and many other species such as the white pelican, great egret, African spoonbill and cormorant find nesting areas within its boundaries. The large, fast running bird, the big bustard, is found only in this park.

Gorée Island

LOCATION
An islet south of Dakar, W 17° 24', N 14° 00'.

DESCRIPTION
Gorée lies at the entrance to the large harbor that is naturally formed by the peninsula of Cape Vert. It is quite small, roughly 540 by 200m (1,800 by 660ft), and is mostly barren and rocky. Most of the island is taken up by the town which was established as a military and trading post. There is a complex of fortifications, a gun battery at the north end, several forts, and a large water reservoir in the south. There are also ruins of a former residential area with a mosque.

SIGNIFICANCE
The history of Gorée is closely connected with the slave trade. Until the abolition of slavery in the French colonies in 1875, the island was a 'warehouse' with more than 10 slave holdings. Slaves were stored here awaiting shipment to the Americas. First occupied by the Dutch in the early 17th century, it was held by the English for one year in 1663, returning to the Dutch, then to the French in 1677. The English managed to wrest control once more, before the island finally fell into French hands for the last time.

TOP LEFT The Sudan bustard
TOP RIGHT Part of the fortifications at Gorée Island

SEYCHELLES

Aldabra Atoll

LOCATION

640km (398mi) off the African east coast, E 46° 25′, S 09° 25′.

DESCRIPTION

Aldabra is a classic coral atoll which has been uplifted above the sea. The atoll consists of 4 main islands of coral limestone, separated by narrow passages and enclosing a large shallow lagoon. The elevation of the atoll rarely exceeds 3m (10ft) above sea level. It contains many diverse habitats, from coral reefs to mangroves.

SIGNIFICANCE

Due to its isolation the atoll has become a refuge for species that have become extinct elsewhere. The unpolluted and undisturbed environment make Aldabra of outstanding universal value to conservation and science. This is probably the sole terrestrial environment where a reptile is the dominant herbivore: the giant tortoise (geochelone gigantea) population of 152,000 is the largest in the world and without doubt the atoll's most outstanding feature.

The giant tortoises of Aldabra

OPPOSITE TOP *Female coco de mer*
OPPOSITE BOTTOM *Black Parrot*

Vallée de Mai Nature Reserve

LOCATION

Praslin Island, E 55° 44', S 04° 19'.

DESCRIPTION

The Vallée de Mai is an 18ha (43ac) nature reserve. Acquired by the government some years ago, it forms the nucleus of the Praslin National Park. The vegetation is lush rainforest with a predominance of palm trees, including five endemic species.

SIGNIFICANCE

Most of Praslin Island, once known as the 'Isle of Palms', has been burnt and cultivated, but this small pocket of palm forest in the valley has been preserved close to its original, primeval state. The flora is rich, with a high preponderance of endemic species. The most notable feature of the park is the famous double coconut which bears the largest seed in the plant kingdom; it can weigh up to 20kg (44lb). Of the distinctive avifauna, the local subspecies of the black parrot is particularly noteworthy, as it is totally dependent on this reserve for its survival.

Profiting from Wildlife Conservation

Ruvuma Village Wildlife Management Program (RVWMP) is part of the Selous Conservation Program (SCP) which is a joint venture between the Governments of Tanzania and Germany.

The prime objective of the program is to conserve, manage and utilize wildlife resources inside the Selous Game Reserve (SGR) and the entire ecological system on the basis of sustainable yield. While the SGR covers an area of approximately 50,000sqkm (19,000sqmi) of south eastern Tanzania, the entire ecosystem incorporates a much larger area of over 80,000sqkm (31,000sqmi), including land in Morogoro, Ruvuma, Lindi and coastal regions. The effective range for certain wildlife species includes the entire ecosystem. In other words under natural conditions, wild animals do not recognize man-made boundaries. As with the animals, it is also accepted in principle that no ecosystem is devoid of human interaction, because people form part of, and influence, the ecosystem and the Selous is not an exception.

It has been observed that the villagers living around the SGR derive many of their means of subsistence from wildlife, ie animals, fish, fruits, vegetables, firewood, mushroom, honey, medicine. A close look at the Wildlife Conservation Act of 1974 however, emphasize excluding, rather than integrating, villagers around SGR, with conservation denying the villagers the right to benefit directly from these resources. Far removed from these expectations of villagers abiding with the law; human-exclusion conservation policy is not working due to the vast size of the protected areas and increased demand for land.

As a result of management ineffectiveness, villagers poach both inside and outside the reserve. Consequently key wildlife species have recently been threatened or exposed to the dangers of extinction. Typical on the list of affected species due to poaching are the African elephant, Lexodanta africana and the black rhinoceros, Dioeros birconis. These two species registered a decline of about 70% and 98% respec-

tively between 1976 and 1989. This drastic decline in species population numbers called for action to research and design a pragmatic approach to conservation through community involvement, enabling them to profit from wildlife in order to sustain resource conservation.

Background

The RVWMP started in 1989. Five villages in the Songea District were selected to serve as pilot areas. The pilot area incorporated the villages of Kitanda, Nambecha, Likuyu Sekamaganga, Mehomoro and Kilimasera. All these selected villages share borders with SGR in the north and boast a human population of approximately 12,000 indigenous villagers and 13,000 refugees from Mozambique.

The land between the reserve and the pilot villages forms important habitats for the elephant sable antelope - Hippatrogus niger, cape buffalo - Syncerus caffer, livingstone eland - aurotragus petersonianus livingstonii and many other typical Brachystegia woodland species. The vegetation cover is characterised by mosaics of habitat types ranging from dense evergreen riverine along the valleys; flood grass areas; seasonal and permanently marshy and swampy areas. The extensive woodland grassland habitats are dominated by tree species of the genus Brachystegia with B. bohemii, popularly called muyombo, being the most dominant. Species of commercial interest include Adina Microcephala and Pterocarpus . These two species are found in localized places which are inaccessible. Otherwise over-exploitation is responsible for their rarity.

In addition to being an important catchment area for major tributaries which join and form Rufiji River, natural ponds which were once rich in aquatic life are found. Recently however, illegal application of pesticides has depleted the endemic aquatic species. The degree of depletion is not possible to assess, because limnological studies have not been carried out in the area.

Source of meat

As mentioned before, the villagers do not keep cattle, therefore wildlife forms an important source of meat. But again, the inhibition of wildlife law as stated earlier, coupled with low income status, together generate constraints for the villagers to acquire legal firearms and buy a hunting licences. This situation precludes villagers from access to legal game meat, a resource whose survival is the result of their traditional ways. Otherwise had the villagers opted for agriculture, there

Female cheetah attacking a Grant's gazelle

would be no wildlife left. Despite their traditional role in saving what remains of the past, the making of conservation laws did not take into account the positive role of the traditional people and instead they were ignored and treated as aliens in their ancestral land. In such a situation commonsense dictates that villagers had only two options; either starve and perish due to lack of protein or violate the law to get the needed meat.

Sustainable Utilisation

'Poaching for the pot' then, was sustainable in the sense that only appropriate tools were available and used to hunt. For instance, muzzle loaders and spears could enable the traditional hunter to kill just enough game for himself and the community. Another feature responsible in ascertaining resource sustainability is the traditional preservation and conservation of wildlife habitats inherently practised by rural communities. This arises from their respect for the bush which is the mother source of life. This unique quality of life is lacking in modern development, which views natural environs as hostile, and in need of taming.

In the eyes of the rural communities the causes of wildlife destruction are the well-to-do people. The villagers, they argue, did not introduce machine guns to the poaching industry. The affluent people did. Their motives were to generate wealth as quickly as possible by 'mining' wildlife resources.

The era of wildlife mining in Tanzania and in particular the Ruvuma region, dates back to the early 1980s. However, large scale elephant poaching and unsustainable utilisation of other wildlife species was first reported in 1984.

Some villagers bordering SGR grew into infamous centers for the nefarious trade in ivory, with villagers assuming the role of primary producers of illegal ivory, while buyers came from different parts of the country and abroad. Whether it is accepted or not, ivory poaching and smuggling was an important source of income for different levels of people.

An aggressive elephant bull

During the era of commercial poaching, relations between rural communities and wildlife employees in the field were cool and hostile, often resulting in overt clashes. Occasionally such hostilities ended in loss of life from either party. A critical review of the overall situation indicated a struggle which neither party could win as long as wild animals remained in the SGR and environs. The poachers, being heavily armed and backed by influential people were accepted by villagers as being the winning side at least while the game was still available in the wild, but eventually they would have been losers once the animals were gone.

The main assumption now is that if villagers benefit directly from wildlife resources, they will support conservation efforts and therefore minimize destruction of the natural environment, thus sustaining wildlife.

This implies that positive results can only come about if the villagers' economic situation improves. It is a fact which must be accepted that hungry people do not have time to think of conservation, particularly when they compare the high standards of living enjoyed by residents in urban centers.

This concept was also sold to the villagers by educating them to the advantages of communal wildlife conservation and sustained yield resource utilization. Recognising their knowledge of adaptive conservation, the villagers were given a mandate to prepare wildlife plans to show how wildlife could be conserved and utilized.

Direct dialogue and public discussions with villagers finally opened up communications between the Project Leader on behalf of the Wildlife Department and the rural communities concerned. Previous hostilities have now been minimized.

Villagers have willingly established wildlife committees and selected some members to serve as village scouts, whose responsibilities include the supervision of sustainable conservation and utilization of natural resources. Village scouts carry out routine patrols, sometimes jointly with Game Wardens and Game Scouts.

Poaching has been completely eliminated in Mohomoro and Kilimasera village areas. In general, villagers in all pilot areas have stopped poaching. The only poaching is done by core poachers, normally from villages not involved in the program. Occasionally they land up in the hands of the village scouts.

Reduction in poaching is apparently resulting in an increased population of big game including elephants. Crop damage is being reported frequently and as a positive gesture reflecting the wildlife authority's commitment to delegate responsibilities, the villagers are fully involved in choosing suitable methods of protecting human life and minimizing crop damage.

Based on the results of two years of operation, the program plans to design and implement programs in three major areas. They are, conservation education to the peasant farmers; sustainable utilization programs to benefit the concerned rural communities; and research on traditional values of wildlife.

If the rural communities have been instrumental in preserving these natural habitats, a phenomenon which is the secret to wildlife species survival, then it is their natural right to benefit directly from wildlife within the legal framework. In short, the success of the program will depend on how fast the government effects changes that will finally give rural communities the right to profit directly from wildlife resources.

IRENEUS F NDUNGURU
Regional Game Officer and Project Leader
Songea, Tanzania

Ngorongoro Conservation Area

LOCATION

East of the Serengeti National Park in the Arusha region, E 35° 30', S 03°15'.

DESCRIPTION

This area is 80,944sqkm (32,400sqmi) of largely savanna grassland. There are several notable geological features, including two huge volcanic craters or calderas, a large volcanically formed lake - Lake Empakaai - and Olduvai Gorge.

SIGNIFICANCE

Along with neighboring Serengeti National Park, Ngorongo forms a huge interdependent ecosystem, containing the largest concentration of wildlife on earth. These huge resources are managed in such a way that the tribal hunters living nearby may benefit without causing any deterioration in the quality of the environment. At Olduvai Gorge, under the leadership of Dr. Louis Leakey and Mrs. Mary Leakey, archeological excavations have unearthed the remains of the oldest known ancestors of man.

RIGHT Lake Empakaai
BOTTOM Black rhinoceros

Selous Game Reserve

LOCATION

Coast Morogoro, Lindi, Mtwara and Ruvuma Regions,
S 07° 17' to 10° 15',
E 36° 04' to 38° 46'.

DESCRIPTION

With 50,000sqkm (20,000sqmi), moderate rainfall and tempera-
tures in a yearly range of 13°-41°C (56°-106°F), this park has a
variety of vegetation zones from dense thickets to open wooded
grasslands. However two broad divisions, east and west, may be
discerned. In the east where grasslands exist, cheetah and giraffe
may be found, while in the west the Miombo woodlands have some
elephants and hartebeest but are generally devoid of plains animals.

SIGNIFICANCE

One of the oldest game reserves in Africa, first gazetted in 1905 at
just 2,500sqkm (1,554sqmi), it has been constantly expanded
while the local population has been evacuated to allow the animals
full reign. This lack of hunting pressure has helped maintain the
area in a natural condition, allowing the animals to wander, free of
further human interference.

We will save ourselves together, or perish together. We no
longer have the choice of which species to protect. They are
all necessary, because each one that disappears is an
irredeemable loss that takes us one step further down the road
to desertification of the planet.

ROGER CANS

Serengeti National Park

LOCATION

*In Mara, Arusha and Shinyanga Provinces, 130km (81mi)
west-northwest of Arusha,
S 01° 15' to 03° 20', E 34° 00' to 35° 15'.*

DESCRIPTION

*Serengeti National Park is 1,476,300ha (3,559,359ac) of largely
uninhabited savannas. The area is famous for its vast plains upon
which huge herds of animals roam, followed by numerous packs of
attendant predators. Water is not in abundance, so the presence of
permanent waterholes in the west leads to massive annual herd
migrations.*

SIGNIFICANCE

*This is easily the most widely renowned wildlife park on earth. It is the
archetypal safari park with immense herds of gazelles, giraffes, wilde-
beests, topi, warthogs, elephants, hippos and black rhinos. Lions,
cheetah and leopards also roam these plains in great numbers. The
movement of some herds can be in lines up to 10km (6mi) long and
presents one of the most awe inspiring wildlife spectacles imaginable.*

ABOVE Massive herds of migrating beasts wear deep ruts in the landscape

Kilwa Kisiwani and Songo Mnara Ruins

LOCATION

Two islands off the eastern coast of Africa:
Kilwa Kisiwani: E 39° 46', S 09° 00';
Songo Mnara: E 39° 47', S 09° 07'.

DESCRIPTION

The ruins at Kilwa Kisiwani include the Great Mosque -12th to 15th century AD, the Palace of Husuni Kubwa -14th century AD, the Arab fort called the Gereza, Makutani - the 'Palace of Great Walls', and several mosques. At Songo Mnara there is a palace, five mosques, a residential area and a cemetery.

SIGNIFICANCE

Kilwa Kisiwani and its dependent neighbor are the remains of the most important medieval city-state on the East African coast. They reached their zenith in the 13th and 14th centuries. These ruins reflect the successes of this maritime power that at one time controlled 1,600km (1,000mi) of coast. This power base declined in the 1500s as the Portuguese arrived but recovered 200 years later.

Kilimanjaro National Park

LOCATION

Kilimanjaro Region in the north, on the border with Kenya, S 02° 50' to 03° 20', E 37° 00' to 37° 43'.

DESCRIPTION

Mt. Kilimanjaro is of volcanic origin and is 5,895m (19,347ft) high. It is encircled by native deciduous forest rising to 2,740m (8,989ft) above sea level. This mountain, much photographed, has the classic pointed shape and is perpetually snow-topped and often shrouded in cloud. In the plains surrounding it are herds of wildlife and upon its slopes are found monkeys, bush pigs, tree hyrix and many small mammals. Leopards and rhinoceros are often to be seen. Facilities for visitors and climbers are well developed with numerous well kept huts on the mountains.

SIGNIFICANCE

Kilimanjaro is the highest summit in Africa. A lone, snow capped peak rising dramatically from the surrounding equatorial plains, it is one of the world's greatest natural sights. This park plays a crucial role in protecting not only this magnificent environment, but also numerous mammals, many of them endangered.

ABOVE *The fort on Kilwa Kisiwani*

Amphitheater Of El Djem

LOCATION

*Approximately 90km (56mi) south of Sousse,
N 36° 00', E 11° 00'.*

DESCRIPTION

*This is a free-standing structure and is not, as was so often the
case, built into or next to a hill. Its state of preservation is excellent
and original, having survived the winds of time and avoided the
restorers' hands. Seating capacity is around 35,000. The facade
has three arched tiers in the Corinthian style. Inside, the podium,
arena and underground galleries are virtually intact.*

SIGNIFICANCE

*This is without doubt one of the largest and best preserved of all
Roman amphitheaters. It was here in 238AD that Gordian was
proclaimed emperor. After the decline of the Roman Empire, it fell
into disuse until becoming a Byzantine fortress. This use was
continued by the Moslem conquerors until well into the 18th
century.*

ABOVE *The amphitheater of El Djem*

Medina of Tunis

LOCATION

City of Tunis, northeastern Mediterranean coast, E 10° 20', N 36° 51'.

DESCRIPTION

*This traditional complex covers an area of 270ha (651ac) and
comprises the central 8th century Medina plus two 13th century
suburbs. There are 700 historic monuments found in this area, including
about 200 palaces and large residences and numerous mosques. The
other notable features are the town gates, the souks (markets) and its
unique urban plan.*

SIGNIFICANCE

*This complex stands on the site of an ancient town which was
mentioned by Pliny the Elder. After the destruction of Carthage in the
8th century, this town was furnished with an arsenal, a port, canal and
outer harbor. During the 12th century it became the capital of
'Aghlabid Afrigiyah' and soon came to be considered one of the greatest
and wealthiest cities in the Islamic world. The tremendously rich
heritage of those heady days is clearly evident today.*

ABOVE *Medina of Tunis*

Carthage

LOCATION

Several kilometers northeast of Tunis, N 36° 51', E 10° 20'.

DESCRIPTION

This site comprises the Acropolis of Byrsa, the Punic ports, a theater, necropolises, a circus, villas, baths and cisterns. The ruins follow the coastline on a north-south axis and are largely incomplete. Major excavations have been attempted but have not been overly successful. On the perimeter of the site the suburbs of Tunis have barely been halted from encroaching.

SIGNIFICANCE

The most distinguished site in Tunisia, due to its long history, Carthage was the great rival of ancient Rome. Until the catastrophic conclusion of the Punic Wars when the city was totally obliterated it was perhaps even greater than Rome. Hannibal and his elephants gave Carthage a decisive edge in the great struggle, but this was squandered. The remains today are mainly from later periods, having been built following the Roman recolonization of the area. Its historical and cultural importance was underlined when the Mayor of Rome declared in 1985 'Carthage must not be obliterated' a reference to the creed attributed to ancient Rome - 'Carthage must be obliterated'

Ichkeul National Park

LOCATION

In the governorate of Bizerta,
N 37° 10', E 09° 40'.

DESCRIPTION

The area of this park is 10,775ha
(26,000ac), with a further buffer zone of
6,000ha (14,000ac). The dominant feature
is the lake which is surrounded by extensive
marshland. Apart from an isolated mountain
811m (2,660ft) high, the landscape is
mainly flat. This lake is the last remaining in
a chain of lakes which once extended across
northern Africa.

SIGNIFICANCE

The international importance of this lake and
its associated marshes and waterways lies in
its use as a stopover point for migrating
birds. More than 185 species have been
recorded, the most numerous being wigeon,
pochard and coot. It is the last surviving
remnant of the ancient northern African lake
chain and therefore is of crucial significance.
The beauty of the landscape, its ecological
formations, the wealth of flora and fauna
combine to make Ichkeul an ecological site,
not only unique in Tunisia but in the whole
of the Maghreb. It is an area untouched by
agricultural disturbances which explains its
continued survival.

FAR LEFT 3rd century Roman villa at Carthage
CENTRE Reed warbler and chicks, Ichkeul National Park
TOP Part of the extensive marshlands at Ichkeul National Park
BOTTOM Wigeon drake, one of the numerous species of migrating
bird found at Ichkeul

Medina of Sousse

LOCATION

East coast, 150km (93mi) southeast of Tunis, N 35° 49', E 10° 39'.

DESCRIPTION

The town of Sousse sits on a hill over looking the Mediterranean Sea. It is surrounded by a fortified wall with towers and crenellations. Shops operate from indentations on the inside of the wall. There are many interesting buildings; the kasbah is perched on the highest point within the walls and has been fully restored. The Kasrnern Ribat is a square fortress with a lofty tower and seven bastions. An unusual building is the Kab wet-el-Kubba (Café of the Dome) which has a square base, a cylindrical body and is topped by a grooved dome. There is a large Great Mosque and a smaller mosque known as Bou Fata'ta.

SIGNIFICANCE

The site of Sousse goes back to ancient days when it was occupied by the Phoenicians and known by the name of Hadrumetum. The fortifications of the present city were built in the 9th century AD. Pirates operated out of the town for many centuries and it has been the scene of many attacks, notably by the Venetians, the Knights of St. John and the French. The multitude of ethnic influences throughout the centuries has left its distinctive mark on this unique old town.

ABOVE Kasrnern Ribat, Medina of Sousse
OPPOSITE PAGE The Great Mosque of Sidi 'Oqba, Kairouan
INSET Ruins of the ancient Punic town of Kerkwan

Kerkwan

LOCATION

*Northeast coast, around 90km (56mi) east of Tunis,
N 36° 35', E 10° 45'.*

DESCRIPTION

*These ruins of an ancient Punic town are relatively intact. They
include the town walls, its residential quarters, a large temple,
several palaces and an extensive sewage system. The necropolis lies
1km (0.6mi) northwest on a rocky hill. It is rectangular in plan,
100m (328ft) wide by 170m (558ft) long. There are more than
200 tombs, all different in layout and size, some with staircases,
and many with painted decorations.*

SIGNIFICANCE

*These ruins are extensive and in excellent order. It is believed that
the city was abandoned during the first Punic War, around
250BC. The necropolis in particular, provides an invaluable
insight into the culture of this advanced civilization .*

Kairouan

LOCATION

Around 130km (80mi) south of Tunis, N 35° 48', E 10° 10'.

DESCRIPTION

*The city covers around 54ha (130ac) and is surrounded by 3.2km
(2mi) of walls. There are several gates, notably the Corte de Tunis
and the Bab Jalladine. More than 80 mosques and 50 mausoleums
line the streets and squares inside. The Great Mosque of Sidi 'Oqba
and the Mosque of the Three Doors are the most important
buildings. There are also baths, souks (markets), the Aghlabites
pools and the Sanctuary of Sidi Abid el Ghariani.*

SIGNIFICANCE

*Kairouan (Qairwan) is Tunisia's Holy City. Legend has it that
'Oqba went out into the desert in 671AD in order to find the site
which would become the center of Islam in Africa. He struck his
spear into the ground and proclaimed 'Here is your Qairwan
(resting place)'. The town is also important architecturally, as its
buildings are some of the earliest in the Islamic world. The Great
Mosque was a model for many famous mosques that followed.*

ZAIRE

Virunga National Park

LOCATION
Close to the borders of Uganda and Rwanda, S 01° 00', E 29° 30'.

DESCRIPTION
This park is a narrow strip of land, 300km (186mi) long and up to 50km (31mi) wide, a total of 8,000sqkm (3,200sqmi) in area. It comprises a zone of extinct volcanoes as well as some that are still active. The landscape varies from lava plains to mountains to alluvial plains around Lake Amin and vast stretches of savanna. There is a great variation in altitude: 798m (2,618ft) in the equatorial forest ranging up to 5,119m (16,794ft) at the glaciers and perpetual snows of Ruwenzori. This has resulted in a similar degree of diversity of ecosystems, in turn responsible for a unique and rich variety of flora and fauna. Many large mammals are found here, such as the mountain gorilla (gorilla beringei), chimpanzee, leopard, lion, elephant, kobus, waterbuck and antelope.

TOP Virunga National Park - hippos and flamingoes
RIGHT Mountain gorillas

SIGNIFICANCE
First created in 1925 as a sanctuary for the endangered species of gorillas, it has been extended several times to its present boundaries. Its essential significance lies in the variety of species found in a relatively limited area. The population of hippopotami around Lake Amin and along the Semliki River is extremely dense and has the potential to outstrip the supply of natural food.

OPPOSITE PAGE Black stork with her young (ABOVE) Mountain gorillas in typical habitat (BELOW), Salonga National Park

Salonga National Park

LOCATION

*In western territories of Monkoto, Bokungu,
Lorilla Dekese and Oshwe,
S 01° 00' to 03° 30', E 20° 00' to 23° 00'.*

DESCRIPTION

*This massive park is in two sections which are
separated by a populated zone. It covers
36,000sqkm (14,400sqmi) of mainly equatorial
rainforest. The climate is hot and humid and it
provides the habitats for numerous flora and
fauna, including many large mammals. There
are many deep valleys and swift flowing rivers.*

SIGNIFICANCE

*This national park is the largest in Zaire and the
second largest in the world. It was transformed
into a national park in order to preserve a large
part of the great equatorial forest which stretches
across the center of Africa. It is in virtually
pristine condition, due mainly to its rugged
terrain and thick, inaccessible forests.
Innumerable species of flora and fauna live in
these great forests, including the endemic pygmy
chimpanzee, several species of monkey, numerous
birds, the hippopotamus and leopard.*

Kahuzi-Biega National Park

LOCATION

West of Lake Kivu, 50km (31mi) from the town of Bukavu, S 02° 10' to 02° 51', E 28° 40' to 28° 50'.

DESCRIPTION

This national park takes its name from two extinct volcanoes, the Kahuzi and the Biega. It is a mountainous area with diverse types of vegetation, characterized mainly by mountain forests and large stands of bamboo. There are also alpine and subalpine meadows, marshlands, peat bogs and some rivers.

SIGNIFICANCE

The fundamental interest of the park lies in its mountain gorilla (gorilla beringei) population. There are several hundred individuals who live mainly in the zones situated between 2,100-2,400m (6,890-7,874ft). Their existence is related to the vast area of forests in the park which provide an ideal habitat for this species. Other fauna include elephant, forest bog, duiker and several species of antelope.

Garamba National Park - northern white rhinoceros (TOP) De Brazza's monkey (TOP RIGHT)
BOTTOM Kahuzi-Biega National Park - Male silverback mountain gorilla

Garamba National Park

LOCATION

In the northeastern area of High Zaire, on the border with Sudan, N 03° 45' to 04° 41', E 28° 48' to 30° 00'.

DESCRIPTION

This is an area of vast savanna, with pockets of forest and several large swamp depressions. The park is crossed by major rivers such as the Dungu, Aka and Garamba. It lies at an altitude varying between 700-900m (2,297-2,953ft), and its climate is characterised by a wet season and a dry season. The trees typical to the park are the Kigelia aethiopica and the Terminalia, both extremely fire resistant.

SIGNIFICANCE

This national park was created as a natural sanctuary to protect its remarkable fauna, particularly its big mammals. It is the habitat of the four largest mammals on earth; the elephant, hippopotamus, white rhinoceros and giraffe. The latter two species were on the endangered list up until very recently. Their numbers are now slowly increasing, due mainly to the provision of this protected environment.

OPPOSITE PAGE Mosi-oa-Tunya - female vervet monkey with her young, (ABOVE) the falls in full roar (BELOW)

Victoria Falls (Mosi-oa-Tunya)

LOCATION

Southern Province of Zambia, Matabeland North Province of Zimbabwe,
S 17° 56', E 25° 55'.

DESCRIPTION

At 1,300km (808mi) from its source, the Zambezi River is interrupted by these falls which descend in several steps a total of about 350m (1,148ft). The falls are 1,708m (5,604ft) wide and send a plume of spray 500m (1,640ft) up into the air which can be seen from 30km (18.6mi) away. After descending the falls, the water of the Zambezi swirls furiously in the 'Boiling Pot' before tortuously traversing the lower gorges, barely one-thirtieth the width of the upper river.

SIGNIFICANCE

When the Zambezi is in full flood, the falls are the largest curtain of water on earth. The whole area below and above the falls is of outstanding geological, geomorphological and hydrological interest. The flora and fauna of the nearby national park is rich in biological diversity. However it is from the enormous width and volume of falling water, that the falls attain their tremendous aesthetic value. The cultural history of the area extends back approximately 50,000 years with several stone artefacts having been uncovered. However, the various interactions between numerous tribes have left no clear or dominant ethnic characteristics. The main human significance lies in the wealth which accrued to the tribes controlling the rich wildlife resources in centuries past.

ZAMBIA AND ZIMBABWE

ZIMBABWE

Khami Ruins

LOCATION

Matabeleland, S 20° 09', E 25° 25'.

DESCRIPTION

These ruins comprise another series of dry stone walled structures. They extend over an area of 108ha (260ac) and sections follow the Khami River. Many artefacts such as beads, ironware, trading goods and golden objects have been unearthed.

SIGNIFICANCE

These ruins are thought to represent a later development of the culture which flourished at the Great Zimbabwe Monument. Carbon dating places their origin at the 15th century, flourishing until the 17th century.

ABOVE The stones of Khami ruins

Mana Pools:
TOP Greater Kudu
RIGHT Nile crocodile
BELOW Elephants grazing

Mana Pools, Sapi and Chewore Reserves

LOCATION

Within the Urungwe District, North Mashonaland Region, S 15° 36' to 16° 24', E 29° 08' to 30° 20'.

DESCRIPTION

There is no permanent human habitation in this 6,766sqkm (2,700sqmi) patch of the Zambezi Valley. The main geographical features are the Zambezi escarpment rising to 1,000m (3,281ft), the flat valley floor, traversed by the sandy Zambezi River, the heavily dissected Chewore Safari Area and the Mupata Gorge, 30km (18.6mi) long. The general course of the Zambezi is along a down-faulted trough, including the various valleys and gorges. Several rivers, mostly dry, lead into the Zambezi basin leaving large areas of alluvial deposits. The various grass and woodlands associated with the largely arid conditions are home to large herds of migratory grazing animals such as zebra, sable, buffalo and elephant and more than 380 bird species. Crocodiles are also found in abundance.

SIGNIFICANCE

Due to the characteristic flooding of the Zambezi and the resultant alluvial build up, the region is not home to large predatory animals. Thus, apart from the threats that man poses, the herds of herbivorous savanna animals are little threatened. As well, the broad open grasslands allow visitors to walk, rather than drive through the parks, as there is little chance of unexpected encounters with ferocious wild animals. The concentration of Nile crocodiles is one of the most important in Africa. Once the danger of over hunting is removed, the mid-Zambezi valley region will become one of the finest breeding areas for the larger mammals and reptiles on earth.

For thousands of years the earth has been generous to us. But now there is drought in Africa and this is not just due to the lack of rain. It is a question of destructive activity. Because governments wanted the foreign exchange, forests were cut down and not replaced. To get fuel, people destroy the trees that are left. This process causes the deserts to grow. The integrity of creation is destroyed for economic reasons.

FATHER JOHN MUTISO MBINDA

The Ancient Secrets of Great Zimbabwe

Deep in the heart of southern Africa, away from the zones of influence of the Islamic and Christian powers, the basins of the Zambezi and Limpopo Rivers were for centuries the setting for a number of brilliant civilizations, the most famous of these being that of Great Zimbabwe. Thanks to painstaking research by archeologists, linguists and anthropologists, the ancient city of Great Zimbabwe, with its cyclopean buildings, is gradually yielding up the secrets of its past.

Whatever the fundamental causes behind the rise of Great Zimbabwe, there is no doubt that it is a most impressive monument. The site is dominated by the acropolis, a long, granite hill covered with enormous boulders. Successive generations of occupants linked the boulders together with stone walls, making small enclosures and narrow passages. The westernmost enclosure is the largest, enclosed by a thick, free-standing stone wall. It contains a long sequence of later Iron Age occupation that provides the basis for subdividing Great Zimbabwe's history into at least three stages.

The most intensive occupation began in about the 11th century; but no stone walls were built until the 13th century, when the small pole-and-mud huts of earlier times were replaced by more substantial mud houses.

The Great Enclosure with its massive free standing walls was built progressively during the following century. It was divided into a series of smaller enclosures, in which the foundations of substantial pole-and-mud houses are to be seen. It was presumably the dwelling place of the rulers of Great Zimbabwe, an impressive and politically highly significant structure.

Great Zimbabwe is a unique site only on account of its scale, for it is the largest of an estimated 150 ruins with between one and five enclosures, at least partially surrounded with free-standing walls and with mud-and-pole huts inside them, built near Zimbabwe and in Mashonaland. The regularly coursed masonry is in the Great Zimbabwe style. Those that have been excavated contain occasional gold objects, copper-wire bracelets, glass beads, and the fire pots and spindle whorls characteristic of the Great Zimbabwe culture.

At Nhunguza ruins there was a single, very large hut, divided into three rooms. One of the rooms was large enough

Great Zimbabwe ruins

to hold a large number of people, a second contained a single seat, a third was 'a completely secluded room that must have contained objects of special value including...what must have been a monolith set in a grooved stone platform'. This unusual structure may well have been the location where a prominent authority held sway.

One has a sense of an extremely strong and unquestioned political and religious authority whose hold over the scattered rural populations was based on some form of unifying faith in the powers of the divine *Mwari* or some other religious catalyst that reached out to every family.

The influence of Great Zimbabwe and its tributary settlements were felt far outside the immediate, relatively limited boundaries of the State itself. The prosperity of Kilwa on the East African coast was closely tied to the fluctuations in the gold trade with Sofala. Already in the 10th century, the Arab geographer al-Mas'udi was writing of Kilwa and the gold trade. Four centuries later Ibn Battuta described Kilwa as one of

Great Zimbabwe Ruins

LOCATION

Masvingo Province, 29km (18mi) south of Masvingo,
S 20° 17', E 30° 56'.

DESCRIPTION

This monument consists of two sites, the hill ruins and the valley
ruins. Both are groups of dry stone wall structures. The total area
covers 722ha (1,741ac) and also includes many Iron Age
artefacts. There is a museum on the site.

SIGNIFICANCE

These ruins date back to 1100AD and are the focus of a unique
culture. Known as the Zimbabwe Culture, this civilization flour-
ished for 350 years until 1450. It is thought that up to 10,000
people lived here. The adjoining article by Brian Fagan delves
deeply into this ancient mysterious civilization .

the most beautiful cities in the world, a town whose prosperity depended on the southern gold trade.

Without question the wealth of the rulers of Great Zimbabwe waxed and waned with the fortunes of the coastal trade. Kilwa itself went through commercial vicissitudes, reaching the height of its prosperity in the 15th century with the reconstruction of the famous Great Mosque. But a century later Kilwa, the east African coast and Great Zimbabwe itself had all declined. By the time the Portuguese arrived at Sofala the coastal trade was but a shadow of its former self.

In the 14th and 15th centuries, however, there was considerable trading activity in northern Mashonaland and the Zambezi valley, which is reflected in some remarkable archeological discoveries. Between the 12th and 14th centuries northern Mashonaland was occupied by the makers of Musengezi ware, subsistence farmers thought to be Shona speakers.

In the north-western corner of Mashonaland and the lower part of the middle Zambezi valley, large settlements and the working and trading of copper assumed great importance. The Chedzurgwe site in the fertile Urungwe district covered over 24ha (58ac) of fine grass land; abundant cattle and game bones testify to the importance of pastoralism and hunting. Copper was made into standardised ingots of two fixed weights; wire bracelets made from copper and tin alloy were commonplace. Textiles were also in use, and extremely fine pottery was made, with a finish and delicacy of decoration on shallow bowls and beakers that is almost unparalleled elsewhere.

BRIAN FAGAN of the UK, is Professor of Anthropology at the University of California, Santa Barbara, USA. An anthropologist and archeologist, he has published many studies on the Iron Age and Stone Age cultures in east and southern Africa.

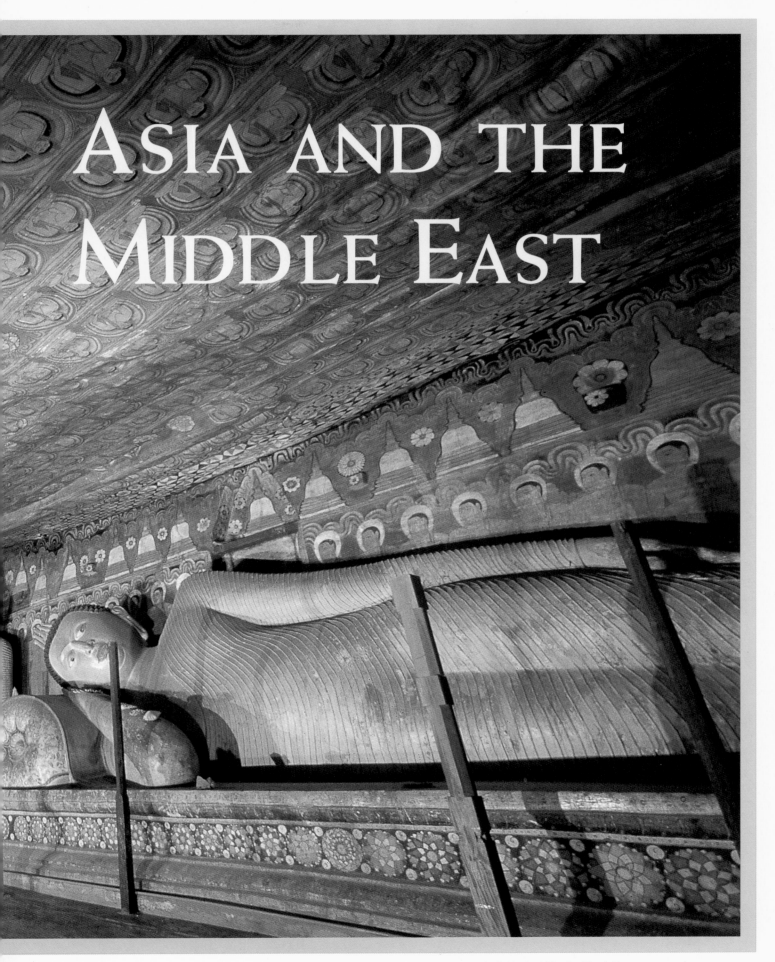

ASIA AND THE MIDDLE EAST

Main cave, the Golden Rock Temple of Dambulla

BANGLADESH

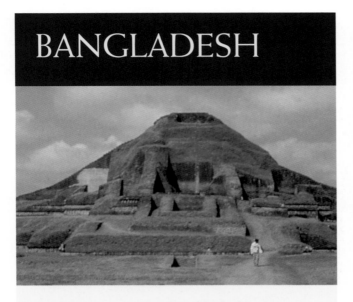

Ruins of the Buddhist Vihara at Paharpur

LOCATION

Paharpur, northeast corner of Naogaon sub division, N 25° 02', E 88° 59'.

DESCRIPTION

A very large brick monastery with outer walls, spreading over 9ha (22ac), now in ruins and partly underground. Over 60 stone sculptures are hidden underground, set into the base of the central shrine which rises to a height of about 20m (65.5ft).

SIGNIFICANCE

It is thought that this monastery, known as 'Somapura Mahavihara', dates from the end of the 8th century AD, when it was founded by Dharmapala, the second Pala monarch. Control of the monastery was wrested from the Palas roughly 101 years later by the Gurjara-Pratiharas. This lasted for another 100 years until the Palas gained control again. They ruled until the 12th century, when the Senas, who were Hindus, gained control. From this time, the monastery slowly declined until being abandoned. These ruins were discovered and recognised as important at the beginning of the 19th century and were placed on the list of protected monuments roughly 100 years later.

The Historic Mosque City of Bagerhat

LOCATION

Immediately east of Bagerhat in the District of Khulna.

DESCRIPTION

There are more than 50 monuments scattered over an area of 6.5sqkm (2.5sqmj). While there is a conservation program in place, at the moment most are in an advanced state of ruin and are overgrown with tropical vegetation. Eight mosques and one tomb complex have been clearly identified under this listing: 1. Shait Gumbad Mosque; 2. Singar Mosque; 3. Bibi Begni's Mosque; 4. Chunakhola Mosque; 5. Khan Jahan's tomb complex; 6. Nine-Domed Mosque; 7. Reza-Koda Mosque; 8. Zindapir Mosque; 9. Ranvijoypur Mosque.

SIGNIFICANCE

Having been the city responsible for minting coins of the independent sultans of Bengal, these ruins bear witness to the accumulated wealth of Bagerhat. The Shait Gumbad Mosque (shown above) in particular reflects this past glory - it is the largest brick construction temple in Bangladesh, and one of the most impressive in the region.

Peking Man Site at Zhoukoudian

LOCATION

Municipality of Beijing, N 39° 44', E 115° 55'.

DESCRIPTION

This has been the site of extensive archeological excavations since 1921. It comprises countless fossils, tools and ornaments, including fossil remains of Peking Man and Upper Cave Man. There is also a cave which was used as a dwelling.

SIGNIFICANCE

The first complete skull of Peking Man, who lived 700,000 to 200,000 years ago, was found at this site. Since then, six other complete skulls have been found, along with numerous fragments of bones and teeth, tools, ornaments and evidence of the use of fire. The site of Upper Cave Man, who lived 18,000 to 11,000 years ago, is nearby. A cemetery was unearthed in a dwelling cave on the site yielding some important bone fragments, including three complete skullcaps.

TOP Peking Man site
ABOVE RIGHT Some of the thousands of life-size terracotta figures at Ying Zheng's mausoleum

The Mausoleum of the First Qin Emperor

LOCATION

Lintong County, Shaanxi Province, N 34° 23', E 109° 06'.

DESCRIPTION

The grounds of the mausoleum are very large, the length of the outer rectangular wall being 6.3km (3.9mi). The buildings are mostly in ruins but many life-size terracotta warriors and horses have been found in a good state of preservation.

SIGNIFICANCE

This mausoleum, easily the largest in Chinese history, was constructed for the first Emperor of the Qin Dynasty, Ying Zheng, in the period 246BC to 208BC. The most remarkable feature of this site is the contents of three large pits that were unearthed just outside the mausoleum grounds in 1974. The first pit contained over 3,000 life-sized terracotta warriors, horses and chariots, all lined up in perfect order, the second and third pits contained a lesser number of similarly life sized soldiers. All of these figures are extremely lifelike and very well preserved.

The Great Wall

Unlike city walls that are built to enclose and protect a small area, China's Great Wall stretches for more than 5,000km (3,100mi) from east to west across the entire width of northern China. As the greatest construction project ever undertaken, not simply in China but in the entire world, the United Nations listed it in 1987 as one of the world's great heritage sites.

The first defensive walls to be built in China appeared in the State of Chu during the 7th century BC. At that time, China was divided into a number of states that were constantly at war with each other. The Chu walls are supposed to have stood at the juncture of present-day Hubei, Shaanxi and Henan provinces and had a total length of about 500 to 600km (310 to 370mi). Chu's example was followed by the states of Qi, Qin, Han, Zhao, Wei, Yan and Zhongshan, each of which erected their own walls.

In 221BC, Qin Shi Huang, the first emperor of the Qin Dynasty, unified China. To protect his empire from the harassment of northern nomadic tribes, he ordered that the walls built by Yan, Zhao and Qin be connected into one continuous wall fortified with watchtowers. Thus the first Great Wall was born, running at Gansu Province's Lintao in the west and ending in the Liaodong Peninsula in the east. During the following 1,800 years, the Great Wall was repeatedly repaired and expanded by more than 20 central and local regimes including the Han, Northern Wei, Northern Qi, Northern Zhou, Sui, Liao, Jin, Yuan and Ming.

The overall length of the Great Wall has risen and fallen with the changing political and military situations of different periods of Chinese history. Some sections built at different times run parallel to each other and occasionally meet and cross. The Great Wall of the Qin, Han, Jin and Ming dynasties exceeded 5,000km (3,100mi) in length, making it the longest in Chinese history. But the aggregate length of all the walls built down the centuries amounts to more than 50,000km (31,000mi). Remains of all these sections can still be found in Liaoning, Jilin, Heilongjiang, Beijing, Tianjin, Hebei, Shanxi, Inner Mongolia, Shaanxi, Ningxia, Gansu, Xinjiang, Qinghai, Hubei and Shandong. In Inner Mongolia alone there exist the remains of 15,000km (9,300mi) of walls constructed over several dynasties.

The construction of the Great Wall was a mammoth task demanding tremendous toil and technical knowledge from countless military strategists and builders. Extending through loess plateaus and desert plains, rising to mountain crests and ridges and descending into river basins, it was largely constructed across terrain already almost invulnerable to outside attack.

The materials used in its construction were all secured locally. Some sections were built of rammed earth. Others were built of giant flagstones, bricks or tamarish twigs and reed mixed with rocks. The construction workers employed to build the wall were principally troops stationed along it, conscripted laborers and prisoners banished to the frontier. According to one inscribed stone tablet found on the wall, each length of the wall was divided up into smaller sections, each of which was in turn assigned to a group of builders.

During the Ming Dynasty, the Great Wall was divided into nine sections guarded by eleven garrisons. A total of one million troops were stationed along the wall. Thousands of beacon towers stood along its length to serve as a means of communicating with Beijing by smoke during the day and with fire at night.

As a defensive work, the Great Wall played an important role in north China's political and economic development. It helped promote economic exchanges between northern and southern China in ancient times. Its western section, built during the Han Dynasty, also successfully guaranteed the safety of traffic along the Silk Road, China's trading link with the West 2,000 years ago.

During the last few centuries, the Great Wall has had little military significance. However, as one of the world's architectural wonders, it deserves to be preserved in as original shape as possible. The Chinese government has designated it for state protection and restored sections at Shanhaiguan, Jiumenkou, Huangyaguan, Jinshanling, Mutianyu, Badaling and Jiayuguan to their former glory, opening them to tourists from China and abroad.

In 1986, China set up the China Great Wall Society and engaged a number of experts to conduct research into the Great Wall. Great efforts have been made to survey and preserve this gigantic monument, and much valuable support and aid has been received from UNESCO and many friends from abroad for China's work in ensuring the continued existence of one of the world's great historic constructions.

LUO ZHEWEN
Vice President of China Great Wall Society

The Great Wall

LOCATION

Crosses many Provinces in northern and central areas,
N 26° to 48°, E 72° to 74° 04'.

DESCRIPTION

Built over a period of more than 2,000 years, the wall stretches out over more than 50,000km (31,000mi) in its entirety. It is in varying states of repair, much of it in ruins, the section built during the Ming Dynasty being in the best state of repair. Construction is generally of earth, stone and brick. The size varies, but it is typically 9m (30ft) high and several meters wide. Numerous towers were built along its length.

SIGNIFICANCE

The Great Wall is without doubt one of the greatest and most famous constructions of the ancient world. Construction began on several fronts sometime during the 7th century BC, when the great kingdoms of the day began erecting walls to protect themselves. During the period 221BC to 206BC, the Emperor Qin had created his Dynasty and began linking up some of the old walls and adding new sections in order to create one great wall. Throughout successive dynasties that followed, the wall was extended and repaired, most notably during the Ming Dynasty. The quality of work performed under Ming was quite astounding and consequently this 5,650km (3,511mi) section of the wall is remarkably well preserved and has been singled out for special protection. Taken as a whole, the Great Wall would have to be described as the greatest building project in human history.

Mogao Caves

LOCATION

At the eastern foot of Mt. Mingsha, Dunhuang County, Gansu Province,
N 40° 08', E 94° 49'.

DESCRIPTION

These caves are man made, having been dug into a 1.6km (1mi)
portion of the cliff at the eastern foot of Mt. Mingsha. There are
numerous caves, all varying in size. The largest is 40m (131ft)
high and 900sqm (10,000sqft) in area.

SIGNIFICANCE

The Mogao Caves hold the richest collection of Buddhist art in the
world. They house more than 2,400 painted sculptures and over
45,000sqm (500,000sqft) of richly colored wall murals. It is
believed that construction of the caves began around 366AD when
a Buddhist monk by the name of Yue Zhun started the first
diggings. The period 581AD to 1036AD saw the greatest activity
in construction when most of the larger caves were dug. By the
16th century they were largely deserted. The most important cave,
the Cave of Scriptures, was discovered in 1900. It contains over
45,000 documents and relics from Buddhist, Taoist, Confucian,
Manichaean and Parsiist Scriptures as well as numerous works of
art and important social documents.

Mount Huangshan

LOCATION

Near the city of Huangshan, Anhui Province, N 30° 10', E 118°
11'.

DESCRIPTION

The protected area itself is 154sqkm (59sqmi) in area, with a
peripheral buffer zone which covers 142sqkm (54sqmi). The
landscape is quite mountainous, with numerous peaks, the most
famous of which is the Lotus-Flower Peak at 1,864m (6,200ft)
above sea level. Large, unusually shaped rocks abound, many of
them resembling animals and mythical figures. The dominant
vegetation is the Huangshan Pine - a species endemic to the area.
The entire area forms the watershed of two major river systems - the
Changjiang and the Qiantangjiang. There are 36 gorges, from
which 36 fountainheads flow into 24 streams. Countless water
falls, deep pools, ponds and springs are to be found, including the
famous Huangshan Hot Spring.

SIGNIFICANCE

This area has been called a 'fairyland on earth': it abounds with
countless unique and wonderful sights. The 'four wonders of Mount
Huangshan', namely, the pines, the rocks, the hot springs and the
seas of cloud which encircle the peaks, form a harmonious whole; a
breathtaking scenic wonder. The great mystical quality to this
area's beauty has led to the development of an entire culture, the
Huangshan culture. Endless paintings, poems, carvings and stories
have been inspired by this, 'the first miraculous mountain on earth'.

ABOVE RIGHT Endemic Huangshan pines set against the distinctive rocks
of the mountain
ABOVE LEFT Tang Dynasty pavilion at the Mogao Caves

Mount Taishan

LOCATION

Central Shandong Province,
N 36° 11′ to 36° 31′, E 116° 50′ to 117° 06′.

DESCRIPTION

Mt. Taishan has 112 peaks, the main one being Jade Emperor's
Peak. There are also 48 caves, 98 cliffs, 102 brooks and many
pools, waterfalls and springs. In addition, there are many cultural
elements to this site, with 22 temples, 97 ruins, 819 stone tablets
and over 1,000 stone inscriptions.

SIGNIFICANCE

The cultural significance of this area complements perfectly the
awesome and majestic beauty of its many forests, peaks, waterfalls,
pools and streams. This mountain rises spectacularly from the
surrounding Shandong Plain and has been considered as a symbol
of heaven for over 3,000 years. For around 2,000 of those years
Mt. Taishan was the destination of the personal pilgrimages of the
Emperors. Ceremonies were held on the summit and each time
something new was left, so that now the mountain is a treasure
trove of ancient religious artefacts and monuments.

Imperial Palace of the Ming and Qing Dynasties

LOCATION

In the center of Beijing, N 39° 30′, E 116° 00′.

DESCRIPTION

The Imperial Palace occupies 150,000sqm (1,665,000sqft) and has
over 9,000 rooms. The entire compound stretches out over 720,000sqm
(7,992,000sqft) and is surrounded by a wall 3km (1.86mi) long and
8m (26ft) high. There are four watchtowers standing at each corner of
the wall and there is a 52m (170ft) wide moat surrounding it. Palace
construction is of timber.

SIGNIFICANCE

Formerly called the Forbidden City, construction on this palace started
in 1406AD and was completed in 1420. It is the largest complete
complex of buildings preserved in China and one of the most significant
preserved wooden structures in the world. The architectural style and
planning employed is distinctive and impressive. A network of
crosslinked primary and secondary enclosures presents an efficient use of
space while emphasizing the importance of the three Great Halls where
official functions and ceremonies were held.

ABOVE Mount Taishan
ABOVE LEFT Inside the imperial throne room

ABOVE *A peaceful valley in Wulingyuan*

*I have spread my
dreams under your
feet;
tread softly,
because you tread
on my dreams.*

WILLIAM BUTLER YEATS

Wulingyuan

LOCATION

*Lies in Wulingyuan District of the city of Dayong,
Hunan Province some 270km
(170mi) from the capital of Changsha,
N 29° 16' to 29° 24', E 110° 22' to 110° 41'.*

DESCRIPTION

*The site covers the entire drainage basin of the Suoxi
Brook and the headwaters of several other streams.
Between the peaks are numerous ravines and gorges,
many containing attractive streams, pools and waterfalls. There are a number of karst features (about
one-third of the site is limestone), notably some 40
caves which are concentrated on the banks of the
Suoxiyu River and the south-east side of Tianzi
Mountain. Many of the numerous brooks and
streams flow underground for long distances. The
vegetation varies with altitude, below 700m (2,300ft)
the community is predominantly evergreen broad-leaf,
between 700m and 950m, (2,300 to 3,000ft) there is
a mixed community of evergreen and deciduous
broad-leaved trees, while above 950m (3,000ft), there
is a community of deciduous broad-leaved trees,
bushes and herbs.*

SIGNIFICANCE

*The most notable feature, dominating about two-
thirds of the site, is the large number of quartzite
sandstone pillars and peaks, of which there are some
3,100, many over 200m (660ft) high. Spectacular
calcite deposits are a major feature of the numerous
caves in the area. Huanglong or Yellow Dragon
Cave is said to be one of the ten largest caves in
China; it is 11km (7mi) long, and includes a
waterfall 50m (165ft) high. There are two
spectacular natural bridges in the area: Xianrenqias
or 'Bridge of the Immortals' is 26m (85ft) long, 1.5 to
1.8m (5 to 6ft) wide, 1 to 2m (3.3 to 6.6ft) thick and
100m (330ft) above the gorge. Tianqiashengkong or
the 'Bridge Across the Sky' is much larger, being 40m
(132ft) long, 10m (33ft) wide and 15m (50ft) thick.
It lies 357m (1,180ft) above the valley floor and
may be the highest natural bridge in the world. 3,000
species of plant occur within the area, including some
600 species of woody plant. There are 116 species of
vertebrates, a number of which are globally
threatened with extinction: Chinese giant salamander,
dhole, Asiatic black bear clouded leopard, leopard
and Chinese water deer.*

Huanglong

LOCATION

Songpan County, north-west Sichuan Province, in the southern part of Min Shan Range, approximately 150km north-north-west of the provincial capital of Chengdu,
N 32° 37' to 32° 54', E 103° 37' to 104° 08'

DESCRIPTION

This 70,000ha (168,000ac) site lies in the southern part of the Min Shan, a rugged mountain range leading from the east of the Qinghai-Tibetan Plateau down to the Sichuan Basin. Above the tree-line there are extensive areas of precipitous mountain scenery, snow-covered for much of the year. The main tributaries leading into the upper waters of the Fujiang River, which has its source at the Snow Mountain Ridge, are found within this area. There are a number of low-temperature hot springs rising from deep groundwater. Huanglong lies close to the inter-section of four floral regions: eastern Asia, Himalaya, and the subtropical and tropical zones of the northern hemisphere. About 65.8% of the site is forest covered, with much of the remainder being above the tree-line.

ABOVE Huanglong -Yellow Dragon Gully
INSET Giant panda

SIGNIFICANCE

This rugged mountainous area is spectacularly scenic and includes several unusual geological features. Xuebaoding, or Snow Mountain Peak, is permanently snow-covered and bears the easternmost glacier in China. Of perhaps the greatest interest is the extensive calcite deposition that has taken place, notably along the 3.6km (2mi) Huanglonggou (Yellow Dragon Gully) where there are several extensive areas of travertine pools. Algae and bacteria proliferate in a number of these pools, giving a wide range of colors from orange and yellow to green and blue. Other karst features include long limestone shoals. Much of the landscape, notably around Huanglonggou, is important in local Tibetan religion, culture and folklore. The Xishen Pubu, or Body Washing Waterfall, is said to have healing properties for those who bathe in its waters, and is traditionally supposed to cure infertility. There are a number of plant species that are internationally threatened, including 16 species of rhododendron. Fauna diversity is high due to the site's location within four floral regions, its wide altitudinal range, and the extensive undisturbed forests. There are 59 mammals, 155 birds, five reptiles, five amphibians and two fish species. Mammals include such notable species as giant panda, Sichuan golden snub-nosed monkey, brown bear, Asiatic black bear, leopard, Pallas' cat, red dog or dhole, red panda, Szechwan takin, mainland serow, common goral, argali and three species of deer. Birds include five species of pheasant, notably Chinese monal pheasant and a number of waterfowl species.

Jiuzhaigou Valley

LOCATION

In Nanping County, Northern Sichuan Province in the southern part of the Min Shan Range, approximately 330km from the Provincial capital of Chengdu, N 32° 54' to 33° 19', E 103°46' to 104° 04'.

DESCRIPTION

The altitude of this 72,000ha (173,000ac) area ranges from 2,140m (7,000ft) to 4,558m (15,000ft). Earthquakes are not uncommon and have been a major influence on the landscape. There are many high altitude karst land forms which have been strongly influenced by glacial, hydrological and tectonic activity. The great majority of the park perimeter follows the mountainous watersheds of several rivers which are part of the Yangtze River system. On the higher mountain slopes, the soils are poorly developed.

SIGNIFICANCE

The best known features are the large number of lakes in the area; many are classic ribbon lakes, at the base of glacially formed valleys, which have been dammed naturally, for example behind rockfalls from avalanches. One of these lakes, Wolonghai or Dragon Lake, has a calcareous dyke running through it clearly visible below the water surface, which, in local folklore, has been compared to a dragon lying on the bottom. There are a number of large and spectacular waterfalls, including Xionguashai (Panda Lake) Fall which drops 78m (250ft) in three steps, and the Zhengzhutan (Pearl Shoal) Fall, which drops 28m (92ft) in a broad curtain of water, 310m (1000ft) wide. The flora diversity is very rich, virgin forests cover nearly 30,000ha (72,000ac) within the scenic area and there have been in excess of 500 plant species recorded. There is also a highly diverse and important range of fauna, with ten mammals, including notable species as giant panda, Sichuan golden snub-nosed monkey, red panda, Szechwan takin, mainland serow, common goral and Thorold's deer.

ABOVE Jiuzhaigou Valley
RIGHT Asiatic black bear

Elephanta Caves

LOCATION

*Elephanta Island, eastern side of Bombay Harbor,
E 72° 56', N 18° 57'.*

DESCRIPTION

*Seven man-made caves are found on this island. The most notable,
the Main or Great Cave, is 39m (128ft) from front to back. There
are many sculptures and carvings inside the caves.*

SIGNIFICANCE

*Originally called Gharapuri, the name became Elephanta after a
massive stone sculpture of an elephant was found by the Portuguese
standing at the southern end of the island. The Great Cave is the
last important monument to stone sculpture in western India. All
the caves are dedicated to Siva, one of the supreme Hindu gods.*

Ajanta Caves

LOCATION

*In the Maharashtra State, Aurangabad district,
N 20° 32', E 75° 45'.*

DESCRIPTION

*These two complexes of Buddhist cave temples have both been dug
in the side of a steep cliff and are connected by a pathway. The
ruins of an old staircase cut into the rock lead up from the
Wagoora River which flows below. Thirty structures were built in
the caves, five are Chaithyagriha (sanctuaries) and the remainder
are Sangharama (monasteries).*

SIGNIFICANCE

*These caves were carved in two distinct periods. The first period
was between 2nd century BC and 2nd century AD, the second
from 5th century AD to 7th century AD. The sanctuaries and
monasteries are remarkable for their attention to detail and for the
countless engravings, sculptures and paintings they contain.*

ABOVE One of thre many sculptures inside Elephanta Caves
ABOVE RIGHT A painting of Gurdharav, Ajanta Caves

The Abode of Gods

The 2,400km (1,500mi) expanse of the Himalaya is the abode of many sky touching peaks, beautiful valleys and lush green pastures. Nanda Devi group of mountains constitutes one of the prominent ranges of Himalaya. The area of national park (now a biosphere reserve) is in the form of an arch.

The crystal clear waters in the river channels and glacial lakes reflect the grandeur and scenic beauty of the surrounding snow clad peaks. The undulating pastures stretching over miles are laden with numerous beautiful Himalayan flowers. The reverence for these Himalayan uplands and its rich flora was a traditional conservation measure enshrined by the myths and beliefs of the local people. Violation of this tradition by humans was believed to earn the wrath of gods by way of being kidnapped or possessed by evil spirits. In 1974, an order was passed to fell a large number of trees in Dasholi block no. 7 near Reni Village which is on the periphery of the Nanda Devi Sanctuary. This move was resisted by the local people in March 1974 and this was called the Chipko Movement. Chipko brought a halt to deforestation not only in this area but also in the entire Rishi ganga and Alakanada valleys. Later the Uttar Pradesh Government formed a high level committee with Dr Virendra Kumar as the chairman. This committee confirmed the vulnerability of the region and gave scientific credibility to the Chipko Movement. The region was thus saved from deforestation. The women of this area came forward as leaders of this movement and clung to the trees contesting that the jungle was their mother and they would not allow it to be chopped by the timber contractors or State Forest Corporation.

The Rishi ganga Valley including the Nanda Devi region is a place of worship for the local people. Most of the mountain peaks are named after gods and goddesses. Nanda Devi is believed to be the presiding deity of this region and is revered as a part of every home. The Nanda Devi basin is called 'Dev sthanam' or the abode of gods. Every year people from the interior of Garhwal and Kumaon gather at a particular place to worship the goddess Nanda. The venue chosen is 900m (3000ft) up, and is located at such a site from where the Nanda Devi peak is clearly visible.

This festival is called Nandashtami and its date falls between 15th August and 15th September every year. This is the time when the lush Himalayan meadows are blooming with a myriad of flowers and human beings bow to the

grandeur and beauty of nature. The newly harvested fruits and flowers are offered to the goddess. The rarest flowers like Brahm kamal are brought in limited number from the higher altitudes and offered to the goddess with prayers. These wild flowers are never plucked by hand; if it becomes necessary to pluck them for medicinal purposes, they are plucked by the mouth, symbolising that the person plucking them is an animal and is ignorant.

The people used to go in this area barefoot. They were prohibited to call out loudly or to wear red and gaudy clothes in this region. This could be related to the sensitivity of this area, many wild animals found here are easily scared and disturbed by the faintest sound. Such precautions, therefore, were essential. Killing the animals and eating meat was prohibited here from mid-January to mid-February and July to August because this is the period of conception and gestation for the animals. All such beliefs acted as conservation rules and the region remained conserved until the middle of this century.

Nanda Devi National Park

LOCATION

Garhwal region of Uttar Pradesh,
E 79° 44' to 80° 02', N 30°16' to 30° 32'.

DESCRIPTION

Situated in the central Himalayas, the entire 630sqkm (156sqmi)
of this park is part of an enormous glacial basin which, with the
exception of Rishi Gorge, is all over 3,500m (11,483ft) in altitude.
The peak of Nanda Devi, which is on the southern rim of the park,
is India's second highest mountain at 7,816m (26,000ft).

SIGNIFICANCE

Wild and largely inaccessible, this area's history is almost totally
devoid of human interference . Strong winds (except in the gorge
which is very sheltered), daily drizzle and regular heavy snowfall
have created a unique climate and hence a distinctive flora and
fauna. Notable amongst the fauna are the musk deer, leopard,
Himalayan black bear and the snow partridge. Flora ranges from
grasslands in the higher areas to forests of birch and conifers in the
gorge.

LEFT Snow leopard cub

The inhabitants of this area have a natural right to these forests, pastures and meadows which were legalised by the State. The cultivation rights were so distributed that there was no place for conflict. Extreme care was taken in dividing the land for cultivation purposes and for the pastures. A very good example of this awareness were two small parks in Rudranath mountains which were very carefully maintained by the local people. These parks, though, were of small size, yet their maintenance through traditional belief system of the local inhabitants was highly conservation oriented. Unfortunately, when the state administration took over these parks and the forest authorities opened them for grazing, they were destroyed in no time. The same can be said about poachers hunting the wild animals. There are many examples when local villagers have helped the state authorities to arrest these poachers.

We believe that merely enacting laws and using force cannot prove successful in conservation. The local people should be taken into confidence and their traditional beliefs

and myths should be re-evaluated scientifically and included in present conservation measures. The villagers who are adversely affected by the conservation plan should be given alternatives which acknowledge that people of this region have played a vital role in conserving nature. It is due to their efforts there now exists a balance between the plant and animal population in this region. If there is any problem it is because of external influences and the difficulty in preventing trespassing.

The reverence and faith of the people in the Himalaya as a symbol of their cultural heritage and an integral part of Indian tradition should be respected and added to the World Conservation Strategy. The local inhabitants and their belief in the sacredness of nature should be made part and parcel of the conservation program.

CHANDI PRASAD BHATT, Chipko Movement
(Translated from Hindi by Rachna Pandit)

Brihadisvara Temple at Thanjavur

LOCATION
Thanjavur District, Tamil Nadu, E 79° 05′, N 10° 45′.

DESCRIPTION
Comprising the principal temple, which is located in the center of a large open courtyard surrounded by a number of smaller shrines, the whole complex has been enclosed by inner double storeyed walls. This is then enclosed by another set of outer walls. The inner and outer complex is again enclosed by a vast brick fortification with a moat, occupying an area of 15ha (35ac).

SIGNIFICANCE
Built by the Emperor Raja Raja who ruled between 985 and 1012 AD, this represents the highest form of temple architecture in southern India. It is laid out on a massive scale and is embellished with many important paintings and sculptures.

*ABOVE The highly decorated ceilings of Brihadisvara Temple
BELOW One of the ancient stupas at Sanchi*

Buddhist Monuments at Sanchi

LOCATION
Madhya Pradesh, E 77° 45′, N 23° 29′.

DESCRIPTION
These monuments consist of several 'stupas' (domed Buddhist shrines), monolithic pillars and temples. They are all situated on a small hill, around 91m (300ft) high, just outside the village of Sanchi.

SIGNIFICANCE
The first monuments were erected during the reign of Asaka, between 272 to 237BC. Construction continued over the years up until the 12th century AD. The later monuments show a distinctive Hindu influence in style.

Ellora Caves

LOCATION

Near the village of Verul Khulatabad Taluka, State of Maharashtra,
N 20° 01', E 75° 11'.

DESCRIPTION

There is a total of 34 caves in three groups, each group the work of a different religious sect: (i) the Buddhist group has 12 caves, including an immense and ornate sanctuary with a magnificent statue of Buddha and a stupa. The remaining caves are monasteries; (ii) the Brahman group has 17 caves and includes an elaborate two-storey cavern with remarkable wall reliefs, as well as a massive temple 82m (270ft) long, by 46m (142ft) wide by 32m (106ft) high; (iii) the last group of five was built by the Jainists and includes some of the most remarkable frescoes to be found in India.

SIGNIFICANCE

These magnificent caves represent one of the most impressive collections of religious architecture and artwork in India. The Buddhist caves are the oldest, dating back to the period between the 5th and 7th centuries AD, the Brahman caves were excavated between the 7th and the 10th centuries, while the Jainist caves go back to the period from the 10th to 13th centuries.

The Sun Temple at Konarak

LOCATION

Puri district of Orissa, E 86° 06', N 19° 54'.

DESCRIPTION

Now in ruins, this temple was originally designed in the form of the chariot of the Sun God. It had a tower almost 60m (200ft) high and a massive porch covered with many carvings and sculptures of lions, elephants, human figures and floral decorations.

SIGNIFICANCE

Constructed during the 13th century, this temple was dedicated to the Sun God. It has been described as 'the most richly ornamented building in the whole world.'

RIGHT Manas Wildlife Sanctuary
INSET Wreathed hornbill

How are we going to be non-violent to nature unless the principle of non-violence becomes central to the ethos of human culture?

MAHATMA GANDHI

Manas Wildlife Sanctuary

LOCATION

In the districts of Barpeta and Kokrajhar, 41km north of Barpeta Road township, N 26° 37' to 26° 50', E 90° 45' to 91° 15'.

DESCRIPTION

This sanctuary occupies a 39,100ha (94,000ac) core area of the Manas Tiger Reserve. It lies in the foothills of the Outer Himalaya and is low-lying and flat. The Manas River flows through the western portion, where it splits into three separate rivers, and joins the Brahmaputra River further south. These and other rivers running through the tiger reserve carry an enormous amount of silt and rock debris from the foothills, which has led to the formation of extensive alluvial terraces. Deep layers of boulders and sandy soil are characteristic of the region. The vegetation is comprised of various types of moist forest, with extensive alluvial grasslands in the west which cover about 50% of the sanctuary.

SIGNIFICANCE

Manas is noted for its spectacular scenery, with a variety of habitat types that support a diverse fauna, making it the richest of all Indian wildlife areas. The sanctuary represents the core of an extensive tiger reserve that protects an important migratory wildlife resource along the West Bengal to Arunachal Pradesh and Bhutan borders. Its wetlands are of international importance and it is also the single most important site for the future survival of the pygmy hog and hispid hare. A total of 55 mammals, 36 reptiles and three amphibians has been recorded. Mammals include golden langur, capped langur, Hoolock gibbon, clouded leopard, tiger (the second largest population in India with 123 recorded in 1984), leopard, golden cat, fishing cat, leopard cat, marbled cat, binturong, sloth bear, wild dog, Ganges dolphin, Indian elephant (with up to 2,000 in the tiger reserve and more than 1,000 moving freely between Indian and Bhutan Manas reserves), Indian rhinoceros, pygmy hog, swamp deer, sambar, hog deer, Indian muntjac, water buffalo (probably representing the only pure strain of this species in India), gaur, giant squirrel, hispid hare and Indian pangolin. Over 300 species of birds have been recorded including the threatened Bengal florican, great pied hornbill, wreathed hornbill and other hornbills.

Taj Mahal

LOCATION

Just outside Agra, N 27° 10', E 78° 02'.

DESCRIPTION

This mausoleum stands on a marble plinth, roughly 100m (330ft) on each side and 7m (22ft) high. It is square in plan with chamfered corners and a large arch on each side. A massive double dome sits on top of a pinnacle that reaches almost 80m (260ft) above the ground. Four minarets stand at each corner of the plinth. The building was decoratively and skilfully completed with colorful, individual flower-petal motifs cut from marble and inlaid in the interior and exterior.

SIGNIFICANCE

Construction began in 1632 upon the decree of Mogul Emperor Shah Jahan in memory of his wife. According to inscriptions, it was built by a Turk to the design of an architect from Lahore. 'Taj Mahal' is a corruption of 'Mumtaz-i-Mahal' which means 'chosen one of the palace' The building itself was completed by 1643, using 20,000 workers each day. The entire complex took another 11 years to complete. The Taj Mahal is without dispute one of the most beautiful and impressive buildings in the world today.

Churches and Convents of Goa

LOCATION

Goa, E 73° 50', N 15° 33'.

DESCRIPTION

There are seven churches at Goa, all the product of different religious orders. All are similar in plan, so far as the various components like the belfry, altars, choir and sacristy are concerned. The Church of St. Cajetan is modelled on the original design of St. Peter's Church in Rome . The Church of Bom Jesus with its facade, decorated with Ionic, Doric and Corinthian pilasters, shows the application of the classical order. All churches were built of locally available red shale and coated with lime to protect them from weathering.

SIGNIFICANCE

Many of these churches built between the 15th and 17th centuries were inspired by Roman churches which had a touch of the Renaissance with baroque interiors. The result in Goa was an interesting blend of styles with numerous unique features.

Hampi Monuments

LOCATION

Karnataka, E 76° 30', N 15° 02'.

DESCRIPTION

There are several temple complexes, all products of different times and different kings. The temples contain shrines with ornate carvings and fine bas-reliefs. There is a fortified citadel, which encloses many non-religious buildings, like the queen's bath, the king's palace enclosure, the Lotus Mahal, the mint, the Sandanayakh enclosure, a water pavilion and the elephant's stable.

SIGNIFICANCE

Construction of the temples and citadel took place between 1377 and 1576AD. This was the time of the reign of the Vijayanagar Dynasty who were great defenders of the Hindu faith and its rich culture. The result was a unique art and architecture that attained new heights of splendor.

Mahabalipuram Monuments

LOCATION

Tamil Nadu State, E 80° 10', N 12° 35'.

DESCRIPTION

There are four features to this listing: the monoliths carved out of solid granite rock, caves cut into the hills used as temples, bas-reliefs or sculptured scenes carved into rock faces and the structural temples.

SIGNIFICANCE

These monuments date from the period 630-800AD and were built under the patronage of the great Pallava rulers. Many of them contain valuable inscriptions and carvings, revealing a wealth of information about these grand civilizations.

ABOVE *Achyuta-raya Temple, Hamp Monument*

ABOVE *This stone embankment was erected in 1984 to protect the monuments at Mahabalipuram*

Kaziranga National Park

LOCATION

Situated in Nagaon and Golaghat districts on the southern bank of the Brahmaputra River at the foot of the Mikir Hills, 8km from Bokakhat,

N 26° 30' to 26° 45', E 93° 05' to 93° 40'.

DESCRIPTION

Kaziranga lies in the alluvial flood plains of the Brahmaputra River. Its habitat is predominately riverine, consisting primarily of tall, dense grasslands interspersed with open forests, interconnecting streams and numerous small lakes or 'bheels'. Much of the area is submerged annually by the flood waters of the Brahmaputra. The rich soils have been built up by alluvial deposits from the Brahmaputra and its tributaries. Grasslands predominate, especially in the west, with tropical wet evergreen forests and tropical semi-evergreen forests covering about a third of the park.

SIGNIFICANCE

Kaziranga is renowned as one of the finest and most picturesque wildlife refuges in southern Asia. It protects the world's largest population of Indian rhinoceros, which has increased from a few dozen in 1908 to some 1,080 in 1984, and 1,100 in 1988. It also contains about 15 species of India's threatened mammals. Other mammals include capped langur, a small population of hoolock gibbon, tiger, leopard, sloth bear, Indian elephant, Ganges dolphin, otter, wild boar, water buffalo, gaur, sambar, swamp deer, hog deer and Indian muntjac. The numerous water bodies are rich reservoirs of food and thousands of migratory birds, representing over 100 species, visit the park seasonally from as far afield as Siberia. The avifauna in total comprises over 300 species. There is a grey pelican rookery near Kaziranga Village. Other birds of interest include black-necked stork, lesser adjutant stork, Pallas's fish eagle, grey-headed fish eagle, Bengal florican, swamp partridge, grey peacock-pheasant, great pied hornbill, green imperial pigeon, silver-breasted broadbill and Jerdon's bushchat.

Khajuraho Monuments

LOCATION

Madhya Prabesh, E 79° 56', N 24° 51'.

DESCRIPTION

This listing comprises three groups of temples. All have an entrance porch, vestibule and sanctuary. They are erected on a lofty platform terrace with a high basement-storey which supports the walls of the temple with balconied windows. The roof consists of a series of graded peaks resembling a mountain range. The temples also contain erotic sculptures which reveal the aesthetic as well as the sexual charms of the body.

SIGNIFICANCE

These grand and powerful temples were constructed between the 9th and 12th centuries. They are outstanding examples of Hindu temple architecture.

ABOVE LEFT Indian elephant

Keoladeo National Park

LOCATION

Situated in eastern Rajasthan, 2km south-east of Bharatpur and 50km west of Agra,
N 27° 07' to 27° 12', E 77° 29' to 77° 33'.

DESCRIPTION

This 2,873ha (7,000ac) area comprises flat marshland situated in the Gangetic plain, artificially created in the 1850s and maintained ever since by a system of canals, sluices and dykes. Water is usually fed into the marshes twice a year from Ajan Bund dam which is south of the park. The area is flooded to a depth of 1-2m (3.3-6.6ft) throughout the monsoon (July-September), after which the water level drops. From February onwards the land begins to dry out and by June only some water remains. For much of the year the actual area of wetland is only 1,000ha (2,400ac). In a semi-arid zone, the park is the only area with much vegetation. The principal vegetation types are tropical dry deciduous forest, intermixed with dry grassland in areas where forest has been degraded. Apart from the artificially managed marshes, much of the area is covered by medium-sized trees and shrubs.

SIGNIFICANCE

This is one of the world's finest areas for birds. Some 364 species of bird have been recorded in the park, with a unique assemblage of species. It is the major wintering ground of the western population of Siberian crane. The park's location in the Gangetic Plain makes it an unrivalled breeding site for herons, storks and cormorants and an important wintering ground for large numbers of migrant ducks. The most common waterfowl are gadwall , shoveler , common teal , cotton teal , tufted duck , comb duck , little cormorant , great cormorant, Indian shag, ruff, painted stork, white spoonbill, Asian open-billed stork , oriental ibis, darter, common sandpiper, wood sandpiper and green sandpiper. There is a rich assortment of land birds including warblers, babblers, bee-eaters, bulbuls, buntings, chats, partridges and quails. There are also many birds of prey including the osprey, peregrine, Pallas' fish eagle, short-toed eagle, tawny eagle, imperial eagle, spotted eagle and crested serpent eagle. Mammals include rhesus macaque and langur, Bengal fox, jackal, striped hyena, common palm civeth, small Indian civet, Indian grey mongoose, fishing cat, leopard cat, jungle cat and smooth-coated otter.

ABOVE Keoladeo's rich birdlife includes storks and tufted ducks (INSET)

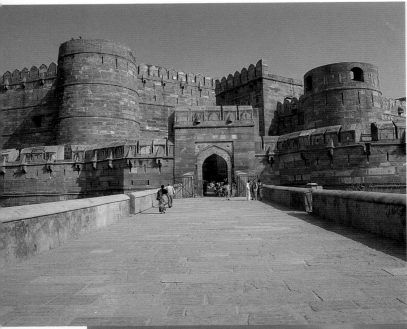

Agra Fort

LOCATION

In the Agra district, N 27° 10', E 78° 02'.

DESCRIPTION

Situated on the west bank of the Yamuna River, this fort is surrounded by 20m (66ft) high sandstone walls that are 2.5km (1.5mi) in circumference. Within the walls are several important buildings, including the Pearl Mosque built by Shah Jahan during the period 1648 to 1655AD and the Jahangiri Mahal built around 1570AD by Emperor Akbar.

SIGNIFICANCE

The Fort was constructed during the period 1564 to 1575 under the reign of the Emperor Akbar. Some of the buildings within were constructed later under the reign of Shah Jahan (1637 to 1655). Many of these buildings have great architectural significance, with the blending of Mogul and Hindu styles and the use of marble and other stone to spectacular effect.

Pattadakal Monuments

LOCATION

Badami Taluk, E 76° 00', N 16° 00'.

DESCRIPTION

The oldest temple here is a massive structure but very simple in design. There is no antechamber and the pillars are plain. Visupaksha is the largest and most important Sravida style temple of the Chalukyan period.

SIGNIFICANCE

Pattadakal was not only popular for Chalukyan architectural activities but also a holy place for royal coronations. Temples constructed here mark developmental stages and the culmination of the Chalukyan style of architecture.

OPPOSITE PAGE *A young male tiger*

Sundarbans National Park

LOCATION
Lies south-east of Calcutta in the 24-Paraganas District of West Bengal and forms part of the Gangetic Delta,
N 21° 31′ to 21° 53′, E 88° 37′ to 89° 09′

DESCRIPTION
The whole Sundarbans area covers some 10,000sqkm (3,900sqmi) of mangrove forest and water (of which some 40% is in India and the rest in Bangladesh), and is part of the world's largest delta formed from sediments deposited by three great rivers, the Ganges, Brahmaputra and Meghna, which converge on the Bengal Basin. The World Heritage site covers 133,010ha (320,000ac). About half of the Sundarbans is under water and the rest of the landscape is characterised by low-lying alluvial islands and mudbanks, with sandy beaches and dunes along the coast. As with the rest of the Bengal Plain, alluvial deposits are geologically very recent and deep, sediment of just the last few million years being as much as 1,000m (3,300ft) thick.

SIGNIFICANCE
This entire mangrove forest is called Sundarban owing to the dominance of the tree species Heritiera fomes, locally known as 'sundari' because of its elegance. The marsh vegetation in this area is found almost nowhere else. The Sundarbans is the only remaining habitat in the lower Bengal Basin for a great variety of faunal species. The tiger population, estimated at 264 in 1983, is the largest in India. The fishing cat abounds, while the only ungulates are wild boar and spotted deer. Aquatic mammals that frequent the tidal waters include the Ganges dolphin, Indo-Pacific hump-backed dolphin, Irrawaddy dolphin and finless porpoise. There is a wealth of water birds, noteworthy residents including Asian openbill stork, black-necked stork, greater adjutant stork, white ibis, swamp francolin, white-collared kingfisher, black-capped kingfisher and brown-winged kingfisher. This area is important for waders, including the Asian dowitcher, a rare winter migrant. The Sundarbans provide important habitat for a variety of reptiles including river terrapin, olive ridley, estuarine crocodile, monitor lizard, water monitor and Indian python . Baghmara Forest Block contains the ruins of a city built by the Chaand Sandagar merchant community approximately 200-300AD. Much later, during the Moghul Empire, Raja Basand Rai and his nephew took refuge in the Sundarbans from the advancing armies of Emperor Akbar. The buildings which they erected subsequently fell to Portuguese pirates, salt smugglers and dacoits in the 17th century. The ruins are evident at Netidhopani and elsewhere.

Humayun's Tomb

LOCATION

Delhi, approximately N 28° 38', E 77° 18'.

DESCRIPTION

The Tomb of Humayan lies in the middle of a splendid garden with a network of pools and channels. The tomb is an irregular octagon, resting on a terraced platform which has small arched cells along its sides. It is crowned by a 42.5m (140ft) marble clad double dome. The center of each side is deeply recessed with large arched vaults. The interior follows the shape of the exterior, with octagonal plans on both floors, and vaulted roof compartments which are connected by galleries and corridors. The structure is of dressed stone, clad in red sandstone with inlaid white and black marble borders.

SIGNIFICANCE

Knowledge of the Islamic garden tomb was brought to India from Persia and central Asia by Humayun and put into practice by the work of his wife and the architect Mirak Mirza Ghiyath. This tomb, commissioned by Humayan's widow in 1569-70, was the first of the Mughal garden tombs, a distinctive symbol of the powerful dynasty which unified much of the sub-continent. It is the burial place of many members of the ruling family and as such is of great historical significance. Construction of the tomb introduced many important architectural innovations which eventually led to the style that culminated in the Taj Mahal.

Fatehpur Sikri

LOCATION

*Uttar Pradesh,
N 27° 05', E 77° 40'.*

DESCRIPTION

The ancient city site is 9.5km (5.9mi) in circumference and is surrounded on three sides by a high wall about 6km (3.7mi) long. There are nine gates and an artificial lake on the northwest side. The city, originally rectangular in plan with a grid pattern of roads and lanes intersecting at right angles, contained a well defined administrative block, royal palaces and the Jami Mosque at the center.

SIGNIFICANCE

This famous deserted city with its impressive red sandstone buildings represents the most spectacular building activities of the rule of Akbar. The Jami Mosque is not only the largest and the most impressive of the whole group of the city monuments, but one of the largest and finest mosques in India.

RIGHT The distinctive red sandstone of Fatehpur Sikri

ABOVE *The minaret and gateway*

Qutb Minar and its Monuments

LOCATION

Dehli, approximately
N 28° 38', E 77° 18'.

DESCRIPTION

This complex includes two mosques, several tombs, an iron pillar, a minaret, and the base of another minaret. The Qutb Minar is the highest stone tower in India. This minaret is constructed of red and buff sandstone, and it towers 72.5m (240ft) above the ground. The diameter of the tower at its base is 14.32m (47ft), tapering up to 2.75m (9ft) at the top. Its five stories are each separated by ornate balconies which are decorated with numerous inscriptions, and the external surfaces of the first three stories are heavily fluted. The Alai Minar is the base of a minaret which was never completed. The Quwwatu'l - Islam (Might of Islam) mosque consists of a courtyard, prayer hall and cloisters. A particularly intriguing monument included in the complex is a 7m (23ft) iron pillar which bears a 4th century Sanskrit inscription.

SIGNIFICANCE

The Quwwatu'l - Islam mosque is the oldest mosque in India. It was built from the remains of demolished Hindu temples and so has historical significance regarding the conversion of many Indians from the Hindu to the Moslem faith. The entire complex is an impressive example of early Indian Islamic art and architecture. The Hindi iron pillar has a value all of its own, bearing testimony to the metallurgical skills of the ancient Indians. Without doubt, though, it is the Qutb Minar which is the most unique item in this ensemble - a beautifully preserved, architecturally eloquent monument to early Islamic India.

Meidam Emam, Esfahan

LOCATION

Within the city of Esfahan, central Iran, N 32° 31', E 51° 39'.

DESCRIPTION

This listing comprises a plaza, 500m (1,640ft) by 160m (525ft), which is surrounded by a two storey facade. The ground floor forms a covered bazaar. There are two mosques, a palace and a large decorated portico within the precincts of the square.

SIGNIFICANCE

During the winter of 1597-1598 Shah Abbas I, the Safavid, moved his capital from Qazvin to Esfahan. The plaza was built in 1612. This, and the construction of the mosques, palace and portico, so embellished the city that it became known as 'Nesfe Jahan' or 'Half of the World'. The plaza itself was named 'Naqsh e Jahan' or 'Image of the World'.

ABOVE One of the two magnificent mosques at Esfahan

Tchogha Zanbil

LOCATION

Khuzestan, E 48° 32', N 32° 01'.

DESCRIPTION

This complex is composed of three concentric mudbrick walls inside which are arranged palaces and temples, with a 'ziggurat' (a pyramidal tower) occupying the central location. The various temples and palaces are all connected by paths paved with bricks.

SIGNIFICANCE

This site was founded in the middle of the 13th century BC by King Untash Napirisha. The complex was, at that stage, foreseen as the new religious center of the Elamite empire, but it was never finished and was abandoned after the death of the king. The site was destroyed by the Assyrians in 640BC. The ziggurat is the largest of its type conserved today.

ABOVE Head of a priest, Tchogha Zanbil

Persepolis

LOCATION

Fars, E 52° 54', N 29° 56'.

DESCRIPTION

The Persepolis complex comprises a terrace built of huge stone blocks. On this terrace several palaces and buildings have been erected. There are 14 main buildings, essentially built of mudbrick. There are some sections of fortified wall remaining around the terraces. Near the site are three rock graves attributed to Artaxerxes II and III, and Darius III, all great Archaemenian Kings.

SIGNIFICANCE

When Darius III ordered a new city to be built, he envisioned it to be a spiritual center of the Empire. The work started around 518BC, continuing under various rulers until 428BC. The site, essentially used for great festivals of the Iranian New Year, was destroyed by the Greeks of Alexander in 330BC when it was burnt to the ground. Some inscriptions authored by Darius, a follower of Zarathustra - the founder of the ancient Iranian religion - still survive. One of them reads: 'I wish to think of justice as long as I can.'

Hatra

LOCATION

110km (68m) southwest of Mosul, N 35° 34', E 42° 42'.

DESCRIPTION

This ancient, fortified city lies in ruins. It occupies an area of about 320ha (772ac). There is an outer clay wall surrounding the town which is surrounded by a 20m (66ft) wide moat. Access is gained by four large gates. There are numerous temples and other buildings inside the walls, with attention focused on a large main temple which stands in the center.

SIGNIFICANCE

From around the 3rd century BC until the 3rd century AD, Hatra was the religious and commercial center for a large area situated between the Tigris and Euphrates Rivers, known as 'Arabaya'. During the 2nd century AD the town became the capital of the first Arabic Royal Dynasty and was the home to the god Shamash. Left in ruins after the great war between the Sassanians and the Romans during the 3rd century AD, Hatra never recovered. Excavations were instigated by the Iraqi Director of Antiquities in 1951.

Right Inside the main temple at Hatra

JERUSALEM

Of enormous importance to the world's three great monotheistic faiths, the history of Jerusalem goes back to the Old Stone Age. By 1400BC, 'Urusalim' (meaning either 'the foundation of the [God] Shalem' or else derived from Sumerian, meaning 'city of peace') had developed into an important fortress under the Egyptians, controlling the surrounding desert, and protecting important trading routes.

It was conquered by King David in 1000BC who made it the capital of the unified tribes and took the Ark of the covenant there, thus establishing it as an important religious center. Under King Solomon, the city developed into an important trading center. In 597BC and 586BC, King Nebuchadnezzar II of Babylon sacked the city, the second time destroying the Temple of Solomon.

After a period of Persian domination the city fell under the control of the Egyptian Macedonian dynasty, the Ptolemies, and then the Seleucids from Syria. The Hasmonaean dynasty re-established Jerusalem as a leading center for Jews from 164 to 64BC, when Pompey entered the city.

Perhaps the most famous period was during the reign of Herod the Great. He gained power in 37BC and proceeded to make profound changes architecturally, culturally and politically. Turning to Rome for assistance, he set about turning Jerusalem into a 'city of marble'. Jesus Christ lived under Herod's rule and was crucified in Jerusalem four years after Herod's death.

After his crucifixion, the Romans destroyed much of the Jewish built city. Following the Jewish war of Freedom in 132AD, the Jews were defeated and Jerusalem was completely levelled. A new city was built, named Aelia Capitolina, and many temples were erected to Roman gods.

Two centuries of 'darkness' followed: then, in 326AD, Constantine ordered the sites of Christ's crucifixion and burial to be recovered. One of them, the Church of the Holy Sepulchre, was built on the site where today a more recent church of the same name is found.

This church, along with many others, was destroyed in 614AD when Chosroes II of Persia captured the city. The Romans recaptured Jerusalem in 629 but were ousted eight years later by Omar. Islamic rule continued for the next 462

years until the Crusaders entered to reclaim the Holy City. It was reconquered by the Moslems yet again 88 years later under Saladin, and remained mostly under Islamic control until 1917, when it was captured by Lord Allenby.

Jerusalem then became the capital of the British mandated territory of Palestine. After the Second World War, the city was divided: the 'old city' passed into the hands of Jordan, while the 'new city' became part of the newly created state of Israel.

During the Six Day War of 1967, Israel occupied the old city. It has remained under Israeli control ever since. Jerusalem was nominated for inclusion on the World Heritage List by Jordan in 1981.

Jerusalem (Old City and its Walls)

LOCATION

N 31° 47', E 35° 13'.

DESCRIPTION

Two hundred and twenty monuments are listed within the old city. The most important area is Haram, where the Mount of the Temple is situated. This is a large quadrangle which has been used by the three great monotheistic religions: Christianity, Islam and Judaism. Other important monuments are the Dome of the Rock, the Church of the Holy Sepulchre and the Wailing Wall.

SIGNIFICANCE

Jerusalem is unique in being a Holy City for three major religions. It has had a great and varied history which dates back to the Stone Age. The most famous period is without doubt during the lifetime of Jesus Christ. Numerous places in the city are traditionally connected with Jesus, the most notable being the Church of the Holy Sepulchre, reputed to have been built on the site of the Crucifixion. Via Dolorosa is considered to be the route on which he bore his cross and the Grotto of Gesthemane is thought to be the cave where he was when he was betrayed by Judas. Mohammed also visited Jerusalem, the Dome of the Rock being the place where it is said his night journey to Heaven began.

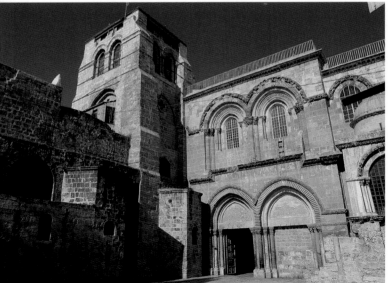

TOP LEFT The Dome of the Rock with the Wailing Wall in the foreground
BOTTOM LEFT Church of the Holy Sepulchre

JORDAN

Jordan's World Heritage sites of Petra and Quseir Amra are dramatic, often awe inspiring examples of the engineering and aesthetic skills developed by the inhabitants of this land. Both are enduring testaments to a sophisticated urbanism which developed and matured in our Arab region on the strength of powerful trans-national cultural interaction with other great civilizations around the Mediterranean basin.

Petra, the older of the two listings, emerged by the 3rd century BC as the capital of the kingdom of the Nabateans - a formerly nomadic Arab people from northern Arabia who, from their heartland in southern Jordan, controlled a pivotal junction along the spice and incense routes for nearly half a millennium. Secured by a double ring of natural fortifications comprising mountains and desert expanses, Petra developed as a spectacularly beautiful city of mostly rock-cut tombs, theaters, temples, funerary banqueting halls, water works and religious high places. To wander through Petra is to step back 2,000 years in time, to a world defined by powerful architectural, aesthetic and religious impulses from the civilizations of ancient Arabia, Egypt, Greece, Rome, the Old Testament kingdoms, and early Christianity. Over 800 individual monuments and structures have survived to this day, largely intact within a natural landscape of chocolate, salmon and cinnamon-colored cliffs and dales - always enchanting visitors from the four corners of the earth with their stunning example of harmony between the glory of God and hand of man. There are only a few very special places in the world which people spend the first part of their lifetime hoping to visit - and, once visited, the rest of their lifetime hoping to return to. Petra is one of them.

Quseir Amra represents a more recent stage in Jordan's history. This 8th century bathing complex provides a fascinating glimpse into our country's diverse cultural heritage; a heritage which conveys a powerful sense of a successful urban tradition through the ages.

It was a message of a human culture which endured and matured because it responded to human needs and lived according to principles which are still relevant to us in modern Jordan.

The most important of those principles was that of human interchange - of free movement, commercial trade, political contacts, technological synthesis and cultural interaction amongst different cultures and nations. The results of such interaction are easily visible at Quseir Amra and Petra in architecture, art, technology, ceramics, political organization and economic activity. Both of these ancient cities prospered for centuries because they were pivotal junctions along international trade routes, linking cultures and people from China and Indonesia in the East to the British Isles and North Africa in the West.

Though Quseir Amra and Petra are physically located in the land of Jordan, we view them as part of the cultural patrimony and aesthetic legacy of all humankind. They constantly remind us that in order to achieve our aspirations for peace, dignity and coexistence among all people today and in the future, we should honor the timeless lesson of the past: that genuine and lasting peace emanates most consistently from constructive interaction among peoples and nations who enjoy stability, liberty and justice. This is the deeper, moral human lesson which we perceive behind the impressive physical monuments of the World Heritage List. It is the legacy of our land, the hope of our children, and the patrimony of all humankind which it is our privilege to preserve in trust for the entire world.

HER MAJESTY QUEEN NOOR OF JORDAN

Petra

LOCATION

District of Ma'an, Jordan, E 35° 26', N 30° 19'.

DESCRIPTION

The site of the ancient city of Petra is one of the most striking on Earth. Its haunting natural setting of hills and canyons was transformed by early inhabitants into something absolutely unique: a city carved out of stone. The area is the center of intense activity with excavations and restorations being continually carried out. The many buildings and monuments include: a theater, a temple adorned with winged lions, baths, a Neolithic village and several frescoes.

SIGNIFICANCE

Petra has a rich and fascinating history. Settlement dates back to 10,000BC and throughout the Iron Age (8th century to 6th century BC) it was an important center. During the Greek and Roman periods it became a major point on the eastern caravan trade route. The seat of a bishop during Byzantine times, Petra was levelled by an earthquake in 363AD. Recovering slightly, its importance again rose during the Crusades until it was finally abandoned. It was rediscovered in 1812 by European explorer Burkhardt.

Quseir Amra

LOCATION

Approximately 85km (53mi) east of Amman, E 36° 34', N 31° 47'.

DESCRIPTION

This complex of baths has three distinct sections; the auditorium, which is 8.5 by 7.5m (28 by 25ft), the pump house and the baths themselves, which are in three rooms.

SIGNIFICANCE

Dating from the rule of the caliph Al Walid I at the beginning of the 8th century AD, this is one of the oldest remaining Islamic baths. The interior decorations are of particular interest, with numerous frescoes covering the walls and the representation of a zodiac on the hemispheric ceiling of the auditorium - the first of its kind.

OPPOSITE PAGE *The old treasury building, Petra*

LEFT *The Siq - the spectacular chasm leading to Petra*

Every part of this earth is sacred to my people. Every shining pine needle, every sandy shore, every mist in the dark woods, every clearing and humming insect is holy in the memory and experience of my people. The sap which courses through the trees carries the memories of red man.

CHIEF SEATTLE

LEBANON

Anjar

LOCATION

In the Bequaa province, approximately N 34° 00', E 36° 00'.

DESCRIPTION

These ruins of an 8th century city consist of a massive rectangular fortification with four large buildings, each having a gate protected by towers. Diagonally opposed gates were connected by 20m (66ft) wide roads. These roads cut the town from east to west and south to north, dividing it in four blocks. Today most of the eastern part of the town has been excavated and reconstructed. There are two palaces, a mosque, some baths, arcades and shops along the main street.

SIGNIFICANCE

Prior to the excavation at Anjar, all of the major periods of Arab history, with the exception of the Omayyad, had been found in Lebanon. With the discovery of these Omayyad ruins, that missing link has been uncovered and now points the way to a fuller understanding of the rich and colorful Arabic history of this region.

Byblos

LOCATION

*Approximately 40km (25mi) north of Beirut,
N 34° 08', E 35° 38'.*

DESCRIPTION

The ruins of this ancient Phoenician city include the perimeter walls with their two gates, the Temple of Baalat-Gebal (the goddess of the city), an L-shaped temple, the Temple of the Ghelisks and the royal tombs. There are also some later ruins dating from Roman times, including two temples, a theater, baths and a colonnade.

SIGNIFICANCE

Reputed to be the oldest continuously inhabited town in the world, Byblos was the major seaport of the east Mediterranean during the 3rd millennium BC. By far the most important trade was in selling cedar to Egypt, where it was used for shipbuilding and extracting oil for embalming. It is believed that the Phoenician alphabet was created here, the oldest known example is found on the sarcophagus of King Ahiram (1200BC). Many large buildings were erected under the Romans. The decline of the city came soon after the departure of the Crusaders.

ABOVE Byblos today

Baalbek

LOCATION

N 34° 00', E 36°12'.

DESCRIPTION

These ruins of the ancient town are centered around the so called acropolis which incorporates the Temple of Jupiter and the Temple of Bacchus. Jupiter is the larger of the two with a massive stairway and entrance to a hexagonal courtyard which then leads to the main court where two huge altars once stood. Bacchus is smaller but much better preserved. Other ruins include the city walls, two temples, a mosque, Roman mosaics and Arab fortifications.

SIGNIFICANCE

In ancient times known as Heliopolis, which is Greek for 'city of the sun' the modern name may be connected with the ancient Canaanite god 'Baal'. The Temple of Jupiter took 200 years to complete and was an important religious center, with its own oracle. The Temple of Bacchus was erected around 150AD. Both temples were dedicated to the 'Heliopolitan triad'. Hadal, the Syrian God of Thunder, equivalent to Jupiter; Atorgatis, the Syrian Goddess of Nature, equivalent to Venus, and a youthful god who was a protector of the crops, equivalent to Hermes. These ruins are an important relic of the so called 'pagan' cults of the time.

Tyr

LOCATION

On the South Coast, N 33° 16′, E 35° 12′.

DESCRIPTION

The archeological site of Tyr includes the Temple of Melkart (Heracles) built in 2750BC and some very important Roman ruins including an arch, aqueduct, baths, theater and the Great Necropolis, containing hundreds of sculptured stones and a marble sarcophagus. One of the largest Roman hippodromes ever found has been excavated here.

SIGNIFICANCE

Founded in 2750BC, Tyr later became an important Phoenician seaport. Originally an island city, Tyr's defences were impenetrable and rebuffed many assaults from Assyrians and Babylonians. Passing under Roman influence, Herod the Great built a temple there in 68BC. During these times, Tyr was famous for its purple silk. A famous visitor was St. Paul, who spent a week there on his way to Jerusalem. Falling into the hands of Moslems in the 7th century, it was reconquered by Christians once more with the victories of the Crusaders in the 12th century. The city was destroyed by Moslems in 1291.

ABOVE Part of the dig at Tyr

Kathmandu Valley

LOCATION

Central Nepal,
N 27° to 42°, E 85° 18'.

DESCRIPTION

The Kathmandu Valley, high in the Himalayan foothills, measures 25 by 19km (15.5 by 12mi). Within the valley there are seven monument zones and over 130 monuments, comprising 61 temples, palaces, public squares, stupas and sacred sites.

SIGNIFICANCE

Throughout history, this small valley has been the political and cultural heart of Nepal. Religious art and architecture, both Buddhist and Hindu, document successive and competing political dynasties of the region. Monuments represent legendary and political history and are sites of veneration by both of the above religious groups. These include pilgrimage centers, shrines, bathing sites, rest houses and open gardens. Many decorations and bas-reliefs on temples can be dated back to the 6th century BC. The Hanuman Dhoku Palace is the current residence of H.M. King Birendra, the 10th ruler of the Shah Dynasty.

Swayambhunath Temple - a view of the stupa (RIGHT), detail of the entrance (INSET)

NEPAL

Royal Chitwan National Park

LOCATION

*Chitwan District,
E 84° 20', N 27° 30'.*

DESCRIPTION

The 932sqkm (373sqmi) of this park are located in the 'Lowland Terai'. This comprises several river valleys and part of the Siwilak Range of the outer Himalayas. The climate of the park is its dominating feature, with dramatic monsoonal flooding regularly changing the landscape. The forest, grasslands and changing rivers make Chitwan one of the most attractive parts of Nepal's lowlands.

SIGNIFICANCE

The park is of prime significance in providing habitats for rare, threatened and endangered species. Its most outstanding feature is its fauna, with some 35 species of large mammals and over 350 bird species reported, one of the highest concentrations of bird species in the world. Some rare species of mammal are found, including the one-horned rhinoceros, sloth bear, wild dog, Ganges river dolphin and the Bengal tiger.

Sagarmatha National Park

LOCATION

Solu - Khumbu district, E 86° 28' to 87° 07', N 27° 45' to 28° 07'.

DESCRIPTION

This park covers 1,244sqkm (500sqmi) of dramatic mountain ranges, glaciers and deep valleys. The lowest point in the park is 2,845m (9,334ft) above sea level, the highest Sagarmatha itself, more commonly known as Mount Everest, which reaches 8,848m (29,029ft) above sea level.

SIGNIFICANCE

There are seven peaks over 7,000m (22,966ft) high which form a 20km (12mi) long barrier. Crowning this massive block is the highest point on the earth's surface - Sagarmatha. As well as being an area of intense geological interest, this park contains an extremely distinctive array of flora and fauna, including juniper, fir and beech forests, several varieties of rhododendron, the musk deer, the snow leopard, the Himalayan black bear and the lesser panda. For the Sherpas, who live within the park, this area is of deep spiritual significance.

RIGHT The mighty Himalayas overlook Royal Chitwan National Park
INSET TOP Blue-eared kingfisher
INSET BOTTOM Indian one-horned rhinoceros

OMAN

Bahla Fort

LOCATION

Sultanate of Oman.

DESCRIPTION

Bahla Fort has a fortified wall, about 12km (7.5mi) long, which encloses the various quarters of the town, as well as most of its cultivated land. In the center lies a large fortified compound, containing a castle with towers which rise 50m (164ft) above the surrounding plain. Most of the compound is constructed of clay and straw.

SIGNIFICANCE

Bahla Fort at various times in the past was the capital of the country. Parts of the vast castle date from pre-Islamic times and were probably originally Persian in construction. The surrounding walls and the large cultivated areas they enclose, are reminiscent of Sumerian cities like the city of Gilgamesh in Iraq. Ibidism, which is strangely confined to Oman and north west Africa, has its deepest roots here.

ABOVE *The tombs at Al-ayn*
INSET ABOVE *Bahla fort*

Archeological Sites of Bat, Al-Khutm and Al-Ayn

LOCATION

In the proximity of the village of Bat, 30km (18mi) from Ibri, E 56° 30', N 23°14'.

DESCRIPTION

There are three separate archeological zones within this listing: (1) Just to the north of Bat, there are the remains of a settlement and of a necropolis . The settlement is comprised of five stone towers and a series of rectangular houses. The necropolis is in two parts; (i) a series of stone tombs scattered along a rocky slope, and; (ii) a much more densely concentrated collection of 'bee hive' style stone tombs. (2) The tower of Al Khutm, 2km (1.2mi) west of Bat. (3) Another group of 'bee hive' tombs at Al-Ayn, 21km (13mi) south east of Bat.

SIGNIFICANCE

These sites date back to the 3rd millennium BC when the area was an important source of stone and copper for Mesopotamia. Some of the tombs in particular, are remarkably well preserved and excavations in this area have proved to be crucial to the understanding of the early history of the Arabian peninsula.

PAKISTAN

Moenjodaro

LOCATION

Sind, E 67° 09', N 27° 03'.

DESCRIPTION

This archeological site of approximately 41ha (100ac) is only one-third excavated. There are two parts; a high artificial mound rising to about 12m (40ft) on the west, and a low much broader city area on the east. Structures include the Great Bath, the Great Granary, the College Square, the Pillared Hall and the Square Towers. Private and public houses, industrial shops and commercial buildings, all built in brick masonry, are lined along the straight streets, which are intersected at right angles by smaller side streets.

SIGNIFICANCE

This site dates back to 2,350BC. The remarkable level of sophistication in the town planning and the drainage system in particular, are unique to such a Bronze Age community. These ruins reveal the workings of the Indus civilization at its zenith.

ABOVE Part of the extensive ruins at Moenjodaro
RIGHT A Buddhist stupa at Taxila

Taxila

LOCATION

Punjab, E 72° 50', N 33° 40'.

DESCRIPTION

This is an archeological site with various ruins including a cave site from the Mesolithic period, a large number of Buddhist monasteries, several medieval mosques and four settlement sites.

SIGNIFICANCE

Taxila is the oldest living city in the Indus region, lying on the historic routes from Central Asia to the Gangetic Plain and from Sinkiang in China to the Arabian Sea. Taxila became a meeting ground for cultures east and west. The romantic ruins are associated with the great historic names of Alexander the Great, the Maurian Emperor Asoka, Bactrian Greek rulers, the Kushana Emperors and the destructive Huns. It also had commercial and cultural contact with the Roman Empire.

Star of the Punjab

I saw Lahore, star of the Punjab, at night, and took its soul unawares. The birds were roosting in the shadow of the banyan trees. The pellucid notes of a sitar were heard, and suddenly a flute joined in.

According to the books, and to hearsay, Lahore is the most beautiful city in Pakistan. The Indus makes the plain of the Punjab gleam with its tributaries, which from earliest Antiquity have brought life and cultural riches with them. Here at this fertile crossroads Lahore was born and grew, to become a key administrative, religious and business center.

Lahore lies on a secondary track of the Silk Road, and is watered by the River Ravi. It assumed its importance in the eleventh century, when it became the capital of the sultans of Rhazni. After a long period of turmoil, destruction and short-lived rulers it became in the 16th and 17th centuries one of the great cities of Mogul India.

Babur, founder of the Mogul empire, made it a star of the first order: under the Mogul dynasty Lahore was adorned with buildings that now form a splendid legacy.

I walked to the moonlit red sandstone Fort. Founded, according to legend, by Prince Loth, son of Rama, it was rebuilt in the 16th century by Babur's descendant Akbar and embellished by his son Jahangir and his grandson Shah Jahan. The twenty or so buildings contained within its ramparts afford an excellent picture of the development of Mogul art over nearly two centuries. Audience chambers and mosques, princely apartments, royal baths and pavilions are disposed around gardens, terraces and ornamental ponds.

I dreamed a while in the Naulakha, a small marble pavilion encrusted with semi-precious stones in floral and geometrical designs. I left the Fort by the Elephant Passage (Hathi Paer); and as I stood in front of the mosaics on the enclosure wall my imagination for a moment conjured up the festivities and pleasures of the court, the elephant and camel contests, and the polo games. Nowadays, in the dry moat, men in dazzlingly white cotton scythe the grass, as though to obliterate the passage of time.

I saw the sun rise over Lahore, and the rosy droplets in the dawn, when the faithful come home from prayers. I saw the sun light up the Shalimar Gardens - the famous 'Garden of Love' laid out by Shah Jahan himself in 1642. He had a canal dug to bring water from the Ravi, to replenish the ponds and irrigate the orchards and beds of roses, cyclamen and iris.

The royal family would have come out on to the three terraces, with their slender marble and sandstone pavilions set amid the delights of the trees, and the music of the birds and fountains, in search of coolness and to be entertained with dances and concerts. At nocturnal festivities the light of camphor-scented candles would have given the trees and waterfalls mysterious shapes.

I saw Lahore unfolding to the light, its women clad in tulip and mango colored fabrics. The men sweltered in the heat. In the Shahdara Gardens I walked to Jahangir's tomb, erected by his son Shah Jahan, who also built the Taj Mahal at Agra, in India. An avenue of venerable banyans and huge fig trees leads to the marble and sandstone mausoleum. On the enclosure wall a plethora of white marble ornament representing bowls of fruit, flowers and ewers is arranged in elegant mosaics.

To reach the heart of the monument I followed a passage decorated entirely with frescoes from wall to ceiling, and found myself in another world. The wind sighed through the cloisters of the cenotaph. All white marble, it bears sacred inscriptions in black marble - the 99 attributes of the name of Allah. Around the plinth run floral mouldings in semi-precious stones - lapis lazuli, amethyst, agate and turquoise - mined in the Karakorum Mountains. How gentle death seems, by the side of this tomb!

Fort and Shalamar Gardens in Lahore

LOCATION

Lahore, N 31° 34', E 74° 20'.

DESCRIPTION

The fort is situated in the northwest corner of the city and is approximately 450m (1,476ft) by 360m (1,181ft) around the base. It is constructed from baked bricks and encloses 21 monuments including the Shish Mahal (Mirror Palace). The gardens are formed in three descending terraces and are surrounded by a high perimeter wall. They cover an area of 16ha (38ac) and contain more than 400 cascades and fountains.

SIGNIFICANCE

Lahore Fort is the only monument in Pakistan which represents a complete history of Mughal (Mogul) architecture. Not much is known of its early history, legend attributes its foundation to the mythical Loh, son of the heroic Rama. The earliest recorded reference to the fort is 1021AD. 'Shalamar' means 'the abode of joy', the perfect name for these magnificent gardens. They were created in 1642 as a haven of peace and relaxation for the emperor while staying in Lahore. Together these two grand monuments represent the zenith of Mughal architecture.

The fort (TOP) and the garden (BOTTOM) at Lahore

I heard the five calls to prayer ring out over Lahore. At the mosque of Wazir Khan, in the heart of the old city, I admired the brilliance of the paradise flowers in the splendid ceramic mosaics of this shrine built in the reign of Shah Jahan. At the Badshahi mosque with its daring marble domes, the sun flooded the huge square court yard in which 60,000 worshippers can pray at once. Its four minarets climb high into the sky like soaring birds.

I saw the burial-place of guru Arjan, fifth prophet of the Sikhs, and the Samadhi, tomb of the illustrious ruler Ranjit Singh - magnificent relics, with their fluted golden domes, of the period (1764-1849) when Lahore was the capital of the Sikh kingdom.

I left Lahore at the time of day when people weave garlands of roses, zinnias and marigolds for the dead. Just before daybreak I betook myself to the poet's tomb, cooled my hands and forehead at a nearby fountain, and murmured to myself these lines by Mohammed Iqbal: 'I would not let my heart become attached to this garden'.

I went my way, free of all ties.

CHANTAL LYARD, French Sinologist, poet and essayist, is a member of UNESCO's cultural heritage division where she is concerned with the implementation of the World Heritage Convention.

Takht-i-Bahi Buddhist Ruins

LOCATION

Northwest frontier Province, E 71° 08′, N 34° 04′.

DESCRIPTION

Located on a rocky hill, this Buddhist monastic complex comprises a court of stupas surrounded by tall niches around the courtyard to enshrine Buddhist statues. Scattered over the hill are residential cells, courtyards, assembly halls, meditation cells and other buildings attached to the monastery. The remains of an ancient town called Sahr-i-Bahlol are found on an elongated, 9m (30ft) high mound, with intermittent stretches of defensive walls.

SIGNIFICANCE

Both the city and the monastic complex date back to at least the 1st century AD. Apparently surviving the period of the Huns, this Buddhist community continued until the 7th century AD. These remains have preserved the character of Buddhist monastic life in those early days.

Thatta

LOCATION

100km (62mi) southeast of Karachi, E 67° 09′, N 24° 07′.

DESCRIPTION

There are two groups of monuments at this site. On the hill, there is an enormous cemetery with hundreds of tombs and gravestones. In the valley below lie the ruins of the old town. There are numerous buildings, the most notable being the Jamia Mosque.

SIGNIFICANCE

This area is one of the richest sources of historical information on the Indus region. The vast cemetery contains the final resting places of princes, scholars and saints of the Sammah Dynasty (14th to 16th centuries, AD), as well as Argun rulers and Tarkhan rulers (16th century). It was also a seat of the Mughal governors until the early 18th century. The Jamia Mosque in the old city area contains splendid brickwork covered with richly colored tiles.

ABOVE The ruins at Takht-i-Bahi
INSET LEFT The vast cemetery at Thatta

Sacred City of Anuradhapura

LOCATION

North central province, E 80° 22' to 80° 27', N 08° 19' to 08° 23'.

DESCRIPTION

The site of the ancient capital city consists of the palace, the Temple of the Sacred Tooth, 13 monasteries, five great water reservoirs and associated settlements, four ancient gates, a rampart and a moat. The city was designed and built in four residential sections, divided according to profession or social status.

SIGNIFICANCE

The sacred city is thought to date back to 500BC, becoming the capital in the 3rd century BC. It played a key role in the development of Buddhist culture, later becoming one of the most important centers of the faith. The stupas or dagobas (a specific type of Buddhist building) of Anuradhapura are particularly well known, especially the Ruaneli dagoba which is on the scale of the Egyptian pyramids and was conceived as an enormous model of the universe. It contains the largest collection of Buddhist relics on the island.

Ancient City of Sigiriya

LOCATION

Matale District, N 07° 55' to 07° 58', E 80° 44' to 80° 47'.

DESCRIPTION

This complex of city ruins is based on a rock approximately 180m (591ft) high. A palace with surrounding buildings sits on the summit. Numerous pathways, some tunnelled through rock, lead down to the plain below where there is a large complex of water gardens to the west and a wall on the east. An inner and an outer moat surround the site which also includes two monasteries and a residential area.

SIGNIFICANCE

Sigiriya, meaning 'lion' takes its name from the staircase to the summit which is built in the form of a lion. Created by Prince Kassapa in the 4th century BC, it was intended to be an inaccessible stronghold for his treasures. After having his father killed, Kassapa ruled as king for 18 years and for this period Sigiriya was the capital. During this time a monastery was founded. After being defeated in battle by his brother, Kassapa killed himself and his brother handed Sigiriya over to the priests.

Sinharaja Forest

Two major ecological zones have been identified in Sri Lanka. The wet zone receiving an annual rainfall of 3,000-5,100mm (118-200in) is confined to the hilly central and south western parts of the country and comprises about 23% of the island. The balance is a relatively flat dry zone receiving under 1,500mm (59in) of rain. Over the last two centuries much of the wet zone has been subject to high population pressures as well as   demand for land for cultivation, leaving a mere 9% of the area under forests.

Amongst the few irregularly distributed tropical lowland rainforests in this region, is a substantially undisturbed and very special forest area of more than 11,000 ha (26,400ac) known as Sinharaja, meaning 'Lion King' in the Sinhala language. The tall canopy of this picturesque forest supports spiralling woody climbers and many epiphytes, including orchids. Ferns, epiphyllous mosses and liverworts are also present. Tall spiny canes find their way to the top canopy in search of light. The streams flowing in the forest and on the valley bottoms carry crystal clear water over well worn rock formations, stones and rounded pebbles. The parent material of the soil in these forests is highly weathered and leached, as a result, the soils are poor in nutrients. The nutrients are mostly contained in the biomass and not in the soil.

In comparison with other forests of Sri Lanka, human activities within Sinharaja forest have been minimal. An aerial photo study in 1957 showed that 15% of the Sinharaja Forest Reserve had been subjected to slash and burn cultivation along the fringes with even a few instances of open pit gem mining within the forest. More recently several places along the fringes have also been cultivated with more permanent economic crops such as tea. Continued cultivation along the fringes in this manner over a long period has led to the establishment of twenty four small settlements around the periphery with a population of about 5,000. Two of these settlements are completely within the forest. About 8% of households in these peripheral settlements are totally dependent on the resources of the forest, others to a lesser degree. Extraction of fire wood and smallwood, production of 'Jaggery' (a form of brown sugar from the phloem sap tapped from the Caryota palm), cutting of cane, collection of medicinal plants and harvesting of wild cardamon are the main resources from the forest.

A section of the Sinharaja Forest was selectively logged in the early 1970s. It resulted in a public outcry and protests by Sri Lankan and foreign scientists against the exploitation of a beautiful and undisturbed lowland rainforest. The status of Sinharaja was re-examined and in 1978 Sinharaja was included in the international network of biosphere reserves established and maintained as a part of UNESCO's Man and the Biosphere (MAB) program.

Based on studies by local scientists, the IUCN and the Ministry of Lands and Land Development of the Government of Sri Lanka formulated a project proposal for the conservation and development of Sinharaja with funding from the governments of Norway (NORAD) and Sri Lanka. About the same time, Sinharaja Reserve, together with a north eastern extension including the Thangamalai plains, was declared Sri Lanka's first National Wilderness Heritage Area. In December 1988, the Sinharaja biosphere reserve was inscribed as Sri Lanka's first natural site under UNESCO's World Heritage Convention thereby giving recognition to its outstanding universal value.

In formulating plans for the management of Sinharaja, one of the problems as regards conservation is the dependence of fringe settlements on a variety of resources available within the forest and the surrounding areas. Future plans have to recognise the needs of the local people as having high priority. Long term solutions have to be found to ensure that the villagers in the course of time will minimize their demands on the forest.

An approach to conservation and management of these areas is being planned to identify a central core area of the forest with no human activity whatsoever, and a buffer zone divided into inner and outer areas. As an extreme measure, relocating some families by providing incentives such as land or alternative employment, mainly to young people, is also being contemplated.

Buffer zone development is mostly confined to the outer buffer zone where private home gardens are located. Direct and indirect benefits to the settlers are planned by increasing awareness amongst local communities of forest conservation, improving agricultural methods such as soil conservation,

Sinharaja Forest Reserve

LOCATION
Sabaragamuwa and southern provinces, E 80° 21' to 80° 34', N 06° 21' to 06° 26'.

DESCRIPTION
Situated in the low wetlands of the southwest, this reserve covers an area of some 8,800ha (21,000ac). The terrain is mostly rolling hills with the highest peak at 1,150m (3,800ft). Rainfall is moderately high and the vegetation is typically tropical rainforest.

SIGNIFICANCE
This is the only surviving area of relatively undisturbed rainforest in Sri Lanka. Of Sri Lanka's 830 endemic floral species, 139 have been recorded in Sinharaja, 16 of which are considered to be rare. A variety of plants known to benefit to man are present, of which palm kitul (for jaggery, a sugar substitute), wewal (for cane), cardamon (as spice), shorea (for flour), dun (for varnish and incense) and weniwal (for medicinal purposes) are used intensively by villagers. Amongst the fauna, endemism is high, particularly for birds, with 19 of 20 species endemic to Sri Lanka present. Endemism among mammals and butterflies is also greater than 50%. Threatened mammals include the leopard and Indian elephant. The endemic purple-faced langur is present. Birds considered to be endangered or rare are Sri Lanka wood pigeon, green-billed coucal, Sri Lanka white-headed starling, Sri Lanka blue magpie, and ashy-headed babbler, all of which are endemic, and red-faced malkoha. The Sinharaja region has long featured in the legends and lore of the people of Sri Lanka. Its name, literally meaning lion (sinha) king (raja), perhaps refers to the original 'king-sized or royal forest of the Sinhalese'.

introducing economic crops and encouraging better health standards. In addition, State sponsored buffer zone activities, such as establishment and maintenance of fast growing timber and fuel species and raising forest plantations with economic possibilities on denuded buffer zone lands are being carried out. The ultimate aim is to develop small-scale industries in the buffer zone which will have significant and sustainable employment and income generating value to the people living in marginal forest communities. While this work is in progress, national and international scientists are continuing studies to learn more about the unique bio-diversity of this forest.

M S RANATUNGA

IUCN Representative, Sri Lanka

Galle

LOCATION

City of Galle, Southern Province, E 80° 25′, N 06° 00′.

DESCRIPTION

This old fortified city is extremely well preserved and is still occupied. It sits on 40ha (96ac) and originally had a moat surrounding its walls which has since been filled in. Three gates are in existence today, one is disused and one was added by the British in 1873.

SIGNIFICANCE

The site was established by the Portuguese in 1543 but the fortifications were not built until 1663 when the Dutch conquered the city. This is by far the best preserved fortified city in south and southeast Asia. It has great historical value in preserving some architectural features of each of three major colonial powers - Portuguese, Dutch and British.

Sacred City Of Kandy

LOCATION

Central province, E 80° 38′, N 07° 17′.

DESCRIPTION

Lying in a valley 488m (1,600ft) above sea level, this old city is surrounded by mountains. Among the many important buildings found here are the temple complex of the Tooth Relic, the massive timber Audience Hall, the large monastery complex of Malwatte Vihara and the Palace of King Sri Wikrama.

SIGNIFICANCE

Established in the 14th century by King Vikramabahu, it later became the island's capital and remained so until 1815. The most important feature of the city is the temple which houses the Tooth Relic of Lord Buddha. Venerated by millions of Buddhists around the world, this temple complex is a treasure house of Kandyan arts.

ABOVE *The temple complex of the Tooth Relic*

The Golden Rock Temple of Dambulla

LOCATION

District of Matale, Central Province, N 07° 59', E 80° 38'.

DESCRIPTION

This Buddhist cave-temple complex is found on a 25ha (60ac) area of Dambulla rock which rises 122m (400ft) above the surrounding plain. There are five caves and the remains of 80 rock shelters within the complex. The main cave temple is about 609m (200ft) in length and 33m (110ft) wide. The caves contain 157 statues of various sizes and over 1,951sqm (21,000sqft) of painted surfaces. Remarkably, the complex is largely excavated - there being few natural caves or shelters.

SIGNIFICANCE

This site has been in continuous use for over 22 centuries, since the time of its initial occupation by a Buddhist monastic establishment, just after the introduction of religion to the island. It is the largest and best preserved cave-temple complex in Sri Lanka and the second largest such complex in south and south-eastern Asia. Of particular value is the art work found on the walls of the caves, notably the exceptionally well preserved 18th century paintings from the Kandy school. Archeological excavations in the area immediately surrounding the rock has revealed evidence of earlier occupation, dating back four millennia.

To see the world in a grain of sand,
And heaven in a wild flower,
Hold infinity in the palm of your hand,
And eternity in an hour.

WILLIAM BLAKE

Ancient city of Polonnaruwa

LOCATION

North central Province, N 07° 52' to 07° 59', E 80° 56' to 81° 02'.

DESCRIPTION

The ruins of this city are most famous for the collection of shrines that are found in The Great Quadrangle. A seven-storeyed brick pyramid, named the Sat Mahal Pasala, the Hata-da-ge, a rectangular masonry structure and the Wata-da-ge, a circular stone shrine are particularly notable.

SIGNIFICANCE

Polonnaruwa was established as the capital not long after the fall of Anuradhapura at the end of the 10th century AD. The greatest building activity was seen between 1059 and 1207 when the three great Polonnaruwa sovereigns reigned - Vijayabahu I, Parakramabahu I and Nissanka Malla. The fine legacy left by this civilization includes many superb bronze sculptures of religious figures as well as a grand and daring architectural style.

SYRIA

Ancient City of Aleppo

LOCATION

Far northwest, N 36° 14', E 37° 10'.

DESCRIPTION

A large city and administrative center, Aleppo sits on limestone hills 360m (1,181ft) above sea level. The old part of the city has many notable features including covered bazaars that are built of stone, an imposing citadel and many mosques. Ruins include the original city walls and gates.

SIGNIFICANCE

The Arabic name is Haleb or halpa which is said to derive from the Semetic word for milk - it is believed that Abraham grazed his cows here. The various ruins and old buildings are an invaluable record of this city's rich and important history.

ABOVE *The old city gates*

Palmyra

LOCATION

Province of Homs, 240km (150mi) north east of Damascus, N 34° 36', E 38°15'.

DESCRIPTION

The ruins of this city cover about 50ha (120ac) and reveal the town plan of the ancient city. Along the principal street there is a double portico which is heavily ornamented. The agora, the senate house and the theater lie to the south. Within the ruins lies a vast complex called Diocletian's Camp, as well as the chief Palmyrene sanctuary.

SIGNIFICANCE

Lying in an oasis of the Syrian desert 390m (1,300ft) above sea level, Tadmor, as Palmyra was known in Arabic, was in ancient times the intersecting point of two great trading routes. Reference to the town was made as far back as the 12th century BC. The original caravan stopover point gradually developed into a large city and an important center for worship to the sun god as witnessed by the ruins of the Great Temple of the Sun.

Ancient City of Damascus

LOCATION

*In the southwest, N 37° 05',
E 40° 05'.*

DESCRIPTION

*Positioned on the rivers of Barada
and A'waj, the old part of
Damascus is partially walled and
lies on the southern side of the
Barada River. It contains the
Great Mosque which was built
within the walls of a 1st century
temple, a Roman citadel, several
souks (markets) and khaus
(trading inns) and the Azam
Palace. There are three distinct
'quarters' to the town - the Meidan,
settled by tribesmen, the Christian
and the Druse.*

SIGNIFICANCE

*Legend has it that 'Dimasqa' was
founded by Uz, son of Aram and
was already a city by the time of
Abraham. It is also known as 'Al
Fayha' - 'the fragrant' - from its
many scented gardens. The history
of this famed city has been
turbulent and dynamic, passing
through the hands of ancient
Egypt, Assyria, Persia, Alexander
the Great, Egypt, Nabataea,
Rome, Arabia, Rome and finally
Arabia again in 635AD. With
such a fabulous history, the antiquities of Damascus will remain
forever invaluable to the heritage of
man.*

RIGHT *Damascus -The Great
Mosque, remains of the old city
walls* (INSET)

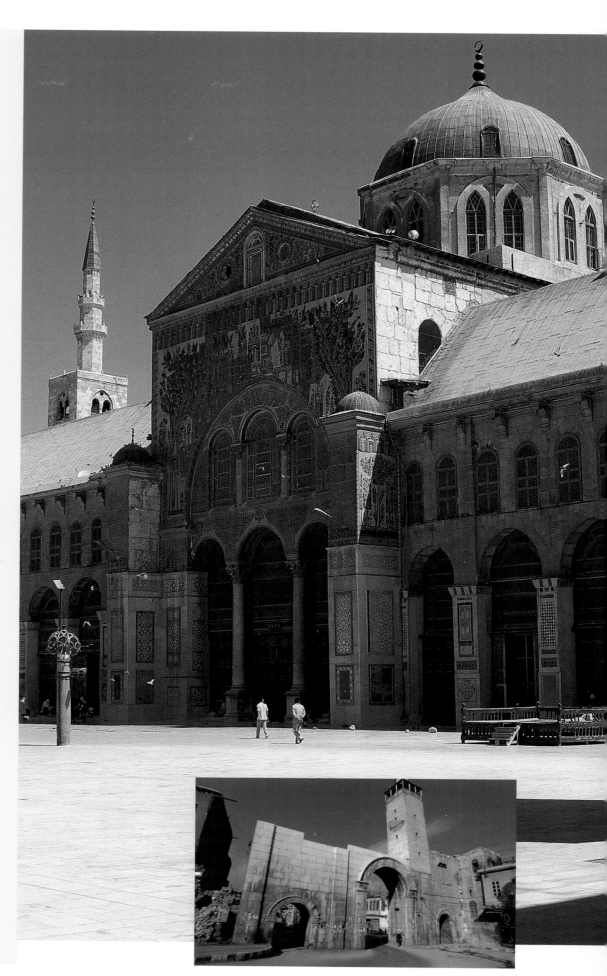

Ancient City of Bosra

LOCATION

Department of Deraa, 100km (62mi) south of Damascus,
N 32° 36', E 36° 40'.

DESCRIPTION

Situated in the fertile valley of the Nukru River the ruins of ancient
Bosra sit on a bed of volcanic rock at an altitude of 850m (2800ft)
above sea level. The remains include the walls and gates, a wide avenue
with colonnades, a theater, baths, markets and in the oldest quarter,
named Vabateau, a monumental gate which leads to the Palace of
Trajan, a cathedral and several mosques.

SIGNIFICANCE

Originally the city of the Arabian people known as Nabateans, Bosra
was conquered by the Romans and made capital of their Province of
Arabia by Emperor Trajan in 106AD. After becoming a Roman
colony, the city fell to the Arabs in 636AD. The Crusaders held it but
briefly in the 12th century. Only a matter of years later a series of
earthquakes devastated the city and it never recovered from the subsequent decline.

ABOVE The theater at Bosra
OPPOSITE PAGE INSET One of many magnificent minarets at Bukhara

UZBEKISTAN

Historic Center of Bukhara

LOCATION

City of Bukhara, approximately N 39° 50', E 64° 00'.

DESCRIPTION

The townscape of the ancient center of Bukhara represents every stage of the city's history over more than one thousand years. The city's main influence has been Moslem and its notable buildings include many mosques, domes and minarets. The 10th century Ismail Samanai tomb is the best surviving example of 10th century Moslem architecture in the world. The most celebrated buildings are from the Sheibanid period, including three major ensembles - the Poi-Kalyan, the Lyabi-Khauz and Hodja-Kalon; as well as several distinctive domes.

SIGNIFICANCE

Bukhara is easily the most outstanding surviving example of a medieval central Asian town which has maintained its original urban fabric and townscape. The site of Bukhara was settled at an oasis on an ancient trading crossroads as early as 2000BC, while the present city dates back 25 centuries. For most of its history Bukhara was under Arabic rule, but it was also sacked by Mongols and taken by the nomadic Uzbek. Despite these changes, the city has maintained its characteristic fusion of central Asian and the Middle Eastern styles with surprising continuity and harmony.

Itchan Kala

LOCATION

The town of Khiva.

DESCRIPTION

Itchan Kala is the historic center of the modern town of Khiva. It is approximately 600m x 400m (2,000ft x 1,330ft) in size and is enclosed by defensive walls. There are four gates and several towers incorporated into these massive 6m (20ft) clay walls. Inside the walls are many buildings including mosques, palaces, madrasahs, mausoleums, bathhouses, residences and shops.

SIGNIFICANCE

It is thought that this town evolved from the initial development of a caravanserai on the site in ancient times. It is known from the Arab chroniclers that Khiva was a great town in the 10th century with an important mosque. It was during the 18th and 19th centuries though, that the town flourished as a center of Khorezmian culture. The original and excellent state of preservation of the numerous monuments and associated artworks found here provide an important living document of the history and cultural development of this area and of central Asia in general.

YEMEN

Old City of Sana'a

LOCATION

Governorate of the capital Sana'a, N 15° 22', E 44° 11'.

DESCRIPTION

Sana'a is a fully contained medieval Arab city. Ancient mosques, souks (markets), houses and towers form an ensemble of rare beauty. There are 103 mosques, 14 caravanserais, 12 bathhouses (hammams) and various palaces. The Byzantine Christian cathedral and martyrium which was built on the personal instructions of the Emperor Justinian is one of the more notable buildings. The city presents an amazingly well preserved collection of winding streets filled with all the character-istic signs of a cultural and religious center.

SIGNIFICANCE

Sana'a is considered to be one of the most ancient cities of the world, and is believed to have been founded by Shem, son of Noah. Due to its long history of foreign occupation by the Abyssinians, Persians, Byzantines and Moslems, Sana'a offers a tremendous variety of cultural and historical monuments, in a state of near-perfect preservation.

Old Walled City of Shibam

LOCATION

Seiyun District, N 16° 00', E 48° 20'.

DESCRIPTION

There are approximately 500 tower houses, three government offices, five mosques and two palaces within the 6m (20ft) high walls of this old and still very active town.

SIGNIFICANCE

An important commercial center throughout its history, Shibam was established after the destruction of Shabwa around 300AD. Floods damaged the new town several times up until 1535AD, when it was almost totally destroyed. A dam was then constructed upstream and new walls were built. The oldest remaining building dates from 904AD, otherwise the town dates mainly from that last great flood. The traditional way of life has been largely preserved.

Historic Town of Zabid

LOCATION

Province of al-Hudayda, approximately N 14° 05', E 43° 11'.

DESCRIPTION

The town of Zabid is built around its oldest mosque, the Mosque of Asa'ir, forming an oval which covers about 135ha (320ac). The town structure comprises mostly narrow streets and alleys, with a few small squares. The houses follow the same traditional pattern, based around open courtyards, with a central rectangular room. Some buildings housed more wealthy residents, and were built up to three stories, incorporating numerous courtyards and elaborately decorated interiors. These buildings are of baked brick though some of the poorer dwellings are made of clay and straw. The front walls of the wealthier houses are magnificently carved, showing exceptional workmanship and talent.

SIGNIFICANCE

Zabid is of outstanding archeological and historical significance for its domestic, religious and military architecture, and for its authentic and complete townscape. It was of great importance throughout the Arab and Moslem world for many centuries because of its renowned Islamic university. As an important religious center, numerous impressive mosques and cemeteries were constructed which remain today. The town is very well preserved, due mainly to the decline of its political and economic power in the 16th century.

ASIAN PACIFIC BASIN

A loggerhead turtle makes its way back to the sea, Shark Bay

AUSTRALIA

East Coast Temperate and Sub-Tropical Rainforest Parks

LOCATION

Eastern coastal regions of New South Wales and southern Queensland, S 28° to 37°, E 150° to 154°.

DESCRIPTION

This listing comprises eight blocks of protected areas scattered over a large area of the east coast. They include: Main Range; Mount Barney Group; Shield Volcano Group; Washpool/Gibraltar Range Group; Iluka Nature Reserve; New England Group; Hastings Group; Barrington Tops National Park. The total area of the World Heritage site is 265,360ha (637,000ac).

SIGNIFICANCE

Rainforests are especially significant in a dry continent such as Australia, where they occupy a small but significant niche in the vegetation landscape. The great diversity of microclimates within rainforests sustains a large range of species. Over 350 trees and shrub species are found in these rainforests, many of them endemic to these areas. The animal population is also extremely diverse, with marsupials such as the mountain brushtail possum, reptiles like the southern angle-headed dragon, and numerous species of frogs, fish and invertebrates. Thirty seven species of bats have been recorded in these rainforests making them an extremely important habitat for these animals.

ABOVE LEFT Adult male koala
ABOVE RIGHT Scaly-breasted lorikeet

We Walked in Wilderness and Shone a Bright Light

It was the morning of January 17th 1983, the last day of the 49th year of my life. The sweet rain which makes South West Tasmania what it is, a wonderland of temperate rainforest had stopped. I looked out from my tent as a wallaby bounded away through the wet undergrowth. It was time for me to go and get arrested and the reason why was all around me: sassafras, leatherwood and myrtle steaming in the sun, a 360° panorama of untouched wilderness. A pink breasted pigeon rose with me to meet the challenge of the day.

One hundred and sixty three days later, on Friday 1st July 1983, the High Court of Australia ruled that the Commonwealth Government had the power to stop the Gordon-below-Franklin dam. Within days the bulldozers and trucks were being dragged back to Strahan on barges that had only months earlier forced their way through our fragile lines of protest.

Without the determination and dedication of the 2,613 people who came to the town of Strahan in a remote corner of south west Tasmania, and the 1,272 of us who were arrested during the Franklin River Blockade, the living heart of a critical area of World Heritage would have been lost forever.

This is a brief timetable of the action which thrust the cause of World Heritage firmly into the arena of international politics.

- 16th June 1982 - Despite mounting public opposition in Tasmania, Australia and across the globe the Gordon River Hydro-Electric Power Development Bill was passed by the Tasmanian Government. The Hydro-Electric Commission (H.E.C.) could legally commence work to destroy Australia's last wild river.

- 26th July - at press conferences in Hobart and Melbourne, announcements were made by the Wilderness Society that the proposed dam site would be blockaded. Liaison with senior police officers commenced.

- 2nd September - large tracts of land were revoked from Wild Rivers National Park and were vested in the H.E.C.

- 16th September - Tasmanian Premier Gray threatened to secede from the Commonwealth if the Federal Government intervened to stop the work on the Gordon-below-Franklin dam.

- 13th November - Wilderness Society meeting agreed that a blockade on the dam site would begin on 14th December if the Federal Government refused to intervene and stop the dam. 15,000 people walk for wilderness in Melbourne.

- 24th November - in response to the blockade plans the Tasmanian Government changed the Police Offences Act so that trespassing would be an arrestable offence.

- 4th December - in the Flinders by-election in the nearby State of Victoria, 40.04% of all the electorate wrote NO DAMS on their ballot papers.

- 8th December - despite its great track record in conservation the Government of Malcolm Fraser said it would not intervene with the dam.

- 14th December - South West Tasmania was given World Heritage Status as the Australian Democrats World Heritage Protection Bill was passed. As promised, the

ABOVE Tasmanian devil - one of Australia's few remaining carnivorous mammals
ABOVE RIGHT The Gordon River

blockade swung into action - 53 people were arrested, 46 refused to accept bail conditions not to return to the H.E.C. land and were remanded in Risdon Gaol, Hobart.

- 16th December - Dr Bob Brown, spokesperson of the Tasmanian Wilderness Society was arrested and remanded in custody.

- 5th January - Bob Brown became a member of the Tasmanian State parliament.

- 12th January - rocks were hurled through the windows of the Wilderness Society's information center in Strahan and their telephone and telex cables were cut, radio equipment was jammed, public telephones in Queenstown and

Strahan were mysteriously out of order. The road to the main blockade camp was blocked by police cars and any protesters who attempted to pass were arrested. Attempts to blockade failed as protesters were pulled from beneath the moving wheels of the low loader and were arrested.

- 13th January - the bulldozer left Strahan at dawn on a barge. At Butler Island at the entrance of the disputed area the boat broke through a blockade of duckies (tiny rubber boats) without slowing down and passed over a submerged diver in flagrant disregard of the Divers Flag. Fifty four people were arrested in the day's actions. Prime Minister Fraser offered Tasmania $500 million to stop the scheme, Premier Gray declined the offer.

- 17th February - the thousandth arrest took place at one of the drill sites.

- 5th March - a Federal Government committed to stopping the dam was elected to power.

- 5th May - the World Heritage (Properties Conservation) Bill was passed in the House of Representatives.

- 18th May - in Hobart all charges of trespass were dropped.

I was just one of those people who walked in wilderness and so helped shine the light of Heritage across the world.

DAVID BELLAMY

Lord Howe Island Group

LOCATION

*Approximately 700km (435mi)
northeast of Sydney,
S 31° 30' to 31° 50',
E 159° 00' to 159° 17'.*

DESCRIPTION

*This listing consists of Lord Howe
Island, Ball's Pyramid, the
Admiralty Islands and associated
islets. All are the eroded remnants
of a volcano. They rise from a
seafloor which is over 2,000m
(6,562ft) deep. The area of the
islands is around 1,540ha
(3,713ac), Lord Howe itself is
1,455ha (3,508ac). All are owned
by the New South Wales
Government.*

SIGNIFICANCE

*Considered to be an outstanding
example of an island group formed
from volcanic activity, these
islands are also spectacularly
beautiful. They harbor a great
diversity of rare and endemic
species, both flora and fauna, and
encapsulate a great diversity of
landscapes. Another feature of
significance is the reef, which is the
most southern coral reef in the
world.*

*ABOVE RIGHT An aerial view
RIGHT LORD Howe wood hen
BELOW Painted sweetlips
INSET TOP Scenic view of the main
island*

Kakadu National Park

LOCATION

S 13°00', E 132°30'.

DESCRIPTION

On the western fringe of the Arnhem Land plateau, Kakadu covers a massive area of over 6,000sqkm (2,344sqmi). The landscape varies from the rugged sandstone of the plateau, down to the lowlands with its red soil and light tree cover and further on to the black-soiled flood plains, muddy tidal flats and mangrove estuaries.

SIGNIFICANCE

The strange and awesome beauty of this ancient land is striking. It is home to some of the most important Australian Aboriginal art, with its 'Mimi' and 'X-Ray' style cave paintings. Some of these date back 18,000 years, making them contemporary with the renowned Palaeolithic cave paintings of Europe. The flora and fauna are extremely rich in their diversity with over 41 species of mammals, 250 of birds, 75 of reptiles, 45 of fish and 10,000 of insects found in the area. More than a quarter of Australia's bird species are found here.

*Above Lotus bird
Center Jim Jim Falls*

Great Barrier Reef

LOCATION

Off the east coast of the state of Queensland,
S 24° 30′ to 10° 41′,
E 142° 30′ to 154° 00′.

DESCRIPTION

The Great Barrier Reef comprises approximately 2,000km (1,243mi) of broken coral reefs (around 2,500 separate reefs), covering an area of 348,700sqkm (136,210sqmi). There are 71 coral islands, or cays scattered throughout its length. The coral is composed of calcium carbonate, being the remains of plant and animal material.

SIGNIFICANCE

The Great Barrier Reef is the world's largest and most complex expanse of living coral reefs. The area is of enormous scientific importance because of the great diversity in life forms. There are over 1,500 species of fish, 400 species of coral, 242 species of birds (109 of which have recorded breeding sites in the area), six species of turtles (including the green and loggerhead turtles which have crucial nesting sites within the reef area) along with many other animal groups. Also of importance are the wide range of algae and seagrasses found throughout the reef. The reef is of considerable historical significance to the Aboriginals and Torres Strait Islanders of the area. There are several important sites, notably on Lizard, Hinchinbrook, Stanley, Cliff and Clack Islands. Also of historical importance are the 30 odd ship wrecks dating from 1791.

ABOVE One Tree Island, one of the numerous coral cays on the reef
INSET ABOVE Giant clam

Uluṟu National Park

LOCATION

Southwest corner of the Northern Territory, S 25° 20', E 131° 00'.

DESCRIPTION

This park is 132,566ha (319,617ac) of arid desert in the heart of Australia. It is owned by the Uluṟu-Kata Tjuṯa Aboriginal Land Trust and leased by the Director of National Parks and Wildlife for use as a national park. The huge monoliths found at Uluṟu (Ayers Rock) and Kata Tjuṯa (the Olgas) are remarkable geological features and stand in stark contrast to the surrounding flat sand plain environment.

SIGNIFICANCE

One of the most famous landmarks in Australia, Uluṟu is an awe inspiring sight. It is no surprise that it has been a place of great mystical significance to the Aboriginals for tens of thousands of years. There are hundreds of painting sites around the base of 'the Rock' and a number of ancient rock engravings. Four secret sacred sites are fenced off and protected by special legislation. Environmentally, the park is extremely important in protecting several unique desert ecosystems.

ABOVE A burning Uluṟu with Kata Tjuṯa in the distance
INSET Sturt's Desert Pea

Tasmanian Wilderness

LOCATION

Central and southwestern regions of Tasmania,
E 145° 25′ to 146° 55′, S 41° 35′ to 43° 40′.

DESCRIPTION

This site is composed of numerous areas, including many islands,
totalling a massive 1,374,000ha (3,312,714ac). There are a wide
range of landscapes, geological features, vegetation and several
important archeological sites.

SIGNIFICANCE

In stark contrast to much of mainland Australia, the area covered by
this listing is extremely rugged. There is much evidence of glacial
activity which has created a myriad of high lakes (including the deepest
lake in Australia, Lake St. Clair), steep gorges and fast running rivers.
The unusual vegetation is a result both of the unique geological condi-
tions and the cool wet climate. There are several ancient species, relics of

bygone eras, like the Gondwanan conifers known only in this area.
There are vast tracts of pristine rainforest as well as many unique
examples of alpine vegetation, eucalypt forests, wet sclerophyll commu-
nities and many varieties of grassland. Notable amongst all this is the
mountain ash, the world's tallest flowering plant, forming a towering
90m (295ft) canopy over the wet sclerophyll understorey. The area is
also of great cultural significance, with some 37 cave sites showing
human settlements up to 30,000 years old. One of the most valuable
prehistoric sites in Australia is Kutikina Cave, one of the first
Aboriginal sites where Ice Age occupation was recognised. Judd's
Cavern is one of the largest river caves in Australia and is richly
decorated with rock art dating from the Ice Age.

ABOVE LEFT Dove Lake, with Cradle Mountain in the background

Wet Tropics of Queensland

LOCATION

Northeastern coastal region of Queensland,
S 15° 39' to 19° 17', E 144° 58' to 146° 27'.

DESCRIPTION

Extending from just south of Cooktown to north of Townsville, there is around 7,000sqkm (2,734sqmi) of tropical rainforest incorporated within the 9,200sqkm (3,594sqmi) of this listing. This represents 90 percent of the total area of wet tropical rainforest in northeast Australia. The geographic range of this region is extremely diverse and subsequently the rainforests here are the most diverse in Australia. From the wet, mist covered and wind blown forests of the Bellenden Ker Range, down to the highly developed forests of the wet lowlands, the landscape is spectacular and harbors a rich array of rare and unusual plant species.

SIGNIFICANCE

This area contains the oldest continuously surviving rainforests on earth. Rainforests only cover 0.2 percent of the total area of Australia - this amounts to around 20,000sqkm (8,000sqmi). Almost 30 percent of that total is incorporated in this listing. It is estimated that some 50 to 100 million years ago, the entire continent was covered with vegetation similar to that found in these forests today. Some of the more striking plants found in these forests include the beautiful and unusual fan palm; many different types of Proteaceae - at least 13 different types out of a world total of 36; over 90 species of orchids, many found in very limited areas; one of the largest cycads in the world, as well as one of the smallest, and the richest concentration of ferns to be found in Australia.

Willandra Lakes Region

LOCATION

Murray Basin, southwestern New South Wales, S 33° 00', E 144° 00'.

DESCRIPTION

Around 6,000sqkm (2,400sqmi) in area, this region incorporates a system of dry lakes which used to be fed from a tributary of the Lachlan River called Willandra Billabong Creek. There are several pastoral leases operating actively within the region, one of which was acquired by the New South Wales Government and is permanently reserved as Mungo National Park.

SIGNIFICANCE

This area has been the source of several important archeological discoveries, including a 30,000 year old burial site, a 26,000 year old cremation site and 18,000 year old grinding stones. Further evidence points to human settlement up to 40,000 years old. Research here has determined that the earth's magnetic field was once at variance 120° with today's field, so the area has importance for world studies of changes in earth magnetism. This is also a site of natural significance in that it is a pristine example of a semi-arid environment, unmodified by glacial or sea-level changes.

ABOVE LEFT *The Daintree coast, where the rainforest meets the sea*
TOP *Hercules moth*
CENTER *Herbert River ringtail possum*
Willandra Lakes:
The eroded landscape of the Walls of China (LEFT)

Shark Bay

LOCATION

Western-most point of the Western Australian coast,
S 24° 44' to 27° 16', E 112° 49' to 114° 17'.

DESCRIPTION

The entire 13,000sqkm (5,000 sqmi) of the shallow bay,
as well as a substantial area of the adjoining mainland, is
included in this listing. The township of Denham,
although within the boundaries, is excluded. Numerous
islands dot the bay, including the larger ones of Dirk
Hartog, Faure, Bernier and Dorre. The landscape around
the coastline varies tremendously, and includes steep
limestone cliffs, vegetated sand dunes, beaches consisting
entirely of small shells, saltpans and rugged rocks.

SIGNIFICANCE

The warm, sheltered waters of Shark Bay are very salty -
the salinity is up to twice that of average seas. One of the
consequences of this is that the waters are rich with blue
green algae, which means that, in turn, the waters are also
rich in a great variety of larger marine life. Humpback
whales use the bay as a migratory staging post during
winter months, more than 10,000 dugongs are to be found
feeding on the plentiful seagrass beds - around 12% of the
world dugong population. Another of the bay's marine
mammals, now world famous for its relaxed interaction
with humans at Monkey Mia, is the bottle nosed dolphin.
Green and leatherback turtles are also plentiful, with
important nesting sites located on Dirk Hartog Island and
Peron Peninsular. Other marine life includes western king
prawns, whale sharks and manta rays; more than 320
species of fish occur in the bay. Especially notable,
although invisible to the naked eye, are the primitive
microbial life forms found in abundance throughout the
bay which constitute a living fossil record. Of particular
interest are the ancient stromatolites of Hamelin Pool.
These unusual structures are built up very slowly over
thousands of years by the accumulation of algae
sediments and constitute a very important fossil record. By
far the dominant life form in the waters is seagrass. The
total area covered by seagrass beds is in excess of
4,000sqkm (1,560sqmi). One in particular, the
Wooramel Seagrass Bank covering more than 1,000sqkm
(390sqmi) is one of the largest in the world and is a
crucial component of the bay's ecosystem. Midden sites
have been found which indicate a history of human
population dating back at least 22,000 years.

ABOVE RIGHT Stromalites at Hamelin Pool
RIGHT Manta ray
INSET Shark Bay mouse

Fraser Island

LOCATION

On the south-eastern coast of Queensland,
S 24° 35′ to 26° 23′,
E 152° 30′ to 153° 30′

DESCRIPTION

This World Heritage site encompasses all of Fraser Island, which is the largest sand island on earth. The dunes of this region are the oldest and highest (apart from Mt. Tempest on nearby Moreton Island) of all known sand dunes.

SIGNIFICANCE

One of the marvels of Fraser Island is the large stands of rare kauri pines and Satinays, brush box and hoop pine, which soar up to 60m (200ft) overhead, yet are growing out of sand. The fragile ecosystems of these forests have been built up over thousands of years. Another remarkable feature is the system of freshwater lakes which are perched up high on the sand dunes. Found in the south of the island, these lakes are made possible in the sandy environment by a lining of organic material which prevents the water from percolating away. The dingoes on Fraser Island are of particular interest, as they are considered to be one of the purest strains in the country. The birdlife is very rich, with over 230 species known to inhabit the area, including some very large and spectacular species such as the glossy black cockatoo, peregrine falcon and sea eagles. Marine life is also abundant, with large populations of various fish species, crabs and prawns. Larger sealife is also found, including substantial numbers of dugongs, dolphins and migrating whales.

RIGHT Some of the famous colored sand formations
INSET One of Fraser Island's pure strain of dingoes

CAMBODIA

Angkor, Roluos and Banteay Srei

LOCATION

Province of Siem Reap, central Cambodia, north of Tonle Sap, approximately N 13° 31', E 103° 45'.

DESCRIPTION

The court of Jayavarman II, 'father' of the Khmer Empire, resided for some years at the site which was half a century later to become the permanent capital of the Khmer Empire. The site was named Yashodapura by his son and later became known as Angkor. The earlier capital, now known as Roluos lies to the south-east and the temple of Banteay Srei about 25km (15mi) to the north-east. Both cities contain many temples and monuments, the most notable of which is the Angkor Vat, dedicated to Vishnu by Suryavarman II in the 12th century. Both cities are distinguished by large water reservoirs.

SIGNIFICANCE

The Khmer style evolved from that of the Indian sub-continent, from which it rapidly became distinct, emerging as an original and influential new style in Asian art and architecture. The art and architecture of these two cities is entirely representative of the development of this style, and of the Khmer empire over the almost 600 year period of its reign. The temple of Banteay Srei is one of a number of indisputable masterpieces found amongst these ruins, a list which must also include Angkor Vat and the Bayon.

TOP Angkor
ABOVE The Temple of Ta Prohm

Unjung Kulon National Park and Krakatau Nature Reserve

LOCATION

West Java and Lampung, S 06° 45, E 105° 20'.

DESCRIPTION

This 76,119ha (182,685ac) park lies at the extreme south-western tip of Java, and comprises a section of the mainland as well the Unjung Kulon peninsula and the islands Pulau Handeuleum, Pulau Panaitan and Pulau Peucang. Coastal features include coral islands and reefs to the north, and spectacular volcanic formations to the west. Vegetation encompasses lowland rainforest, palm forests, dense stands of bamboo, freshwater swamp forests, mangrove forests and grasslands. Krakatau Nature Reserve comprises the central island of Anak Krakatau, the peripheral islands of Rakata, Payang and Sertung and the surrounding coral reefs. Vegetation on this group varies from the early stages of biotic colonization on the still active Sertung to the extensive moss forests of Rakata. Fauna includes the Javan rhinoceros, several large carnivores, ungulates and primates. Around 300 species of birds have been recorded in the area, while the fish population is the richest in Indonesia.

SIGNIFICANCE

The Krakatau reserve presents the world's best known example of island vulcanism. The dramatic explosion of 1883 profoundly altered ecological processes in the area, today providing a remarkable opportunity to study biological colonization and subsequent evolutionary processes on a tropical island. Unjung Kulon peninsula has the most extensive stand of lowland rainforest remaining on Java. There are several threatened species protected by this area, the most notable being the Javanese rhinoceros. This park provides this species with its only remaining viable natural refuge.

RIGHT Some spectacular coral reefs are found in this park
INSET TOP Blue nose angel fish
INSET BELOW Javanese rhinoceros

INDONESIA

The habitats of the tropics are the main repository of Earth's natural diversity - nearly two thirds of all species live there.

ALVARO UMAN

Borobudur Temple Compound

LOCATION

Central Java Province,
S 07° 07', E 110° 10'.

DESCRIPTION

This compound comprises three temples: the main temple of Borobudur and two smaller ones to the east, Mendut and Pawon. The complex is built on several levels around a hill which forms a natural center. The most striking visual feature of this ensemble is the main stupa of Borobudur which rises 35m (96ft) from the ground. Beneath the stupa, the base of the main temple is constructed in five square terraces. Above this are three circular platforms which are adorned by 72 smaller perforated stupas. Stairways provide access to the main stupa. Numerous reliefs decorate each of the temples, and there are many statues of Buddha in various sizes and positions. Construction is of stone and the masonry is to very high standard.

SIGNIFICANCE

Borobudur is one of the world's great Buddhist monuments. It was built around 800AD under orders from one of the Saliendra kings and represents the zenith of Indonesian Buddhist art. The complex was abandoned in the 11th century and was gradually consumed by the surrounding jungle. It was rediscovered in the 19th century and has since undergone two major restoration programs.

ABOVE *A view of the main stupa*
INSET *One of the many stone Buddhas*

Prambanan Temple Compound

LOCATION

Central Java Province,
S 07° 32' to 08° 12',
E 110° 00' to 110° 50'.

DESCRIPTION

This compound is in fact an archeological park, and includes the Loro Jonggrang Temple complex, the Sewu Temple complex and three temples which lie between. The Loro Jonggrang complex is Hindu (dedicated to Siva) and comprises three court-yards adorned with hundreds of temples of various sizes. Many temples are in ruins, but restoration work is slowly reclaiming much of the complex's past glory. The Sewu complex is Buddhist and comprises one main temple and 240 minor temples over an area of 30,500sqm (329,000sqft). There are four entrances, each guarded by giant statues. The three temples, Lumbung, Bubrah and Asu, which lie between the two complexes are in a state of ruin.

SIGNIFICANCE

Loro Jonggrang, constructed during the first part of the 9th century, is the largest Siva ensemble in Indonesia. Its temples are extensively adorned with reliefs illus-trating the life of the 3rd century Hindu hero Rama. The entire compound presents an outstanding example of Indonesian classical art, recalling an era when Central Javanese Culture was at is zenith.

Komodo National Park.

LOCATION

East Nusa Tenggara Province,
S 08° 24' to 08° 50', E 119° 21' to 119° 49'.

DESCRIPTION

This rugged 219,321ha (526,372ac) park comprises a coastal section western Flores, the islands of Komodo, Padar, Rinca and Gili Motong, as well as the surrounding waters of the Sape straits. All three islands are generally rocky, with the occasional sand beach to be found in some of the sheltered bays. The section of coastal mainland is similar in topography, but with an abundance of freshwater, something lacking on the islands. There are extensive patches of coral reef as well as large areas of seagrass beds. The predominant land vegetation, covering 70% of the park, is open grass and woodland savanna. There are also cloud forests on the peaks, tropical forests along the valleys and mangrove forests in some of the sheltered bays. More than 70 species of birds have been recorded within the park. Mammals include primates, ungulates and a number of feral domestic species. The most famous inhabitant is the Komodo monitor, the world's largest lizard.

SIGNIFICANCE

This dramatically beautiful park provides the only significant wild environment in the world for the Komodo monitor. The isolated and rugged nature of the park affords this magnificent and ancient lizard population of 5,700 the best chance of survival, as well offering a rare glimpse of biological evolution work. This area also has geological significance, being at the junction of the Asian and Australian tectonic plates.

ABOVE Crab eating Macaque
INSET The park's most famous resident and namesake
OPPOSITE PAGE INSET Forests of distinctive Siebold's beech cover the mountains of Shirakami

JAPAN

Shirakami-Sanchi (Shirakami Mountains)

LOCATION

In the north of Honshu, 15 km (9mi) inland from the Sea of Japan, N 40° 22' to 40° 32', E 140° 02' to 140° 12'.

DESCRIPTION

This park is all national forest and is located entirely within the Shirakami Mountains which extend over 450sqkm (176sqmi). Almost no logging has been carried out due to its remoteness and the nature of the terrain - these are rugged, steep sided mountains, with summits lying between 1,000 to 1,200m (3,300 to 4,000ft). More than half of the area comprises deep valleys with steep slopes at gradients of more than 30°. Many streams have their sources within the area and it is an important water catchment area. The climate is cool and moist and there is heavy snow during winter. The vegetation is dominated by Siebold's beech (Fagus crenata), which is the typical Japanese temperate forest.

SIGNIFICANCE

The Shirakami mountains are home to 24,000ha (57,600ac) of pristine Siebold's beech forest. This forest is the last beech forest wilderness in Japan and the largest remaining in the east Asia region. Many of the 500 odd plant species found within the area are also typical of Japanese flora. There are several species which are endemic to the area and also many globally threatened species including numerous orchids. All the mammal species found on Honshu, with the exception of two, are found within this park. The Japanese black bear is common, and the forest is also the northern most habitat for primates in the world - the snow monkey, or Japanese macaque is often seen roaming the forests. There have been 87 species of bird identified within the area, including one pair of golden eagles which is designated a National Monument and a Special Bird due to its limited breeding record and endangered status in Japan. There are also three pairs of black woodpecker and one pair of Hodgson's hawk, similarly designated as Special Birds. There is a particularly rich population of insects, with over 2,212 species having been recorded.

Yaku-Shima
(Yaku Island)

LOCATION

In the northern end of the Ryukyu archipelago, across a 60km (36mi) wide strait from Kyushu, N 30° 20', E 130° 30'.

DESCRIPTION

Yaku-shima is extremely rugged and steep. It has the highest mountain in southern Japan, and there are several other peaks over 1,800m (6,000ft) as well as ridges over 1,000m (3,300ft) which surround these central peaks. There are a limited number of walking paths and two huts are maintained.

SIGNIFICANCE

Yaku-shima's vegetation is unique in that it represents the southern limit of at least 200 species of plants. The flora is extremely varied, with more than 1,900 species recorded, 94 endemic to the island. A distinctive feature is the richness of epiphytes, particularly at higher elevations. Of special significance is the indigenous Japanese cedar (Cryptomeria japonica), known colloquially as 'sugi'. Specimens under 1,000 years old are known as 'kosugi', while older specimens, some over 3,000 years old, are known as 'yakusugi'. These majestic warriors of the forest are found at higher altitudes, they are revered as sacred trees and have a high spiritual value; many are known by name and their age and height are recorded. There are 16 species of mammals on the island including the Japanese macaque and the Sika deer. Amongst the 150 odd bird species present, four, including the Japanese wood pigeon and the Ryukyu robin, have been designated as Natural Monuments.

ABOVE Japanese macaque - the world's most northern dwelling primate
RIGHT Forest of Yaku cedar
INSET ABOVE An aerial view

Buddhist Monuments in the Horyu-ji Area

LOCATION

Nara Prefecture, approximately N 34° 42', E 135° 50'.

DESCRIPTION

A total of 48 buildings are included in this site: 21 in Horyu-ji East Temple, nine in Horyu-ji West Temple, 17 monasteries and associated buildings, and the Hokki-ji Pagoda. The plan of the complex is modelled on an ancient Chinese style, featuring an asymmetrical arrangement of the buildings. The structures themselves are remarkable for their intricate bracketing, a highly modified form of post and lintel construction, which enables the heavy tiled roofs to be supported on large wooden columns.

SIGNIFICANCE

Dating from the 8th century, this collection of Buddhist monuments was the first to be constructed in Japan, shortly after the introduction of Buddhism to the islands, and includes a worship hall which is said to house the ashes of the Buddha. Included in the complex are 11 buildings which are the oldest surviving wooden buildings in the world. The adaptation of Chinese architectural styles which the buildings of Horyu-ji initiated, proved to be profoundly influential on subsequent religious architecture throughout east Asia. The complex also represents a significant stage in the spread of Buddhism.

Himeji-jo

LOCATION

Hyogo Province, approximately N 34° 46', E 134° 38'.

DESCRIPTION

Himeji-jo is an archetypal 17th century Japanese castle complex. It comprises two concentric circles of walls and moats, enclosing turrets, keeps and Samurai residences. There are 83 buildings in total, all constructed of timber. At the center of the complex is the 'Tenshu-gun', consisting of three small keeps connected to a main keep. This elaborate structure, built on a low hill, is protected by a complex construction of plastered earth walls with many watch-towers and gates, and is visible from every part of the complex.

SIGNIFICANCE

Himeji, also known as the Castle of the White Heron, is the finest surviving example of a feudal castle from the Shogun period. Almost all of its kind were destroyed, and the few remaining seriously altered through later modifications. The mastery of the woodwork is astounding and the beauty of contrasting white plaster with wood and stone is exceptional. The castle is a symbol of functional feudalism and military might, and owes much of its excellent state of preservation to the practical considerations of its later keepers.

ABOVE *Himeji-jo framed by blossoms*
INSET *Part of Horyu-ji west temple complex*

NEW ZEALAND

Te Wāhipounamu
(South-West New Zealand)

LOCATION

Southland, Otago, Westland and Canterbury districts of the South Island, E 166 00' to 170 00', S 43 00' to 46 35'.

DESCRIPTION

This massive park covers around 2.6 million ha (6.2 million ac). It is an amalgamation of the previous sites of Fiordland and Mt. Cook/Westland National Parks, as well as incorporating Mt. Aspiring National Park and a large area of former State forest. The landscape varies tremendously; it includes the deeply indented, glacially cut mountains of Fiordland, more than 450km (280mi) of largely isolated coastland, 28 of New Zealand's 29 mountain peaks over 3,000m (9,842ft), three of the most spectacular glaciers to be found anywhere - Franz Josef, Fox and Tasman - sand dunes and rocky estuaries. The vegetation includes evergreen temperate rainforest, alpine tussock grasslands, herbfields, fellfields, wetlands and bogs. Fauna comprises mainly birds and invertebrates, many of which are endemic.

SIGNIFICANCE

Southwest New Zealand covers almost ten percent of the total land mass of New Zealand and it is the ten percent of the country which is least modified by human influences. The area demonstrates the world's finest remaining examples of Gondwana flora and fauna in their natural habitats. Distinctive flora, such as the extensive forests of southern beech and podocarps, are all a reflection of this ancient Gondwana origin and New Zealand's 80 million year isolation. The fauna is likewise distinctive. Most notable are two species of kiwis, the kea - the world's only alpine parrot, its forest relative, the kaka and the rail or takahe - a rare and endangered flightless bird which is now confined to a limited area of Fiordland.

INSET The kea - the world's only alpine parrot

Tongariro National Park

LOCATION

Tongariro and Wanganui regions, North Island,
S 38° 58' to 39° 25', E 175° 22' to 175° 48'.

DESCRIPTION

Covering 795sqkm (300sqmi), this park is situated on the central
volcanic plateau of the North Island. The altitude ranges from 500m
(1,665ft) to 2,797m (9,314ft) at Mount Tongariro - the highest peak
in the North Island. Both glacial and volcanic landscapes are to be
found, and the vegetation includes tussock/grassland and forests of
hardwood and beech. There are three ski fields within the park, although
the area affected by tourism covers only two percent of the total area.

SIGNIFICANCE

This area is linked with the arrival of the first Maoris from the Pacific.
The name 'Tongariro' is derived from 'Tonga', meaning 'fire' and 'riro'
meaning 'carried away'. These sacred mountain tops were given to the
New Zealand Government by the local Maori people in 1887 and
formed the nucleus of New Zealand's first national park. This extensive
natural area also has strong ecological significance. There is a long
history of vulcanism in the area, including volcanoes that are still active
today. This has produced a diverse range of ecosystems and highly
scenic landscapes which are invaluable from both scientific and aesthetic
viewpoints.

Baroque Churches of the Philippines

LOCATION

Four churches: Church of the Immaculate Conception of San Agustin, District of Intramuros, City of Manila; Church of Nuestra Señora de la Asunción, Municipality of Santa Maria, Province of Ilocos Sur; Church of San Agustín, Municipality of Paoay, Province of Ilocos Norte; Church of Santo Tomás de Villanueva, Municipality of Miag-ao, Province of Iloilo.

DESCRIPTION

The Church of the Immaculate Conception of San Agustin has a plain, box-like exterior. The interior walls are lined with paintings dating from the 19th century which overlay much older murals. Both sides of the nave are lined with chapels. Other distinctive features include a dome, stone barrel vault and arched vestibule. Built in brick, the Church of Nuestra Señora de la Asunción is situated on a hill and is completely surrounded by a defensive wall. Unusual features include a 'convento' which is parallel to the church facade and a separate bell tower. The Church of San Agustín was built to withstand earthquakes. It is heavily buttressed, and the lower part of the apse and most of the walls are constructed of coral stone blocks. The massive coral stone belltower sits some distance from the church. The Church of Santo Tomás de Villanueva stands at the highest point of Miag-ao, its towers serving as lookouts. The church is squat and heavily built and features a highly decorated and fanciful facade.

SIGNIFICANCE

The Church of the Immaculate Conception of San Agustin was the first church built on the island of Luzon in 1571, immediately after the Spanish conquest of Manila. This early structure was built from wood and palm fonds and was replaced six years later in 1587 by the stone structures which became the headquarters of the Augustinians in the Philippines. The church was the only structure in the area of Intramuros to survive the liberation of Manila in 1945. The Augustinian mission at Santa Maria which the Church of Nuestra Señora de la Asunción now represents has served as a base for the Christianization of the north of the Philippines since 1765. The success of the mission may no doubt in part be attributed to the unusual siting of the church on a hill, combined with it being surrounded by a defensive wall; measures which ensured its longevity. The Church of San Agustín at Paoay is considered to be the finest example in the Philippines of what is known as 'earthquake baroque'. Construction commenced in 1694 and was finally completed in 1710. The present building of the Church of Santo Tomás de Villanueva was constructed between 1787 and 1797 after being twice destroyed by Moslem pirates in 1741 and 1754. It was designed as a fortress to withstand further incursions, and is considered to be the most outstanding surviving example of 'fortress baroque'.

ABOVE Church of Santo Tomás de Villanueva

Tubbataha Reef Marine Park

LOCATION

*In the middle of the Central Sulu Sea, 181km (110mi) south-east of
Puerto Princesa City, Palawan Province,
N 08° 45' to 09° 00', E 119° 45' to 120° 04'.*

DESCRIPTION

*This extensive Marine Park comprises the only two atolls in the
Philippine archipelago, North Reef and South Reef. They are separated
by a 8km (5mi) wide channel. North Reef has an oblong shape and
comprises a continuous reef platform 16km (10mi) long and 4.5 km
(3mi) wide. It encloses a sandy lagoon which is around 24m (80ft)
deep. One of the most notable features is North Islet, a coral sand cay
which is an important breeding site for many bird and turtle species.
South Reef is triangular in shape and much smaller . It also encloses a
sandy lagoon, and features a coral sand cay, South Islet. This area is
exposed to both the south-west and north-east monsoons. Rough seas
are experienced much of the year: from July to October with the southwest monsoons, and then again from November to March during the
north-east monsoons.*

SIGNIFICANCE

*Tubbataha is one of the most biologically diverse coral reef systems in
South-East Asia and is of great importance for the sustenance of
fisheries as well as providing important breeding sites for several bird
species. The terrestrial flora is limited; only four species of trees occur,
and there are also only four species of grasses. Only two coconut groves
exist in the park. The marine flora is much more varied, with extensive
seagrass beds in the shallower parts of the reefs and lagoons and 45
different species of macroalgae. At least 46 different species of birds have
been observed, including brown boobies, red-footed boobies, common
noddy, sooty tern and crested tern. Marine turtles nest on some of the
beaches, including hawksbill turtle and green turtle. There is a very rich
fish population, with 379 species having been recorded. Black-tip shark
and white-tip shark, manta rays and eagle rays are common. Several
different clam species occur, including crocus clam, giant clam, scaly
clam and horse's hoof clam.*

THAILAND

Historic City of Ayutthaya

LOCATION
Ayutthaya Province, N 14° 20', E 101° 33'.

DESCRIPTION
The remains of this city, the second capital of Siam, are situated on an island at the junction of the Lopburi and Pasak rivers. The oval-shaped city was once enclosed by 12km (7.5mi) of fortified walls, only segments of which remain. The ruins of the old royal palace are located at the center of the island and at the heart of the present day historical park. To the north, is the largely intact palace of the crown prince which houses a museum. Numerous wat (monasteries and temples) are scattered throughout the city, some of these pre-date the establishment of Ayutthaya as the capital.

SIGNIFICANCE
Ayutthaya was established as the capital of Siam, after the decline of the Sukothai kingdom, on March 4th, 1351 by King U-Thong and remained so until 1767 when it was razed by the Burmese. Throughout these four centuries of rule, the city experienced rich and varied relations with many countries, including neighbors such as Vietnam, Cambodia, Indonesia, Laos, Malaysia and Burma as well as Europe, China, Japan and Persia. This enormous depth of influence resulted in the development of extremely complex forms of art and architectural styles which are so distinctive of Thai culture today.

Ban Chiang

LOCATION
Province of Udon Thani, approximately N 18° 22', E 101° 44'.

DESCRIPTION
This settlement on the Khorat plateau dates from around 3600BC. Three main periods of habitation have been recognised: the Early Period, from 3600BC to 1000BC; the Middle Period, from 1000BC to 300BC; and the Late Period, from 300BC to 300AD. The main excavations have taken place at the perimeter of the modern village of Ban Chiang. A large number of burial sites from all three periods, with rich finds of grave goods and ceramics, have been unearthed. It is thought that the major part of this site remains untouched under the modern village.

SIGNIFICANCE
Ban Chiang is without question the most important prehistoric site yet discovered in south-east Asia. Previous to the discovery of Ban Chiang it was believed that prehistoric south-east Asia was relatively under developed. These excavations have redefined our view of south-east Asia and the people of the region have been proved to have had a vigorous cultural past. The distinctive red-on-buff pottery of the region is particularly notable for its fine beauty. Within this site's strata lies the earliest evidence of farming and of the manufacture of metals in the region.

Thung Yai-Huai Kha Khaeng Wildlife Sanctuary

LOCATION

Kanchanaburi, Tak and Uthai Thani Provinces, on the Burmese border,
N 14° 56' to 15° 48', E 98° 27' to 99° 28'.

DESCRIPTION

The neighboring wildlife sanctuaries of Thung Yai and Huai Kha Khaeng together cover an area of 320,000ha (790,700ac). Both are generally hilly with many permanent and seasonal streams dissecting the landscape into small valleys and plains. A distinguishing feature of Thung Yai is the large central land plain from which it takes its name ('big field'). There are numerous small lakes, and swamps, both permanent and seasonal, as well as many limestone sink holes. The forests vary, with evergreen on the higher slopes, and mixed deciduous and bamboo across most of the lower areas. Almost 4,000 people live within the area.

SIGNIFICANCE

This is one of Thailand's least accessible and hence least disturbed areas. It supports numerous endemic species as well as at least 28 rare or endangered species. More than one-third of Southeast Asia's mammal species are present, while the dry tropical forest which is typical here is the most complete in Southeast Asia. It is also an area at the cross roads of several biogeographic zones - it contains elements of each of the Sino-Himalayan, Sundaic, Indo-Burmese and Indo-Chinese zones. Its importance in preserving two large watersheds for the region cannot be overstated.

TOP *One of the sanctuary's more spectacular residents*

The energies of our system will decay, the glory of the sun will be dimmed, and the earth, tideless and inert, will no longer tolerate the race which has for a moment disturbed its solitude. Man will go down into the pit, and all his thoughts will perish.

ARTHUR JAMES BALFOUR

Historic City of Sukhothai

LOCATION

Sukhothai and Kamphaeng Provinces, N 16° 21' to 17° 26', E 99° 27' to 99° 48'.

DESCRIPTION

There are three former cities in this listing, all now archeological sites: Sukhothai, Si Satchanalai and Kamphaeng Phet. All have walls and moats, special forested areas outside the walls which were for the use of Buddhist monks, and numerous Buddhist temples constructed of brick. It is thought that the royal palaces that once graced the sites would have been constructed of timber and hence left no traces. The remains of kilns are found outside the walls of Sukhothai and Si Satchanalai, once used to produce the famous Sangkalok ceramics. Sukhothai shows the remains of an intricate system of canals, reservoirs and ponds which was typical of Khmer settlements before the rise of the Sukhothai kingdom. The other two cities were built on rivers and adapted their layout to take advantage of the water flow.

SIGNIFICANCE

During the 12th century, people from Yunnan in China settled in the northern parts of the Khmer state. They were known as Thai, meaning 'free men' and they quickly organised themselves into small communities. The first Siamese state, the kingdom of Sukhothai, was formed after a Thai prince married a Khmer woman, rebelling against the controlling powers. This prince's second son, Rama the Strong, became a powerful sovereign, achieving numerous military victories, which brought with them much new territory. He invented the Thai alphabet, introduced strict Buddhist influences, and organised a social order based on the vanquished Khmer neighbors. So the Sukhothai culture was born and rapidly developed. These three towns present a remarkable record of the emergence of the Siamese culture.

Hue Monuments

LOCATION

Province of Thua Thien-Hue, approximately N 16° 33', E 107° 30'.

DESCRIPTION

The capital city of South Vietnam during the 17th and 18th centuries and the capital of united Vietnam from 1802-1945, Hue is a most distinguished city. Its impressive walls form three concentric boundaries, the outer forming an irregular hexagon, while the inner forms two squares. The first city consists of administrative and public buildings, while the inner city, which is also protected by a moat, contains royal residences and religious temples: the Palace of Supreme Harmony, The Queen Mother's Palace, the Mieu Temple and the Royal Reception Hall. The Forbidden Purple City around which the city is built was the King's own residence and had great ceremonial and spiritual signifi-cance, but is now mostly in ruins. The buildings of the city are highly decorative with straight edged rooves of yellow or blue cylindrical tiles resting on gilded pillars and rafters with brick walls, the whole being raised on a podium with wooden trusses.

SIGNIFICANCE

Hue is a paragon of Vietnamese culture. It has obvious historical signif-icance, and great architectural value. The city's rich cultural heritage is remarkable; it was built in harmony with the Vietnamese religious philosophy, incorporating in its planning and construction the elements: earth, wood, metal, fire and water; the cardinal points: center, east, west, north and south; and the five primary colors: yellow, white, blue, black and red. The building of the city also took into account the natural features of the site using the Perfume River as its main axis. As such, it is a remarkable demonstration of the power of the vanished Vietnamese feudal empire, and an outstanding example of an eastern feudal capital.

ABOVE The tomb of Emperor Khai Dinr
INSET Statue detail

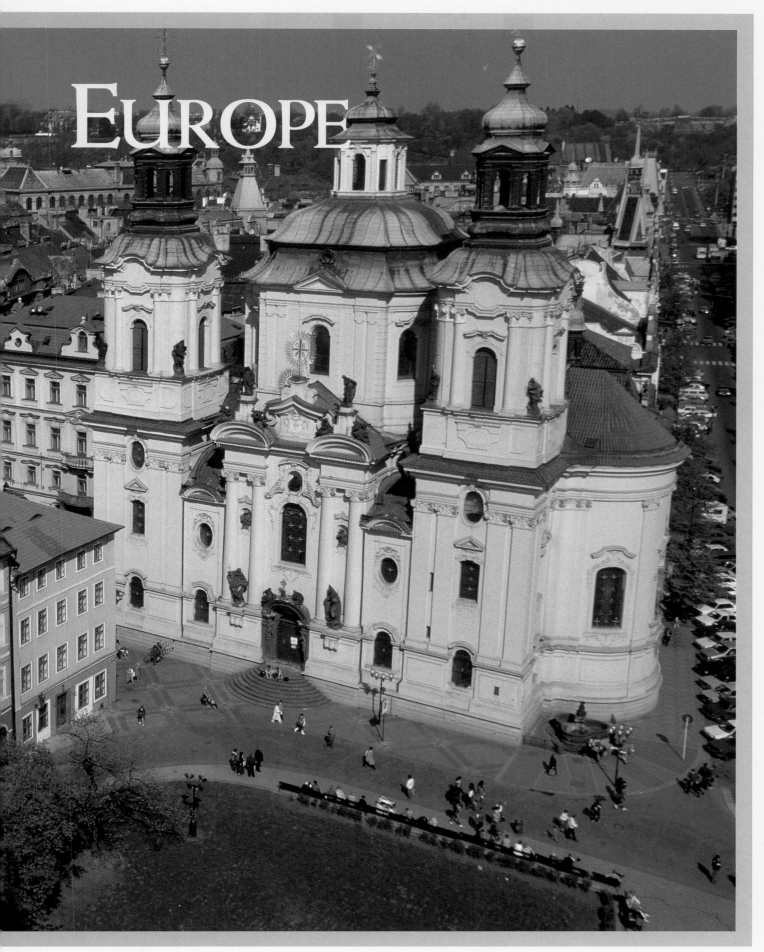

EUROPE

Historic Center of Prague

Butrinti

LOCATION

Region of Saranda, approximately N 39° 52', E 20° 00'.

DESCRIPTION

This ancient city, known to the Greeks as Buthros, comprises archeological remains, buildings and monuments, dating from the Greeks in the 7th century BC to the Venetians in the late 14th century. The most interesting ancient Greek monument is the theater, which is quite well preserved. From the Paleochristian era, there are the Roman public baths, featuring beautiful mosaic tiled floors, and the baptistery, which was built inside the baths and rebuilt in the 9th century.

SIGNIFICANCE

The site of Butrinti has been inhabited since prehistoric times. When a Greek colony was established over 2,600 years ago, fortifications were erected around the town. Later Roman occupation saw the emergence of a city, which, during the Christian era, became a bishopric, resulting in the construction of numerous religious monuments. The period from the 7th century until the 12th century saw many struggles and the affluence of the city declined. There was a short era of prosperity under Epirus in the 13th century, but the city was not to last much longer, and it was abandoned whilst under Ottoman rule at the end of the 14th century. The fact that the city was abandoned before later periods of building excess took hold, means that Butrinti today is able to provide clear evidence of its development from an ancient Greek colony to a city of the Middle Ages, making it an invaluable archeological conservatory.

ALBANIA

TOP Ruins of the theater at Butrinti
BELOW European bison
RIGHT Red deer

Belovezhskaya Pushcha and Bialowieza National Parks

LOCATION

*In south-west Belarus, and north-east central Poland,
N 52° 43´ to 52° 48´, E 23° 48´ to 23° 56´.*

DESCRIPTION

*This joint listing between Belarus and Poland forms an exceptionally
large park by European standards. Total area is around 93,000ha
(223,000ac), with 87,600ha (210,000ac) in Belarus and 5,316ha
(12,800ac) in Poland. This region is situated in between the hydrological basins of the Black Sea and the Baltic Sea. There are numerous
glacial formations with deep sandy deposits overlaying clay and loam
covered bedrock. The park is almost entirely covered by forest - 88% of
the land area is vegetated with conifers and broad-leafed trees, by far the
largest extent of old growth virgin forest in lowland Europe.
Belovezhskaya Pushcha was declared a National Park in 1991,
previous to that the Pushcha was managed and protected as a hunting
reserve. The adjacent Polish forest was designated a national park in
1932. In recognition of the fact that nature knows no boundaries, and
that the Byelorussian forest and the Polish forest are in fact one and the
same, the Director of the Belovezhskaya Pushcha is a member of
Bialowieza National Park's Scientific Committee. There is also a trans-
frontier committee which meets intermittently to discuss the management
of environmental problems.*

SIGNIFICANCE

*The entire area is unique in that it remains largely undisturbed by
human intervention. This small remnant is the only forest of its kind to
be found in Eastern Europe. Much of the flora and fauna is rare and it
is one of the few places where the origins of European ecology can be
studied and understood. It is this uniqueness, along with the location of
the site, which combines elements from Scandanavia/Siberia as well as
southern Europe, that has resulted in a biodiversity that is exceptionally
rich for this part of the world. There is an extensive population of free
ranging European bison, a major feature of the area which led to the
World Heritage inscription of the Polish portion of the forest in 1979.
More than 900 vascular plant species are known in the area, including
26 trees, 138 shrubs, 210 lichen, 80 liverwort and 1,500 fungi.
Broadleaved trees include, linden, oak, European hornbeam and
European ash. Also found in the park are coniferous pine and spruce.
There are also meadows and small patches of wetland scattered
throughout the park. The fauna is typical of European forest communities - what is left of them anyway - with 55 species of mammal,
including the European bison, wolf, European lynx, otter, red deer, roe
and wild boar. More than 200 different bird species live in the park
from 'mound birds' to boreal species and raptors. Of these, 90 species
nest and breed within the park. There are more than 8,000 species of
insects, along with 212 birds, eleven amphibians and seven reptiles.*

BULGARIA

Srebarna Nature Reserve

LOCATION

Srebarna Lake is located on the Danube flood plain, 19km (11mi) west of the town of Silistra in Silistra province, 1km (0.6mi) south of the Danube (which forms the border with Romania), N 44° 05', E 27° 07'.

DESCRIPTION

This reserve is 600ha (1,447ac) in area and comprises a freshwater lake which is situated on the flood plain of the River Danube. The lake was connected to the Danube until 1949, when the connection was blocked. This prevented the annual flooding which is so crucial to the lake ecosystem and the level of lake fell one meter per year. This situation was stabilised when the connection was recreated by canal in 1978. The land in the immediate surroundings is marshy, and just beyond the boundaries are low hills.

SIGNIFICANCE

The reserve was set up primarily to protect the rich avifauna - nearly 180 bird species (half of the Bulgarian avifauna), including 80 migratory species. There are 99 breeding species, including the only Bulgarian colonies of Dalmatian pelican, white-tailed eagle, glossy ibis , white spoonbill and little cormorant. The reserve is the only nesting place in Bulgaria for great egret, and there are five other species of heron with some 1,000 nests. Otter are occasionally found. Srebarna is the only natural tract of land of any considerable extent to be protected in north-eastern Bulgaria, a floristic region of the Ukraine-Kazakh biotic province. Members of the reed community (Phragmites communis) occupy two thirds of the reserve and form a thick barrier around the lake. Water lilies and a number of rare marsh plants are also found.

LEFT Some of Srebarna's rich birdlife - mute swans and a bearded tit feeding her young (INSET)

Pirin National Park

LOCATION

In the Pirin mountains, south-west Bulgaria, south of Razlog and Bansko, between the valleys of the rivers Strouma and Mesta, N 41° 40', E 22° 50'

DESCRIPTION

Covering 40,060ha (96,000ac), this park was created in 1934 when 2,900ha (7,000ac) were set aside as a reserve. Sixty percent of the park is coniferous forest and its altitude ranges from 1,000 to 2,915m (3,280 to 9,560ft) above sea level. There are around 70 glacial lakes scattered throughout the mountains and much of the landscape is glacially formed.

SIGNIFICANCE

This beautiful and rugged mountain landscape is a relic of the ancient glacial times of Europe. The presence of limestone rocks, the more southerly position of the range and closer proximity to the Aegean, coupled with its relative isolation, have made Pirin Mountain a most important refuge. Forests in the park are mainly coniferous, including endemic Macedonian pine, Bossnian pine, silver fir, Austrian pine, spruce and Scots pine. The flora of Pirin, comprising as it does many rare species, is of great interest and beauty; there is a mixture of central European, alpine, Balkan mountain and sub-Mediterranean species, but in addition there are some endemic species not found elsewhere (about 30 local endemic species). In all there are about 70 Bulgarian endemic species. There is a wide variety of animal species including many endemic species and glacial relicts among the invertebrate fauna. Threatened bird and mammal species include brown bear, wolf, pine marten, rock marten, polecat, badger, otter, wild cat, red deer, roe deer, wild boar, alpine chamois, golden eagle, hazel grouse, eagle owl, black woodpecker, and three-toed woodpecker.

ABOVE A forest of beech
INSET Badgers, one of the threatened species in Pirin

Ancient City of Nessebar

LOCATION

On the Bulgarian coast of the Black Sea, 30km (18.6mi) north of Burgas, N 42° 07', E 27° 39'.

DESCRIPTION

Situated on a 24ha (58ac) peninsula, the fortified City of Nessebar is connected by an isthmus to the mainland. The archeological sites cover twice the area of the peninsula and are mostly under water.

SIGNIFICANCE

These ruins represent over 2,000 years of history. Perhaps the most interesting are the earliest - the remains of an acropolis, a temple and an agora from the Hellenistic period. There are several important churches dating from the 10th century up to the 14th century AD. Later remains of importance include some fine examples of wooden architecture from the period of the Bulgarian Resistance.

Boyana Church

LOCATION

The Boyana district of the City of Sofia.

DESCRIPTION

This church has three sections, the eastern church, the middle or Kaloyan Church and the western church. All differ in architectural style and were built in different eras, but still manage to form a harmonious whole.

SIGNIFICANCE

The eastern church is the oldest construction, dating back to the 10th century, it was part of the royal court at Boyana during medieval times. The Kaloyan Church can be more accurately dated by its frescoes which were completed in 1259, while the western church was built around 1845, the time of the Bulgarian national uprising. Over 900 years of Bulgarian history are represented in this remarkable building.

ABOVE Fresco detail, Boyana Church

Madara Rider

LOCATION

Department of Shumen, eastern Bulgaria.

DESCRIPTION

This carving of a man on a horse is chiselled out of the solid rock of the Madara Plateau. A lion sits at the horse's feet and a dog follows behind. There are also Greek inscriptions carved in the rock.

SIGNIFICANCE

This sculpture is believed to represent the victory of a sovereign over his enemies. It dates from the 8th century, during the early years of the founding of the Bulgarian State. The inscriptions relate events that occurred between 705AD and 831AD. The detail and workmanship shown on this sculpture are remarkable.

Thracian Tomb of Kazanlak

LOCATION

The town of Kazanlak, in the Department of Stara Zagora, central Bulgaria.

DESCRIPTION

This tomb is situated at the southern slope of a burial mound and is composed of three chambers. The main part of the construction is the burial chamber, a brick construction in the shape of a beehive, 3.25 m (11ft) in diameter, with a corridor.

SIGNIFICANCE

This tomb is important because it differs significantly from other tombs of a similar age. The main distinguishing features are the beehive shape of the burial chamber dome and the outstanding quality of the fresco artwork which decorates the walls and ceilings. The most interesting fresco, the 'funeral banquet' alone deserves recognition as a landmark in the history of painting.

TOP *Madara Rider*
BELOW *Ceiling fresco at Kazanlak*

Rila Monastery

LOCATION

Rila mountain, E 23° 06', N 42° 07'.

DESCRIPTION

The main building is a rectangular fortress with two entrances. It comprises the monks' residences, four chapels, guestrooms, the kitchen, the 22m (72ft) high Khreljo Tower, the main church of the Dormition and the Orlitza Convent.

SIGNIFICANCE

The monastery was founded in the 10th century AD by followers of St. John of Rila. It is one of the more significant religious complexes in Europe. There are numerous works of art within its walls, including some superb 14th century frescoes, Byzantine paintings and intricate wood carvings. Perhaps the most important feature of this monastery is the crucial role it has played through the years in protecting and nurturing the Bulgarian culture, faith and language.

As we approach the year 2000, we would do well to think back a thousand years to the Dark Ages. At that time, monks hand-copied ancient manuscripts to preserve knowledge. A millenium later, species and their genetic manuscripts - whole biological libraries and the ecosystems that sustain them - are disappearing every day. Like the ancient scribes, we cannot predict the ultimate value of what we are trying to save. We only know that, collectively, the threatened biological treasures of our planet are resources we cannot afford to lose.

PARKS IN PERIL, Nature Conservancy

Thracian Tomb of Sveshtari

LOCATION

Razgrad District, northeastern Bulgaria.

DESCRIPTION

Only discovered in 1982, this tomb has three chambers and is constructed of stone blocks. It forms a mound some 80m (262ft) in diameter and almost 12m (39ft) high. The main burial chamber is particularly well preserved and is in the style of a dwelling with several interesting features, including four Doric columns, ten sculptures of females which are attached to the wall and support the architraves, two stone beds for the deceased couple and a frieze on the wall which depicts the deceased.

SIGNIFICANCE

This tomb dates back to the 3rd century BC and is one of the best preserved of surviving Hellenistic tombs. It is a unique monument to Thracian culture and to Hellenistic art.

Rock-Hewn Churches Of Ivanovo

LOCATION

The village of Ivanovo, 16km (10 mi) from Ruse, northeastern Bulgaria.

DESCRIPTION

Here we find a number of churches, monasteries, chapels and cells cut into the rock along the Rusenski River. There has been some serious damage inflicted to some of these monuments by rock slides. Five of the churches are preserved in reasonably good order.

SIGNIFICANCE

These carved monuments date from the time of the second Bulgarian State, 1187AD to 1396AD. Their construction was initiated by Joachim, then a monk, but later to become Joachim I, the first Bulgarian Patriach when the Bulgarian Church was restored to independence in 1235. The five preserved churches are decorated with outstanding frescoes, especially in the church of 'Tsarkvata', where the frescoes are considered to be some of the finest surviving examples of Byzantine art.

CROATIA

Old City of Dubrovnik

LOCATION

Adriatic coast of Croatia, N 42° 38', E 18° 06'.

DESCRIPTION

Covering 15.2ha (36.6ac), this listing includes all the buildings erected from the 12th to 16th centuries within the walls. The area is precisely defined by fortified walls, former moats and the steep coastline. The city was developed as a continuously evolving whole, with various documents showing the concern with controlling new building, based on the general city plan. A broad central square/main street, the 'Plazza', has all main north-south lines running perpendicular to it. Even following the great earthquake of 1667, the existing structural unity of the stone built city was maintained during its reconstruction. Major landmarks are the 'Castellum' which joins the rocky foundation of the city to the main coastline, the rector's palace, the cathedral and several fountains, public squares and public buildings.

SIGNIFICANCE

Due to the well preserved documents relating to various planning initiatives, Dubrovnik presents an almost intact record of medieval urban development both in conception and realisation. In many ways the city is the epitome of 'metropolitan' life, totally planned to fit its earlier role as a transport and economic hub. It exhibits both the characteristics of a political power base and an ecclesiastical seat. The town is permanently protected from any modern redevelopments.

Dubrovnik: the Crisis Continues

'Since wars begin in the minds of men, it is in the minds of men that the defences of peace must be constructed'. These words open the preamble to the constitution of UNESCO. But the 'minds of men' is at the same time the most sensitive and the most resistant material. Recent events in different parts of the world show that we do not learn anything from history: after millions of human lives were lost in the two world wars which shocked mankind by the scale of disaster they produced, armed conflicts continue to explode for the sake of some abstract ideas, money, oil, but in fact for the sake of power.

Constitutions, laws, and international and other agreements have value only when they are respected. Unfortunately however, people obsessed with the idea of power tend to forget the promises they made and the responsibilities they

accepted in the past. They neglect laws, ignore dignity, and become oblivious to beauty.

Dubrovnik, this pearl of the Adriatic coast, has managed to retain its rich and diverse identity over the centuries. It survived earthquakes and fires, tidal waves, an epidemic of plague, and several wars. But neither natural nor man-made disasters could wipe this remarkable city from the map. As the legendary Phoenix, it rose from the ashes and continued to prosper, gradually becoming one of the most famous cultural centers of Europe.

In 1979 the Old City of Dubrovnik was inscribed on the World Heritage List as a 'unique creation of medieval architecture and town planning, which has exerted considerable influence not only within a small area but on the greater area of the Adriatic coast and the Balkans'. Four years earlier, in 1975,

having ratified the World Heritage Convention, the Government of Yugoslavia assumed its national and international obligation to safeguard the property concerned 'as part of the world heritage of man-kind as a whole'.

From the very beginning of the tragic events in Yugoslavia, another international instrument came into effect in the territory of this country - the Hague Convention for the protection of cultural property in the event of armed conflict. This convention applies to movable and immovable property in the event of declared war or of any other armed conflict between two state parties and also 'in the event of an armed conflict not of an international character occurring' within the territory of a state party. This convention was ratified by the Government of Yugoslavia.

Already in September 1991, before the bombardment of Dubrovnik began, the Director-General of UNESCO, Mr Federico Mayor, in his public appeal invited all authorities concerned to respect the rules imposed by international conventions protecting cultural heritage. For a few weeks it seemed that this appeal was heard and taken into account so that monuments located in the former Yugoslavia, particularly nine sites inscribed on the World Heritage List, were not damaged. Nevertheless, in the course of the fall of 1991 the Secretary General of the United Nations and the Director-General of UNESCO repeatedly addressed the authorities concerned as well as the international community, warning them against the devastating consequences of the war in the Yugoslavia. On the 25th October the General Conference of UNESCO dedicated a session to the discussion of the situation in Yugoslavia and the danger it represents for Dubrovnik. In its resolution on this subject the General Conference urged 'the opposing forces to withdraw from the city of Dubrovnik which is included on the World Heritage List and whose splendor belongs to the whole of humanity'.

Unfortunately, all these efforts did not lead to any improvement of the situation and after several bombardments in October-November, the day of the 6th December 1991 became known as the Black Friday. At dawn, the city of Dubrovnik was attacked by heavy artillery. UNESCO observers in Dubrovnik reported that the city had suffered from this attack: 30% of buildings in the old city have been destroyed or seriously damaged, including the Pile Gate, a Dominican monastery and a Franciscan monastery, Saint Blaise Church, Palace Sponza, a Serbian church, the Rupe museum, and the facades of the buildings in the avenues

Sponza Palace, Dubrovnik

in Carthage (Tunisia) took a decision to inscribe the Old City of Dubrovnik on the World Heritage List in Danger. (I should like to clarify that putting a site on this special list must not be regarded as a sanction against it or the country where it is located. On the contrary, it is a way to draw even more public attention to the current state of the site concerned and to provide exceptional measures for its salvation and preservation in the future.) Simultaneously, elaboration of the plan of action for the most urgent restoration began with participation of UNESCO Secretariat and international experts.

In the framework of this urgent assistance, the Director-General announced to the Mayor of Dubrovnik that UNESCO had allocated US$200,000 for the restoration of the historic city. Later, another US$49,000 was allocated by the World Heritage Committee. A meeting of national and international experts was organized by UNESCO, the Institute of Protection of Historical Monuments and the Institute of Restoration of Dubrovnik. The participants of this meeting elaborated a plan for urgent restoration work. Since 60% of the roofs of the old city had been damaged, it was decided that they should become an object of priority operation before winter. For this purpose 270,000 tiles were purchased by UNESCO and sent by lorries to Dubrovnik..

In spring of 1992, while occasional bombardments of Dubrovnik continued, it was Bosnia-Herzegovina which became the 'hot spot' of the conflict. Once again, the Director-General of UNESCO launched an appeal for the peaceful coexistence of the different communities of the country in order to save 'our most precious heritage - which is each human life', as well as to protect the most beautiful creations of humanity. Mr. Mayor underlined the threat to a number of cultural and religious sites, some of which are more than 400 years old and represent the history and sacred values of Islamic, Catholic, Orthodox and Hebrew communities who live in the territory of Bosnia-Herzegovina.

At the time of writing, the war in the former Yugoslavia is still going on. People continue to be killed and deprived of their homes. Blood and tears are still being shed and the future seems sombre. And yet the hope exists that one more time common sense will take over and the Phoenix will again rise from the ashes.

Bernd von Droste
Director, World Heritage Center

Stradun and Prijeko, some of which date back to the thirteenth and fourteenth centuries. Altogether, about 1,000 buildings were to a greater or lesser degree damaged by the shelling.

The moment this news was announced, the Director-General addressed a cable to General Veljko Kadijevic, Federal Minister of Defence, which said, in particular: 'I solemnly demand that you give an immediate order to your armed forces to stop any hostile action against the city, in the name of international law and in respect for humanity and the world community'. Again no result. Later that month the World Heritage Committee at its 15th session which was held

Historic Complex of Split with Diocletian Palace

LOCATION
Adriatic Coast of Croatia, N 43° 30', E 16° 26'.

DESCRIPTION
The massive Palace of Diocletian, built from the late 3rd century to early 4th century AD, covered more than 30,000sqm (333,000sqft). It is rectangular with peripheral towered walls and double gates. The remains of the imperial apartments to the south are built on a substructure supporting 50 vaulted rooms. There are temples and baths, the remains of porticos, servants' dwellings and the open entrance hall containing the Mausoleum of Diocletian. Within the well preserved Roman palace are several monuments and architectural complexes, dating from the Middles Ages to recent times. These include Romanesque monuments from the 12th and 13th centuries, Gothic palaces, medieval fortifications, baroque and Renaissance buildings. Outside the palace, the medieval town contains numerous churches such as those containing the sculptures of St. Anastasius and St. Arnir. Several baroque and Renaissance edifices can be found, though often having been substantially altered.

SIGNIFICANCE
Built specifically for Emperor Diocletian's retirement, this palace is one of the largest in Europe and the best preserved of all Roman monumental buildings. It is of inestimable value in the study and conservation of ancient structures. The town outside the old palace provides invaluable records of the series of rulers that followed the collapse of the Roman Empire.

ABOVE The entrance to the mausoleum
RIGHT Campanile of St. Doimus Cathedral with Diocletian's Palace in the foreground

National Park of the Plitvice Lakes

LOCATION

Croatia, N 44° 52', E 15° 36'.

DESCRIPTION

The Korana River flows through this park which covers 192sqkm (75sqmi) of spectacular forest, lakes and streams. More than 20 lakes and countless waterfalls, the highest 80m (260ft), cover this luxuriant landscape. The water has a high concentration of calcium carbonate which leaves many formations called travertine dams - naturally formed dams which grow around 1cm (0.4in) per year.

SIGNIFICANCE

This park contains a unique system of lakes and waterfalls, all part of the natural flow of the Korana River. The profuse growth of moss-like material over thousands of years has formed natural dams along the river's flow, creating a series of deep lakes, all connected with waterfalls. When in full flow, this system is one of the natural wonders of Europe. The wooded hills overlooking the water are a refuge for bears, wolves and many rare birds. This is one of Europe's last virgin forests.

CYPRUS

RIGHT Ruins of Aphrodite's Temple, Paphos
BELOW Fresco detail, Archangelos Michael at Pedhoulos, Troodos

Painted Churches in the Troodos Region

LOCATION

Troodos Region,
N 34° 58' to 35° 00',
E 32° 49' to 33° 02'.

DESCRIPTION

This listing comprises nine churches: 1. Ayios Nikolaostis Steyis at Kakopetria; 2. Ayios Ionnis Lambadhistis Monastery at Kalopanayiotis; 3. Panayia Phorviotissa at Nikitari; 4. Panayia tou Arakou at Lagoudhera; 5. Panayia at Moutoullas; 6. Archangelos Michael at Pedhoulas; 7. Timios Stavros at Pelendria; 8. Panayia Podhithou at Galata; 9. Stavros Ayiasmati at Platanistasa.

SIGNIFICANCE

All nine churches are in a good state of preservation, but their styles and dates of construction vary. The earliest was built in the 11th century. The paintings represent different styles of art, including that of the 13th century crusaders, 12th century Constantinople, 15th century Middle East, Italian Renaissance and a style influenced by medieval manuscripts.

Paphos

LOCATION

Paphos district, southeastern coastline,
N 34° 39' to 34° 46',
E 32° 24' to 32° 37'.

DESCRIPTION

The World Heritage area of Paphos comprises three sites; the coastline that is the legendary birthplace of Aphrodite; Aphrodite's sanctuary at Kouklia village; Aphrodite's sacred city at Kato Paphos town.

SIGNIFICANCE

All three places were of tremendous significance in the ancient world. Aphrodite, the Greek Goddess of Love, was born, according to Homeric legend, when she emerged from the foaming sea at the very spot cited in this listing. The Sanctuary of Aphrodite at Kouklia was mentioned by Homer and other ancient authors and is considered to be the most important of the many that were built in the ancient world. The sacred city has many impressive buildings, including the ruins of a theater, a gymnasium, an odeon, baths, a necropolis, catacombs and early Christian basilicas.

CZECH REPUBLIC

Historic Center of Cesky Krumlov

LOCATION
Southern Bohemia on the banks of the Vltava River, approximately N 48° 49', E 14° 28'.

DESCRIPTION
Cesky Krumlov straddles the Vltava River at the site of an ancient travel route which was a channel of east-west communication for centuries. The castle of the Vitkovici family, planted firmly on one side of the river, dates from the 13th century, the core being a Gothic 'Hradeck' with a high round tower. Added to this base were constructions of Renaissance and baroque styles, the whole being converted into a baroque chateau in the mid-18th century with the addition of a garden, the Bellaire summer palace and a theater. Facing the castle, on the other side of the river, is a medieval town which extends out from the traditional town square. The town was a wealthy one and contains many prestigious houses.

SIGNIFICANCE
Cesky Krumlov is an outstanding example of a medieval central European town owing its architectural significance to its history of economic importance. The peaceful and prosperous history of the town and its castle has preserved many magnificent examples of architecture from the 13th to the 19th centuries. The wealth of the region attracted great artists and contributed to the building of both residential and ecclesiastical buildings of exceptional quality. The natural setting of the town in a scenic bend of the Vltava river also adds to the site's rich scenic beauty.

Historic Center of Prague

LOCATION

Central Bohemia, approximately N 50° 03', E ° 14 25'.

DESCRIPTION

There are three separate elements to the historic center of Prague: the old town (Staré Mesto), the lesser town (Malá Strana) and the new town (Nové Mesto). The old town was established in the late 9th century on top of a much older settlement, dating back into prehistory. It was built initially on the left bank of the river, where Prague Castle now stands, but soon after expanded down towards the river. During the next century, the town grew rapidly, becoming the capital of Bohemia. Many of the earlier wooden structures were replaced with stone, as Staré Mesto emerged. Nové Mesto was established in the mid 14th century, when the town experienced another period of rapid growth and a defensive wall was erected. Today, Prague is rich in monuments from all periods of its history; notably Prague Castle, the Cathedral of St. Vitus, Hradcany Square, the Gothic arcaded houses around the old square, and the late 19th century buildings and plan of the Nové Mesto.

SIGNIFICANCE

The integrity and authenticity of Prague is remarkable. More than 1,000 years of urban development is represented throughout the Historic Reservation which covers more than 866ha (2,100ac) and over 3,500 individual buildings. Today Prague is one of the most beautiful cities in Europe, both in terms of its dramatic setting and the high standard of restoration which has been carried out on its rich inventory of historic monuments.

ABOVE A view of the old town from Charles Bridge

Historical Center of Telc

LOCATION
Moravia, near the south-western border with Bohemia, approximately N 49° 11', E 15° 29'.

DESCRIPTION
Situated on a hilltop, the city is built around a market square which is shaped like an elongated triangle. There are numerous stone houses and a church from the 14th century, as well as a late 15th century Gothic castle, a Renaissance castle, a distinctive triangular market place, and a baroque Jesuit college and church. The profusion of architectural styles can be seen most clearly in the 14th century Church of St Jacob: the basic twin-aisled layout has seen added a Renaissance choir (1638), a Gothic tower and a baroque dome (1687).

SIGNIFICANCE
Telc fortunately avoided major refurbishment in the 19th and 20th centuries, and so today retains its authentic nature. Settlements such as Telc were established in areas of thick forest for reasons of political control and economic expansion. It is a magnificent example of the planned settlements of medieval Europe, preserving the original town plan and highlighting the town-castle relationship which was so crucial. The market place particularly is of great cultural significance, as well as being a feature of great beauty, surrounded as it is by well preserved Renaissance buildings and a variety of facades.

Fortress of Suomenlinna

LOCATION
Province of Uusimaa, N 60° 09', E 24° 57'.

DESCRIPTION
Suomenlinna is a bastion fortress, comprising a series of fortifications on six islands just off the coast of Helsinki. Construction of the walls is of granite, while the 190 buildings are brick. The area of the islands is 73ha (175ac). Four of the islands constitute a virtually enclosed fortress. In the middle there is a dockyard which was formed by blasting the seabed and damming between the islands. The administrative center, the Great Courtyard of Susisaari, is also in the middle.

SIGNIFICANCE
Work began on the construction of Sveaborg ('Swedish Fortress') in 1748, under orders from the Swedish Parliament. It was the largest construction project in Sweden in the 18th century, at the peak of activity the construction crew totalled more than 6,500. It was conceived to control entry into Helsinki and to provide a safe winter harbor. The name was changed to Suomenlinna ('Fortress of Finland') following Finland's declaration of independence in 1918. The unique conception and construction of this well preserved fortress provides a fascinating and invaluable study in military architecture.

Old Rauma

LOCATION
Gulf of Botnia, Province of Turku et Pori, approximately N 61° 07', E 21° 30'.

DESCRIPTION
Rauma today is a modern city, but the old center is intact and has been very well preserved even though it was decimated by fire in the early 17th century. The principal monuments of the old center are the Franciscan Church and the City Hall.

SIGNIFICANCE
Rauma is a remarkable example of an old Nordic timber city. It was originally built around a Franciscan monastery - the 15th century church which was attached to it still survives. It soon developed into an important harbor: now one of the oldest in Finland. The town is typical of the architecture of old northern European cities and it is without doubt one of the most beautiful and extensive examples that has survived.

FORMER YUGOSLAV REPUBLIC OF MACEDONIA

Top The small Monastic Church of St. John Bigorski is perched upon a rock overlooking Lake Ohrid
Bottom A view across the lake to the town of Ohrid

Ohrid and its Lake

LOCATION

Southwest Macedonia,
N 40° 54', E 20° 37'.

DESCRIPTION

The lake is 294sqkm (118sqmi) in area and belongs to a large group of lakes in the Adriatic basin. It is situated 694m (2,277ft) above sea level and is fed by underground springs. There are numerous archeological sites from the Neolithic and Bronze Ages as well as from the Illyrian period scattered around the area. The medieval fortified city of Ohrid is on a hill over-looking the lake. Many churches and monasteries are preserved, St. Pantelejmon with the tomb of St. Clement, St. Naum and St. Sophie's Cathedral being the most important. Some Islamic monuments mark the 500 years of Turkish rule.

SIGNIFICANCE

Ohrid is one of the oldest Slavic cultural and religious centers in the Balkans. Clement, who was a 9th century follower of the two prominent Byzantine missionaries, Cyril and Methodist, founded an important education center here. It was the capital of the first Macedonian Slav Empire of Samuilo, from 976 to 1014. Its most precious treasure is the world renowned collection of Byzantine icons from the 11th to 14th centuries. This collection is the second most important in the world after the Tretiakov Gallery. The lake is also of great importance, both culturally and ecologically. Its archeological sites are numerous and the lake itself supports several rare species of flora and fauna.

Stone portal, Chartres Cathedral

A Reference for all Humanity

The wonders of the ancient world numbered only seven. Things are no longer so simple. Our planet, having been totally chartered and mapped, contains an evergrowing number of buildings and sites listed under World Heritage, which reflects a concern for preserving our cultural roots.

In France, the notion of heritage is quite ancient, dating back to Italian influences of antiquity. Nowadays, laws protect and maintain not only artistic treasures but also urban zones, factories of social significance and machines. In fact, the idea of preservation follows and embraces the great changes due to wars, revolutions and agrarian reform.

Our commitment to historical monuments stems from the Revolution and from the Romantic period. Within days of the First World War, we were lamenting the destruction of the Arras squares and discovering the importance of civil architecture. The Second World War brought with it the obliteration of the old quarters of Rouen, Tours and Le Havre. As a result, laws have been drafted to protect areas of historical importance. Profound economic changes of the sixties were as destructive as both wars, resulting in the transformation of much of the countryside into desert and the neglect of numerous small towns, in particular the industrial areas of the north and east of France.

Consequently, a greater interest in both monuments and urban structures developed. This interest in our heritage has entered our consciousness and made a large impact. It goes

If all the elements of heritage preservation benefit a nation, they should also benefit society at a universal level.

The World Heritage List represents more than an honor list for a particular country. Rather, it should be an anthology contrasting the exceptional and the marvellous, to be used as a reference for all humanity.

Lascaux, Carnac and Mont Saint-Michel are fine examples of the exceptional, while Chartres, Vézelay or Versailles represent the marvellous. The perfect expression of the spiritual life-blood of a society can only be assured if the authenticity of a site is undeniably preserved. Is it not true that the aura of a particular place is linked to the emotional impact of having our consciousness raised? Can we separate Cologne Cathedral from Goethe, Notre Dame from Victor Hugo, the Colosseum from Chateaubriand and Chartres from Peguy? Isn't this the value of World Heritage work?

La Douce France should also figure on a World Heritage list. Yet where does the cultural begin and the natural end? Auvers-Sur-Oise, Saint Victoire Mountain and the sunflowers around Arles should be kept for the world to cherish.

One of the major duties of World Heritage is to place the preservation of what belongs to everyone in the hands of those who are dedicated to this monumental task. The Parthenon, the Dogon Statues and the Temple of Angor are all living testimony to this feat. Yet, the idea of international scientific co-operation along the lines of a Doctors Without Borders concept would be a strong show of heritage unity. I believe that France would play a major role in this area.

André Malraux dedicated many prophetic pages to the imaginary museum of mankind. It is vital that mankind strives to preserve the works which constitute our own, real heritage.

MR. JACK LANG
Former Minister for Culture, France
Translated by Nick Baker

Royal Saltworks of Arc-et-Senans

LOCATION

Franche-Comté, N 47° 03', E 05° 04'.

DESCRIPTION

The saltworks complex consists of the director's villa at the center, with the factory buildings arranged in a semi-circle around it. There are two large workshops either side of the villa, where the salty brine was processed in massive vats. The raw material was pumped some distance to this complex through a system of wooden piping.

SIGNIFICANCE

In 1776 these saltworks were built according to a grand scheme designed by master 18th century architect, Claude-Nicolas Ledoux, that would have seen an entire city built around them. Unfortunately they never operated entirely successfully and changed hands quite a few times. The current owners, the District of Doubs, bought the works in 1927 and soon after launched a campaign to restore them. Today it houses an information center concerned with future trends and is open to the public.

Chateau and Estate of Chambord

LOCATION

In the Loire Valley, N 47° 37', E 01° 32'.

DESCRIPTION

The estate of Chambord is entirely owned by the State. It is situated on the Cosson River and occupies an area of over 5,000ha (12,055ac). A 32km (20mi) wall with six gates surrounds the entire estate. The chateau dominates the site. It is rectangular in plan, the sides being 770m (2,526ft) by 156m (512ft). Four large cylindrical towers sit at each corner of the building.

SIGNIFICANCE

Originally built as a hunting lodge, the chateau was completely rebuilt by Francis I and Henry II. It subsequently passed through many royal and noble hands, including Stanislaw I, Louis XV and Napoleon. It was purchased by the State in 1932. Today the chateau is considered to be one of the true marvels of Renaissance architecture. Particularly famous are the roof, a forest of elaborate chimneys and ornate lanterns, and the spiral staircases which wind around each other without touching.

Pont du Gard

LOCATION

Languedoc-Roussillon, N 43° 56', E 04° 32'.

DESCRIPTION

A sandstone bridge, just under 49m (161ft) high, the Pont du Gard is constructed with three levels of arches. The first level has six arches, the second level eleven and the top level 35. The largest of the arches, under which the river flows, is almost 25m (82ft) wide.

SIGNIFICANCE

Remarkably large for this style of construction, this bridge formed part of a 50km (31mi) long aqueduct which was built around 20BC to supply water to the town of Nîmes. The harmony of the design, the amazing state of preservation and the sheer vastness of this aqueduct bridge provides a superb monument to the daring of Roman engineering.

Fix your eyes on nature - follow the path traced by her.

———————————

JEAN-JACQUES ROUSSEAU

Church of St. Savin-sur-Gartempe

LOCATION

In the Poitou region, department of Vienne.

DESCRIPTION

The main body of the church is 70m (230ft) long and is complemented by five chapels. It is crowned by a 94m (310ft) lanced tower. Ten columns decorated with animals and demons correspond to the chapels which are arranged in a semi-circle around the center. Two old rectangular crypts are found under the altar and one of the chapels. Most of the monastic buildings have disappeared except a building east of the church.

SIGNIFICANCE

A monastery was first founded on this site in 811AD by Charlemagne. Construction of the abbey commenced around 200 years later. It suffered a tortuous history, being destroyed several times, until the Benedictine monks of St. Maur rebuilt it in 1640. There are several exceptional murals within this complex, notably those dating back to the 11th century which depict scenes from Genesis and Exodus.

Strasbourg - Grand Ile

LOCATION

Strasbourg, Alsace, N 48° 33', E 07° 40'.

DESCRIPTION

The protected sector of the city is an island in the middle of the town. The river Ill surrounds it, forming channels around the district known as 'petite France'. This old quarter is very striking with its numerous timbered houses along the channels. Several covered bridges cross the waterways. The most remarkable building is the famous Gothic cathedral built in red sandstone over a period of eight centuries, (11th to 19th), on Place Kleber. The facades are richly decorated with carvings and statues and the church is enhanced by a beautiful 142m (466ft) high spire.

SIGNIFICANCE

This island is the site of the original town, which was a Celtic settlement. After the Romans captured it, the town passed to the Franks who gave it its present name in the 5th century AD. Seven centuries of German domination began in 842 when the 'Strasbourg oaths' were taken between Charles the Bald and Louis the German. This town's fame lies in its rich and often bloody history resulting from its strategic importance, its striking architectural heritage and its crucial role as a center for artistic and intellectual endeavors, especially through the renowned University of Strasbourg.

Amiens Cathedral

LOCATION

In the town of Amiens, province of Picardy, Department of Somme.

DESCRIPTION

The cathedral is 133m (435ft) long and 65m (213ft) wide. It is built on three levels, reaching a height of 42m (138ft) with large arcades covering half of the interior. On the western side are two large towers, a rose window, and a magnificent array of stone sculptures, including a 13th century Christ and a scene of the Last Judgement. The enormous interior is striking for the purity of its lines and the carved wood choir stalls.

SIGNIFICANCE

Built on the site of a Romanesque church of 1220, the cathedral is the largest in France. The imposing structure with its tri-level construction is acknowledged as the finest example of a Chartrian Grand Basilica. The vast collection of statues is remarkable for its diversity and quality.

Place Stanislas, Place de la Carrière and Place d'Alliance In Nancy

LOCATION

Nancy, Lorraine.

DESCRIPTION

Apart from the three squares, there are many buildings, monuments, statues, fountains and facades, including: Hotel de Ville, a vast palace, Arc de Triumphe, a main arch with two lower flanking arches, Café de Foy, a former medical college and Palais de l'Intendance, now a military residence.

SIGNIFICANCE

In 1751, Stanislaw, the father-in-law of Louis XV, conceived the plan to link the old town and the new town by means of a 500m (1,640ft) long vista which would be formed by creating these three squares. The result was a magnificent blend of classical and baroque architecture which today stands as a testimony to 18th century urban planning.

ABOVE Neptune's Fountain, Place Stanislas

Mont St. Michel

LOCATION

On the borders of lower Normandy and Brittany.

DESCRIPTION

This monastery is perched on a small granite outcrop 80m (263ft) high, linked to the mainland by a 19th century causeway. On the islet there is a fortified Gothic abbey and a small village with one street named Grande Rue. There is a church crowning the mount with a large spire which rises 152m (500ft) above the surrounding sea.

SIGNIFICANCE

The monastery was founded in 96AD by 12 Benedictine monks, as a sanctuary dedicated to St. Michel. The early Romanesque church of Notre-Dame Sous-Terre dates from that period. It was an important pilgrimage center for many kings. The monastic community had a great sphere of spiritual and artistic influence as demonstrated by the numerous beautifully illuminated manuscripts found here. Mont-Saint Michel is one of the most dramatic sites in Europe, particularly when the famous tides course into the bay.

Saving a Sanctuary of Prehistoric Art

The prehistoric painted cave of Lascaux is situated near the little town of Montignac in the Périgord region of south-west France. The whole area is rich in prehistoric sites, but it is in the limestone cliffs which run beside the winding course of the Vézère river that the ancient rock shelters and caves are most abundant.

The Lascaux cave was discovered on the 12th September 1940 by four children from Montignac while they were playing among the pines and chestnut trees on a steep slope above the river a kilometer or two outside the town.

The opening of the cave, barely 800mm (31.5in) square, was half hidden beneath a layer of dead leaves. It plunged vertically into the hillside, ending in a pile of debris and rubble.

In the next few weeks, the undergrowth surrounding the entrance was cleared, and an enormous pit several dozen meters wide was dug in front of the hole. The excavations provided virtually direct access to the grotto which, because of the animals depicted on its ceiling and walls, was to become known as the Hall of Bulls.

Access to the cave had probably never been easy. After the last of the cave artists had left, rocks falling from the roof gradually piled up and sealed off the grotto for thousands of years. Air currents and water infiltrating through the debris caused little damage, except possibly during the period at the end of the Ice Age, when geologists believe that the calcite hollows known as gours were formed. The calcification of the surface of the cone of rubble, the formation of stalactites, and the infiltration of sand and clay washed down by glacial meltwater must have consolidated the barrier at the entrance. Studies would later show the importance of this barrier in preserving the frescoes on the walls of the cave. The roof of the limestone vault, between six and eight meters thick, was covered by a layer of impermeable clay. As a result, the paintings, including the 'unicorn' situated less than 10m (33ft) from the original passageway, remained in a perfect state of preservation.

The listing of the site as a historic monument on the 27th December 1940 enabled the French authorities to intervene on what was a piece of private property, and the owner was wisely persuaded to erect a wooden door at the entrance to the cave. However, this was mainly to prevent uncontrolled access by the public, not to preserve the grotto's 'micro climate' the significance of which was still unsuspected.

Major operations at Lascaux did not begin until World War II was over, and it was not until the 14th July, 1948 that, with a stone staircase, a bronze door, an entrance hall and a paved pathway through the grotto which had been equipped with protective barriers and lighting, Lascaux was opened to the public.

The scenes portrayed in color on the brilliant white calcite crust are a supremely beautiful and impressive display of Palaeolithic art, with their remarkably skilful use of the relief of the cave walls to depict animals caught in mid-movement, and their highly individual mixture of perspectives and profiles. The conservation of the frescoes called for scrupulous care and constant supervision.

In July 1955, the curator noticed that during peak visiting periods condensation colored by pigments from the frescoes was dripping from the walls and ceiling. Scientific investigation established that this was caused by the carbon dioxide exhaled by the visitors.

In 1958, an air conditioning system was installed. The air in the cave was sucked through a filter to remove dust, decarbonated, and cooled to a constant temperature of 14°C (57°F), while the humidity was kept close to dew point (95-98%). This electronically regulated system was hooked up to a turnstile which recorded the number of visitors entering the cave.

It proved so successful in eliminating condensation and purifying the atmosphere that the owner was authorised to keep it running at full power at the height of the summer tourist season, when on some days over a thousand visitors filed through the grotto.

In September 1960, the curator noticed a green spot, so tiny as to be scarcely perceptible, on the ceiling of the cave. Despite the application of a treatment recommended by the Pasteur Institute, tests the following year showed that more spots had appeared. And so, in March 1963, the Minister of Cultural Affairs, André Malraux, appointed a special committee of scientists from a wide range of disciplines to investigate the problem and propose solutions. It took over ten years of dedicated efforts and close collaboration between scientists from over a score of laboratories before the frescoes were finally saved.

The closure of the cave, on the 20th April 1963, was no solution to the problem. The colonies of microscopic plant organisms which were the source of the danger continued to spread, and within a few months had increased from three to 720. Laboratory tests revealed the presence of many species of algae, as well as growths of ferns, mosses and fungi. Shock treatment was clearly required to eliminate these sources of pollution.

After making sure that the paintings would not be harmed, the scientists rid the cave of bacteria in the air by spraying the cave with antibiotics. The algae on the walls, which had by now spread out in to 1,350 colonies, were gradually destroyed by spraying with solutions of formalin, in concentrations of 1:10 on the cave floor, 1:20 on the bare rock, and 1:200 on the paintings. After two years of treatment, the micro-organisms had been totally wiped out, but in order to prevent further contamination, visits were limited in number and duration, and the intensity of the lighting was considerably reduced. Regular analysis of the bacteria and the algae in the atmosphere and on the floor of the cave, and inspections of the walls and ceiling have made it possible to limit precautionary measures against new outbreaks to a minimum.

Scarcely had the biological attack been repulsed, however, than a new threat to the paintings materialised. The right-hand wall of a smaller cave which is decorated with stags, began to disappear under a fine crust of calcite crystals. The same thing began to happen, to a lesser extent, to the unicorn in the main grotto.

The pigmentation of the paintings was examined in depth and content, and the temperature of the soil was studied by infra-red radiometry. At the same time, the temperature at various points on the cave walls was measured to within 1/100th of a degree, and the volume of the enclosed space was accurately determined (1,778 cubic meter or 63,000 cubic feet). Aerodynamic studies were carried out to detect the existence of microclimates through data provided by electronic equipment which recorded in minute detail the temperature, humidity, carbon dioxide content and barometric pressure.

The processing of all the data obtained over several years led the scientific committee to decide on a course of action designed to preserve as far as possible the 'natural' climate of the cave, and more particularly to prevent changes in temperature, humidity and carbon dioxide content.

Decorated Caves of the Vézère Valley

LOCATION

Near the town of Les Eyzies, in Dordogne, N 45° 00', E 01° 00'.

DESCRIPTION

There are sixteen sites within this extensive prehistoric listing which follows the course of the Vézère River. Near the town of Les Eyzies, there are four grottoes, three rock shelters and six sites of fossil deposits. Scattered at various places nearby are three other grottoes.

SIGNIFICANCE

These sites date way back into prehistory and show signs of continuous occupation for up to 100,000 years. This extraordinary length of occupation has left an exceptionally rich legacy of ancient artwork, artefacts and fossils. It was here that the first remains of Cro-Magnon Man were found. Such a wealth of information has emanated from these sites that the area is considered by many to be the single most important prehistoric site yet uncovered.

ABOVE Detail inside Font de Gaume cave, Vézère Valley

Air entering the cave is now chilled; excess carbon dioxide of natural origin is tapped at its source (the so-called 'Wizard's Well') and pumped out of the cave. Partitioning of the cave into several compartments also helps to stabilise the temperature, humidity, and carbon dioxide content. No more than five visitors, who must be bona fide scientists, may enter the cave on any one day. The cave is completely sealed on two days each week.

Eighteen years after the cave was closed to the public, the wall paintings of Lascaux have been saved from what had seemed to be certain destruction.

MAGDALEINE HOURS

Roman and Romanesque Monuments of Arles

LOCATION

Arles, Provence, N 43° 41′, E 04° 38′.

DESCRIPTION

The historic section of the township of Arles contains eight buildings or monuments from Roman times or later that are of importance: 1. the arena - a very early amphitheater; 2. the ancient theater; 3. an underground gallery called the Crypto-Porticus; 4. the Thermae of Constantine - old heated baths; 5. miscellaneous ruins that include stonework from the protective wall of an old fortress; 6. a necropolis called the Alyscamps; 7. the Church of St. Trophime; 8. Montmajour Abbey.

SIGNIFICANCE

Some of the earlier buildings, such as the ancient theater, date from the reign of Augustus, around the end of the 1st century BC. At this time Arles was a thriving shipyard and enjoyed substantial material prosperity. By around 400AD Arles had become the second city of the Roman Empire and an important religious center. Later buildings, like the Church of St. Trophime, are typical of Romanesque architecture.

ABOVE Roman arena at Arles

Chartres Cathedral

LOCATION

Chartres, 100km (62mi) southwest of Paris.

DESCRIPTION

This massive Gothic cathedral is 130m (427ft) long, 45m (148ft) across and 36m (118ft) high. The highest spire is the Clocher Neuf, at 113m (371ft), while the Clocher Vieux is 105m (344ft) above the ground. There are seven side chapels and the entire structure is supported by numerous methods of internal and external buttressing.

SIGNIFICANCE

The Cathedral of Notre Dame in Chartres was founded in the 11th century AD by Bishop Fulbert on the site of an older church. It was destroyed by fire in 1194 and the cathedral that stands today was built in the mid 13th century. This cathedral is considered to be one of the outstanding examples of high Gothic architecture. Its 13th century stained glass, the statuary of the portals and the Renaissance choir screens are all unique. The view of the irregular spires against the horizon is one of the most famous sights in France.

Cistercian Abbey of Fontenay

LOCATION

In the Cote d'Or department, Burgundy, E 04° 24', N 47° 39'.

DESCRIPTION

The Abbey of Fontenay is situated at the bottom of the valley of the Egraves. It is a self contained complex of two buildings. The first is a lodge and chapel for visitors, while the second, a monastic complex, comprises a church, refectory and cellars. There is also an infirmary built upon the banks of the river along with a black-smiths' works.

SIGNIFICANCE

Founded in 1188, Fontenay quickly developed into one of the most prosperous of the Cistercian monasteries. It became a royal abbey and had as many as 300 monks in the 14th century. Its position as one of the foremost religious centers in France continued until its decline during the Hundred Year's War.

ABOVE The courtyard at Fontenay

Palace and Park of Versailles

LOCATION

Versailles, west of Paris.

DESCRIPTION

The palace grounds are 100ha (241ac) in area with magnificently landscaped gardens created between 1661 and 1668 by Le Notre. The palace itself consists of three sections in the form of two flanking wings and an extended open rectangle, the interior of which forms two courtyards, the Cour de Marbre and the larger Cour Royale. The interior is notable for its reception hall and 'Galerie des Glaces'.

SIGNIFICANCE

Originally built in 1624 as a hunting lodge for Louis XIII, the palace was enlarged around 1682 for Louis XIV and became his seat of government. One of its more remarkable features is the 'Galerie des Glaces', a magnificent hall 76m (250ft) long and 10m (33ft) wide which is illuminated by 17 large windows on one side and enhanced by 17 panels of 400 mirrors on the opposite wall. This palace is associated with two monumental events; the French Revolution and the signing of the peace treaty in 1919.

ABOVE The Hall of Mirrors, Versailles

Roman Theater and Triumphal Arch of Orange

LOCATION

Orange, Provence, N 44° 08', E 04° 48'.

DESCRIPTION

Standing to the north of the town of Orange is the Triumphal Arch comprising three archways, the outer pair smaller in size. Nearby is the large Roman theater built under Augustus having a southern facade 103m (338ft) long with a 38m (125ft) high wall. The mighty statue of the Emperor Augustus is in a central niche with the lower five rows of the 10,000 seat auditorium having been restored.

SIGNIFICANCE

The arch commemorates the founding of the colony of Arausio (Orange) and numerous land and naval battles. Its decorations and military trophies are extremely well preserved giving detailed records of several campaigns. The immense scale of the southern facade, which is virtually complete, makes this theater unique in the world of Roman architecture.

Palace and Park of Fontainebleau

LOCATION

In the Ile de France area, Department of Seine-et-Jarne, N 48° 24', E 02° 42'.

DESCRIPTION

This large and rambling palace has a very complex plan due to its long history of extensions and renovations. Some of its more notable features include the massive main entrance, 115m (378ft) by 112m (368ft), known as the Cour des Adieux, and the horseshoe shaped staircase which leads to the first floor apartments. To the east of the palace, there is an 84ha (210ac) area of parkland.

SIGNIFICANCE

Fontainebleau is rich in royal history. Originally built as the royal hunting lodge in 1137 under St. Louis, Phillipe IV was born here in 1268. After being abandoned in the 15th century, Francois I gave it new prosperity by making it his residence. It was further extended between 1594 and 1609 by Henri IV. Napoleon chose the palace as his first imperial residence and restored it extensively.

Scandola Nature Reserve and Capes Girolata and Porto

LOCATION

Situated in the communes of d'Osani (Scandola Nature Reserve), Ota, Partinello, Piana and Serriera of South Corsica and Commune Galleria of Haut Corsica,
N 42° 14' to 42° 25', E 08° 37' to 09° 00'.

DESCRIPTION

The reserve is divided into two sectors: the Elpa Nera inlet and the peninsula of Scandola. The World Heritage site covers 12,000ha (28,800ac) on land and 4,200ha (10,080ac) of marine habitat. The area has a varied and rugged relief on marine and shore habitats. The jagged and sheer cliffs contain many grottos and are flanked by numerous stacks and almost inaccessible islets and coves. The combination of the red cliffs, some 900m (3,000ft) high, sand beaches, headlands such as Cape Osani and the Peninsula of Elbo, and the transparent sea, make the area exceptionally beautiful.

SIGNIFICANCE

Scandola Nature Reserve contains a rich pelagic, sedentary and migrant fauna including several dozen pairs of a rare subspecies of shag, some peregrine falcons, osprey, bearded vulture and Eleonora falcon with Cory's shearwater and Audouin's gull occurring in the littoral zone. The marine environment contains considerable numbers of spiny lobster and a wide range of invertebrates and fish. All the classic zones of marine algae for this part of the Mediterranean are represented and a number of species, including red algae, occur which are not recorded elsewhere in the region. There are also some Roman sites of significance, and the remains of a Genoese fortification system.

Cathedral of St Stephen, Bourges

LOCATION

Département of Cher, approximately N 47° 07', E 02° 23'.

DESCRIPTION

This site has been of religious significance to Christians from the 3rd century AD, when Gaul's first Christian community was established. The construction of this cathedral began in 1195, and continued throughout the 13th century. It was built on top of an 11th century Romanesque basilica, and a small crypt from that structure still survives. The form of the cathedral is basilican, with chapels surrounding the nave, and it boasts exceptional sculptures on the north and south doors as well as a remarkable depiction of the Last Judgement on the western facade. The stained glass is also of exceptional quality.

SIGNIFICANCE

The overall beauty and harmony of this very original cathedral is the product of careful planning and continuous construction, as well as aesthetic sensitivity. Unlike most great Gothic cathedrals, St Stephens was built with a view to its entirety and not added to piecemeal over the centuries. Its principal claim lies in its striking beauty, combining as it does a superior management of space with harmonious proportions and interior decorations of style and grace.

Banks of the Seine, Paris

LOCATION

Paris, Ile de France, N 48° 50', E 02° 21'.

DESCRIPTION

The section of the Seine in this listing is based on the age-old distinction between Paris upstream and Paris downstream: upstream is the port and the center of commercial river traffic, while downstream - the area encompassed by this listing - is the heart of aristocratic Paris. This area is bounded by Pont de Sully and Pont d'Iéna and includes Ile de la Cité and Ile Saint-Louis. There are numerous significant buildings and places along these banks, including: the Louvre Palace and Tuileries Gardens, Place Saint-Germaine-l'Auxerrois, Place de la Concorde, The Hôtel des Invalides, the Grand Palais and Petit Palais des Champs Elysées, Ecole Militaire, Champs-de-Mars, the Eiffel Tower, the Palais de Chaillot and the Trocadéro Gardens.

SIGNIFICANCE

This world renowned riverside ensemble constitutes a remarkable example of urban architecture where the differing architectural styles of this great city's dynamic history are harmoniously and grandly displayed. The astounding density of masterpieces found in this area is not repeated anywhere around the world. Several of them were standard references for the spread of particular styles - such as Notre Dame which inspired countless Gothic constructions, or the Place de la Concorde and Invalides which both exerted considerable influence on the urban development of European capitals.

Notre Dame Cathedral, Tau Palace and the former Abbey of Saint-Remi, Reims

LOCATION

The town of Reims, region of Champagne Ardenne, approximately N 49° 17', E 04° 02'.

DESCRIPTION

This listing comprises three religious buildings in the old town of Reims. The predominantly Romanesque abbey dates back to the 11th century, when construction commenced on the site of St. Christopher's chapel. The cathedral of Notre Dame is classically Gothic in style; it replaced an older Carolingian church which was destroyed by fire in 1211. Construction was completed by the end of the 13th century. The archiepiscopal palace was built between 1498 and 1509.

SIGNIFICANCE

Christianity was established in Reims by the middle of the 3rd century, when a bishopric was founded there. Several of the town's bishops were canonised, the most famous being St. Remigius (St. Remi). He anointed Clovis, the King of the Franks in Reims. Later kings desired to be anointed there with oil from the sacred phial which according to legend was sent from heaven by a dove for Clovis. This phial of oil was delivered from the abbey, where it was stored, to the cathedral, where the consecration took place. Later, a banquet was held in the palace, which was the episcopal see. So it may be seen that these buildings form an historical ensemble of considerable significance as they all played a role in the construction of the French sovereign. Architecturally they are also of considerable significance; Notre Dame is viewed as a masterpiece of Gothic art, while the abbey's perfect lines have exerted influence upon many subsequent churches, particularly in Germany.

ABOVE *Notre Dame Cathedral, Reims*

You brought it to my attention everything that was made in God; down through centuries of great writings and paintings. Everything lives in God; seen through architecture of great cathedrals down through the history of time; is and was in the beginning and evermore shall be.

VAN MORRISON

Vézelay, Basilica and Hill

LOCATION
In Burgundy, about 150km (93mi) west of Dijon.

DESCRIPTION
Known in France as the 'Eternal Hill', the fortified village of Vézelay, perched on a hill above the Burgundy countryside, is dominated by the magnificent abbey church of la Madeleine, built mainly in the Romanesque style. The interior is striking for its simplicity and the exceptional quality of its capitals.

SIGNIFICANCE
The abbey was first founded around 875AD. After a short decline in the 11th century, it prospered due to the rumor that the body of Marie Madeleine was buried in the church. The nave dates from that period, around 1140AD. The three door portal was carved between 1125-1130 and is a remarkable example of early Romanesque art. In 1146, the Second Crusade was preached here by Saint Bernard, and in 1217 the first Franciscan building in France was established on this site.

LEFT View over the Bascillica

GERMANY

Conservation: the task ahead

Anybody who has followed politics in Europe knows that, as from the 3rd October 1990, the 'German question' has been resolved: Germany has been reunited! For more than forty years people and nature were physically separated by the 'Iron Curtain'. Politically, there were two German states in existence. That is why the German Federal Republic had already entered into the agreement to protect the world's natural and cultural heritage on 23rd August, 1976, while it took the German Democratic Republic until 12th December, 1988, to join.

St. Mary's Cathedral, Hildesheim

During the period of separation after the Second World War, the United Nations has been of special significance to Germany: through their programs and agreements they brought both German states into early negotiations through bonds of common responsibilities. In future we will remember this with gratitude.

The Second World War had grave consequences for Germany's common cultural heritage. The enormous damage done to the cathedral and monastery at Hildesheim and to the castle in Potsdam has only in very recent times been able to be partially repaired.

At the same time, our monuments throughout the country are threatened by new dangers. Extensive air pollution is causing worrying damage to old and new materials alike. It is becoming increasingly necessary to reorganise, conserve and restore monuments which have existed for hundreds of years.

To assist in this work, the Ministry of the Environment, through the Environment Department, maintains a co-ordination and advisory branch concerned with environmental damage to monuments. Through exchange of information, this branch encourages co-operation in the protection of monuments.

The fundamental contribution to environmental policy concentrates on reorganization , conservation and restoration. As a result of careful environmental policy - utilising protective measures for soil, air and water as well as climate - extensive damage from emissions will be avoided. Only in this way is it possible to permanently protect cultural and natural values.

That is why I would like to see, within the frame work of both the World Heritage Convention and the relevant EEC conventions, clear political emphasis placed on the fight against pollution which crosses international boundaries.

I greet the publication of this book with great enthusiasm. It pictures the unique heritage of our common natural and cultural past, and in so doing leads us to the realisation of the importance of both national effort and international co-operation.

It especially pleases me that nine of Germany's cultural monuments have fulfilled the requirements for acceptance and so have been included on the World Heritage List. I see however, that we, despite our multi-faceted and beautiful countryside, have not as yet nominated any natural sites for World Heritage inclusion. In this I see a great and rewarding challenge for the future.

PROFESSOR DR. KLAUS TOPFER
Federal Minister for the Environment, Conservation and Reactor Safety

Aachen Cathedral

LOCATION

*The town of Aachen, around 100km (62mi) west of Bonn,
approximately N 56° 00', E 06° 00'.*

DESCRIPTION

*The central structure of this building is the original palace cathedral.
This is in the Carolingian style, it is octagonal in shape and is crowned
by a large dome or cupola. An important feature is the bronze cast main
portal, known as 'Wolf's Doors'. Several substantial extensions have
been made over the centuries including the present day town hall and the
choir hall, which are both in the Gothic style. Also an addition, the
Hungarian chapel to the southwest contains a rich collection of art.*

SIGNIFICANCE

*This cathedral was built under Charlemagne's direction during the
period 790 to 800AD by his master builder, Odo. It was the first
church of Charlemagne's 'Empire' and its construction was considered
by his contemporaries to be a 'miracle'. The illustrious Emperor was
buried here and it continued after his death to serve as the place of
coronation for more than 30 succeeding German kings and emperors.
The cathedral possesses numerous sacred relics which are brought out
for public display once every seven years.*

INSET Charlemagne's throne

Historic Monuments in Trier

LOCATION

Province of Rhineland-Palatinate, N 49° 45', E 06° 47'.

DESCRIPTION

This beautiful old town abounds with historical monuments. Of the numerous Roman buildings, the most impressive include the amphitheater, which seated 30,000 people; the remarkable Porta Nigra, a massive fortified gate, 30m (98ft) high; the ornately decorated Barbara baths; and the nine piered Moselle bridge. Later monuments include the Romanesque Trier cathedral, an early Gothic church named the Church of Our Lady and the old town hall.

SIGNIFICANCE

Trier is the oldest town in Germany. It was founded in 15BC by the Romans and soon after became known as 'Roma secunda'. The collection of Roman monuments is certainly without parallel in Germany and is barely rivalled elsewhere. The later monuments are also of significance; the Church of Our Lady is thought to be the oldest Gothic church in Germany.

TOP *View into the Roman amphitheater*
BOTTOM *The Porta Nigra*

Pilgrimage Church of Wies

LOCATION

In Steingaden, Upper Bavaria, N 47° 40', E 10° 50'.

DESCRIPTION

Situated in a large expanse of meadow, this harmonious rococo style church is roughly oval in shape. The interior is rich and colorful, with countless ceiling and wall paintings, highly ornamental stucco work and many statues. The steeply walled altar dominates the room and the focus is on the ornate pulpit.

SIGNIFICANCE

The church is a famous center of pilgrimage. It was built upon the spot where a local woman is said to have found a wooden figure of Christ crying. After hearing about this miracle, several famous artists gave their services in the construction of the church. These works, which include pieces by Albrecht, Bergmuller and Mages, make this church very important in the world of European art.

Augustusburg and Falkenlust Castles at Brühl

LOCATION

Between Cologne and Bonn, in North Rhine-Westphalia Land.

DESCRIPTION

Augustusburg has three brick-built wings with two adjoining orangeries (hot houses for oranges). The facade is composed of a series of embrasures and pilasters with ornately decorated sculptures. There are a number of large rooms, including that of the Prince Elector of Cologne, called the Yellow Room. The castle is set in gardens with many symmetrical flower beds leading to an ornamental lake. The main alley is lined with lime trees, leading to Falkenlust. Falkenlust is a two storey, rough-rendered brick building in the country style. There are two adjoining exhibition rooms. Set in a small park, it was used as a base for Prince Elector, Clemens August to practice his favourite sport, falconry.

SIGNIFICANCE

Construction of Augustusburg commenced in 1725. It remained the residence of the Prince Elector until 1794. For the next 21 years it was the property of France until it became the official residence of the Prussian Royal Family, and afterwards of the German Kaisers. It has been a museum since 1918. Falkenlust was built from 1729 on, and was conceived as a large country residence. It was constructed to allow the Prince Elector, Clemens August, to practise his favourite sport of falconry. It has been a government museum since 1960. The two buildings which originally housed the Prince Elector's falcons are now used for exhibitions. Both castles are considered to be exquisite examples of rococo architecture.

ABOVE Falkenlust Castle

Palaces and Parks of Potsdam and Berlin

LOCATION

Potsdam County and Berlin, N 52° 24', E 13° 02'.

DESCRIPTION

Here we have a large ensemble of palaces and parks from the 18th and 19th centuries. The centerpiece is Sans-Souci Palace. This is a three-winged masonry building of one storey, with a central courtyard bounded by a colonnaded porch. There are extensive grounds adjacent, including a large terraced vineyard, several large guest residences, a Chinese tea house and numerous objects of garden architecture. Numerous other palaces, churches, guest houses and gardens are to be found in the immediate vicinity of these central palace grounds.

SIGNIFICANCE

These buildings and gardens were designed and constructed by the best available architects, craftsmen, builders and artists of the day. They represent the zenith of the 18th and 19th century north German rococo styles. The preservation of this entire ensemble in such original condition, plus the retention of this rich collection of artwork in its original setting, presents a unique and invaluable record of the artistic, architectural and social history of those times.

ABOVE LEFT Sans Souci Palace
ABOVE RIGHT Cathedral and Residence seen from across the Regnitz River, Bamberg

Historic Center of Bamberg

LOCATION

Northern Bavaria, N 49° 54', E 10° 50'.

DESCRIPTION

The historic center covers a total of 250 ha (600 ac). It incorporates the three areas of settlement that coalesced when the town was founded. These are: Bergstadt, with its cathedral and precincts, the former Prince-Bishop's residence, and the burgher area with the vintner's settlement and parish church; the Inselstadt, founded in the 12th century with a market and pre-urban settlement and defined by the two arms of the Regnitz River; and the Theuerstadt, a late medieval area of market gardens with scattered houses and large open spaces.

SIGNIFICANCE

Bamberg is a magnificent example of a central European town with an early medieval plan which has managed to retain a high level of authenticity. The street layouts of the three areas still display their medieval features and numerous ecclesiastical and secular buildings have been carefully restored. The architecture of this town had strong influences on both north Germany and Hungary in the Gothic period, whilst its Baroque elements are closely linked with developments in Bohemia.

St. Mary's Cathedral and St. Michael's Church at Hildesheim

LOCATION

Hildesheim, Lower Saxony, N 52° 15', E 09° 48'.

DESCRIPTION

St. Mary's is in the center of the town of Hildesheim, while St. Michael's is found on a hill-top a little to the north-west of the center. St. Michael's is architecturally the more interesting, being exceptionally broad and built in ashlar masonry. It has four slender towers with three apses projecting from the eastern end. The flat ceiling is supported by typical Saxon column-piers with arcade arches alternating in red and white stone. This ceiling is of wood and has a representation of the 'Tree of Jesus' painted on it.

SIGNIFICANCE

St. Michael's was founded by Bishop Bernward who, later canonized, is buried there. The painted ceiling is of great beauty and is a unique example of 12th century art. The gold cross and candelabras to be found in St. Mary's are of exceptional quality. These examples of the famed Hildesheim metalwork were executed by St. Bernward.

ABOVE St. Mary's Cathedral: interior detail showing bronze column

Speyer Cathedral

LOCATION

Speyer, Rhineland-Palatinate, N 49° 20', E 08° 25'.

DESCRIPTION

This is a large cruciform sandstone basilica with three main naves. Its design is distinguished by the considerable incorporation of arches (vaulting). There are several other important features including two octagonal towers, a series of large, rounded arched windows and extensive gabling of the ceilings. The interior walls are decorated with spectacular frescoes.

SIGNIFICANCE

This church has had a colorful and chequered history. Construction of the original cathedral began under Emperor Konrad II in 1030AD and continued until 1061 when it was consecrated by Henry III. In 1082 Henry IV commenced reinforcing the structure as well as constructing towers and an apse. The entire building was gutted by fire in 1689 when the French soldiers of Louis XIV attacked during the Palatine War of Succession. Restoration and extensions proceeded during 1772-1784, but damage was again inflicted by French hands in 1794. Further restoration and the addition of some beautiful frescoes were completed between 1846-1858. Most recently, extensive renovations were completed in 1968 and the cathedral now stands as a superb example of an early Romanesque basilica with equally impressive Gothic additions.

Hanseatic City of Lübeck

LOCATION

Schleswig-Holstein, N 53° 51', E 10° 43'.

DESCRIPTION

The center of this old Hanseatic seaport is dominated by its seven church towers. St. Mary's is the most famous of these Gothic churches. Of the remaining buildings, the town hall, which dates from the Middles Ages is the most well known. One of the distinctive features of the town is its rows of well preserved houses, all adorned with ornate facades.

SIGNIFICANCE

The historic center of this fine old city represents the best preserved example of a typical medieval northern European townscape. Particular importance is given to St. Mary's Cathedral, one of the finest examples of early Gothic architecture in Europe, and to the town hall, which is famous for its staircase and its intricate wood carvings.

Abbey and Altenmünster of Lorsch

LOCATION

The town of Lorsch, Hessen, approximately N 49° 49', E 08° 40'.

DESCRIPTION

This listing incorporates three principal elements: the site of the original monastery at Altenmünster (an island on the river), the monastery which was built on the riverbank to replace the earlier one, and the Carolingian gatehouse which is part of the later monastery. Within the largely intact walls of the later monastery, various buildings have been preserved: a nave of a Romanesque basilica, residential and administrative buildings, a tithe barn, and a bailiff's house and lodge. The gatehouse is well preserved and includes an impressive collection of wall murals and sculptures.

SIGNIFICANCE

The first monastery was established around 764-765AD. The first Abbot was the Bishop of Metz who donated the relics of St Nazarius, which he had acquired from Rome. As its reputation grew, so did its population, resulting in plans for a new monastery which was duly built and consecrated in the presence of Charlemagne in 774. Improvements were made over the next century, culminating in it becoming, at the death of Louis II the German, the burial place for the Carolingian kings. This complex today represents a rare architectural and cultural document of the Carolingian era.

Würzburg Residence

LOCATION

District of Lower Franconia in the State of Bavaria,
E 09° 56′, N 49° 47′.

DESCRIPTION

Surrounded by extensive gardens, the central building, the Corps-de-Logis, is decorated with sandstone statues in a severe classical baroque style. The state rooms have lavish decor culminating in the imperial hall with its triple flight staircase. There is a development throughout the residence from the early 18th century decorative style to the mature rococo outside. The court gardens are skilfully laid out to take advantage of the area which is limited by the bastions of the city fortifications.

SIGNIFICANCE

The residence, and especially the imperial hall, are amongst the greatest examples of European baroque architecture. The ceiling paintings in the hall are regarded as the high point of that art in Europe, while the Prince-Bishop's Court Church has great decorative works from painter Rudolph Byss, stuccoist Antonio Bassi and sculptor Wolfgang van der Auvers.

The Maulbronn Monastery Complex

LOCATION

Land Baden-Württemberg

DESCRIPTION

The basic medieval layout of this monastery complex, which is typical of the Cistercian tradition, is intact. The church especially is typical of early Cistercian architecture, with its two-storey Romanesque nave and low chevet leading to a transept which has three rectangular chapels off each arm to the west. Throughout the 13th century, many of the wooden buildings were rebuilt in stone. The fortifications which surround the complex consist of a 850m (2,800ft) outer wall and an inner wall, with a ward between them. The monk's refectory and lay dormitories are the only structures which have undergone significant alterations since the Reformation - in order to adapt them for use as a Protestant seminary. Several post-monastic buildings are included in the listing, including the former hunting lodge of the Duke of Württemberg, and the Ducal stables. Also included is an elaborate system of water reservoirs, irrigation canals and drains.

SIGNIFICANCE

The Maulbronn Monastery was founded by twelve monks from the Cistercian abbey of Neubourg in the middle of the 12th century and today it is the most complete surviving example of a Cistercian monastic establishment in Europe. The medieval Gothic style found here was very influential throughout Germany and much of Europe. The construction of the church particularly, was of fundamental importance in the spread of the Gothic style. The hydraulic schemes for which the Cistercians are well known are richly exemplified in the water complex of Maulbronn. The monastery and its hydraulic system are in extremely good condition, and the changes made by the monastery's more recent Protestant inhabitants have only added to the complex's historical interest.

Rammelsberg Mines and Historic Center of Goslar

LOCATION

In the Harz Mountains of Lower Saxony

DESCRIPTION

The remains of the mining industries at Rammelsberg are remarkably complete and representative of every period from the 10th century until the 20th century. Included are 10th century waste heaps, 12th century ore transportation tracks, numerous tunnels, various mining structures and installations, quarries, water wheels, administration buildings, ventilation shafts and miners' residences. Only one kilometer north west of the mining site is the old town of Goslar. This town achieved great prosperity through revenues from mining, financing the construction of the late medieval townscape which is so well preserved today. Among the notable monuments are: the Imperial Palace and Palatine Chapel of St. Ulrich; the Frankenburger Church; the Frankenburg miner's settlement; and the market place fountain.

SIGNIFICANCE

Rammelsberg Mine has been a source of metals for human use since the 3rd century. Copper, lead, zinc and gold were all found, but silver was the richest plunder. It was partly due to the silver deposits that the Imperial residence of Emperor Henry II was built at the base of the mountain at the beginning of the 11th century. The town of Goslar which subsequently grew around it, became rich and powerful due to the mine. Both the town and the mine have grown over time, and remained economically powerful well into the 20th century. The mine was still in operation until full and final closure in 1988. One of the earliest and most continuous industrial mining towns in the world, Goslar and its mine are of great historical interest. Rammelsberg is a veritable museum of mining techniques and equipment. The wealth generated by the mine also contributed to the quality of the growing town center and the beauty and extravagance of its many notable buildings and constructions.

GREECE

...The whole Greek world, past, present and future, rises before me. I see again the soft, low mounds in which the illustrious dead were hidden away; ...I see the geometrical pattern of nature expounded by the earth itself in a silence which is deafening. The Greek earth opens before me like the Book of Revelation.

HENRY MILLER, COLOSSUS OF MAROUSSI

Delos

LOCATION

The island of Delos is part of the Cyclades group in the central Aegean,
E 22° 56', N 37° 33'.

DESCRIPTION

This listing comprises the entire island of Delos, which is a protected archeological zone. It is only 5km (3mi) long and 1,300m (4,330ft) wide, but contains a fabulous collection of ancient monuments, sites and associated articles. There are three harbors which were all used in ancient times, an ancient town, a sacred precinct which was dedicated to Apollo and which includes several temples, many residences and an agora.

SIGNIFICANCE

According to Homer, Delos was the birthplace of Apollo, who, next to his father Zeus, was the most feared of the ancient Greek gods. Hence the island was from early times a sacred place and an important religious sanctuary. The other factor that has contributed to the fame of this island is its location. Occupying such a central position, it was inevitable that Delos would develop into a major trading center. These two factors combined to make this tiny island one of the most important destinations in Greek antiquity. The enormous wealth of information available from the numerous archeological sites on Delos provide an invaluable record of a great and varied history that spans almost 3,000 years.

Pythagoreion and Heraion of Samos

LOCATION

The north-east coast of the Island of Samos, approximately N 37° 50', E 27° 00'.

DESCRIPTION

This site is clearly defined by the surrounding mountains. It comprises the ancient city of Pythagoreion and the classical temple of Heraion. There are town fortifications which date back to the classical period, and excavations have revealed much of the original street plan. There are public buildings, an aqueduct, Roman baths, a sewage system, sanctuaries and temples, an agora (market place), houses and a stadium. One of the most famous features of the site is the Eupalineio, a 1,040m (3,400ft) tunnel which runs through the mountainside, designed to bring water to the city. The temple of Hera also included in the site has been rebuilt several times, each rebuilding showing great innovation and ambition. This complex includes altars, smaller temples, stoas, and statue bases, all included inside the sanctuary, along with the remains of a 5th century Christian basilica.

SIGNIFICANCE

The remains at this site, which has been left in ruins for a millennium, are amongst the most impressive and complete in the Greco-Roman world. They are most notable for two outstanding engineering and architectural structures - the Eupalineio and the Heraion. The technological mastery displayed at the Eupalineio served as a model for subsequent engineering and public works, while the Temple of Heraion is regarded as fundamental to a deeper understanding of classical architecture.

Delphi

LOCATION

In Boetia, Central Greece, E 22° 30', N 38° 29'.

DESCRIPTION

The site of Delphi is situated at the foot of the southern slope of Mt. Parnassos between the Phaedriades. It includes: 1. the Sanctuary of Athena Pronaia (5th century BC) with its temple and famous tholos (rotunda 4th century BC); 2. the ruins of the gymnasium, with baths, palaestra and chystos (covered colonnade); 3. the Sanctuary of Pythian Apollo, with the Sacred Way and its treasuries, the Temple of Apollo, the theater (4th century BC); 4. the Castalian Fountain, in which the Pythia purified herself; 5. the stadium, situated in the highest part; 6. the ancient city and its two necropolises, spread between the two sanctuaries.

SIGNIFICANCE

Delphi was considered to be the center of the ancient Greek world. Mythology tells the story of how Zeus released two eagles, one from the east and one from the west. They met at Delphi and the spot was marked by a stone in the temple. The Oracle of Apollo at Delphi was one of the most famous in the ancient world and became one of the more prestigious pilgrimage centers of the times. Destroyed in 373BC by an earthquake, it was later rebuilt and restored by the Roman Emperor Hadrian. Modern excavations commenced on the site in 1892 and have since revealed a wealth of invaluable information.

ABOVE Temple of Athena Pronaia

Mystras

LOCATION

In the province of Laconia, on the Peloponnese, west of Sparta, E 22° 21', N 37° 04'.

DESCRIPTION

These ruins are of a medieval town built on a 621m (2,050ft) high hill at the foot of Mount Taiyetos. The upper town consists of the Frankish fortified castle at the summit, the Palaces of the Despots, Seigneurial residences, several monasteries and the Church of St. Sophia. All are surrounded by a wall which has two gates. The lower town is surrounded by a second wall and is centered around the 13th century Cathedral of St. Demitrios. There is also a monastery and the 14th century Church of Pantanassa.

SIGNIFICANCE

Mystras was fortified by the Franks in 1249 and became the site of a Byzantine military government between 1262 and 1348. It was the capital of the Despots of Morea from 1348 and 1460. The city was conquered by the Turks in 1460 and the Venetians in 1687. It was a flourishing trading center thanks to its silk worm industry and was populated until 1830. King Otto built the new town of Sparta, sparking the decline of Mystras. Fine examples of Byzantine architecture and wall paintings have been preserved amongst the ruins.

Epidaurus

LOCATION

Nafplia Province, N 37° 30', E 23° 07'.

DESCRIPTION

The Sanctuary of Apollon Malaetas and Asklepeion was the cultural center of the ancient city state of Epidaurus. The sanctuary was a medical center dedicated to healing and convalescence. There is also an extremely well-preserved theater; the ruins of richly decorated temples, dormitories, hotels and banquet halls.

SIGNIFICANCE

Regarded as the starting point of healing-practices in ancient Greece, the sanctuary was renowned throughout the classical world. The theater was famous for its stunning acoustics and in many ways this site is considered to have been of primary importance in the development of modern civilization. The tholos here is one of the finest buildings to have survived from classical times.

ABOVE The theater at Epidaurus, famous for its remarkable acoustics

Medieval City of Rhodes

LOCATION
One of the Dodecanese group of islands, N 36° 22', E 25° 56'.

DESCRIPTION
A fortified medieval city, its outer walls are very well preserved. Inside can be found the Collachium, the fortified castle of the Knights, as well as the Palace of the Grand Masters and several inns or residences. There is also the hospital of the Knights and the remains of a 3rd century BC temple to Aphrodite.

SIGNIFICANCE
Founded in 408 BC, Rhodes was a prestigious city in the 3rd and 4th centuries BC, and became part of the Eastern Empire in 395 AD. Independent in the 13th century, it was conquered in 1309 by the Knights of St .John of Jerusalem who first took refuge on the island in 1306. They were defeated by the Turks in 1523. Today the old city is remarkably intact and so provides a valuable record of the civilizations that founded it and subsequently controlled and enriched it.

Meteora

LOCATION
District of Thessaly, N 39° 43', E 21° 38'.

DESCRIPTION
This is a group of seven monasteries, all perched high up on some very unusual rock formations. These formations jut straight out of the surrounding Thessalian plain, the highest soaring up to 400m (1,312ft). The names of the monasteries are: Saint Nikolas Anapafsas, Roussanou, Transfiguration of the Saviour, Varlaam, Holy Trinity, Saint Stephen and The Ascension of Jesus Christ. All of the monasteries are rich in artwork, with numerous paintings, frescoes, sculptures and relics, many of great importance.

SIGNIFICANCE
'Meteora' in the Greek language means literally 'suspended in the air'. The description could not be better, especially when viewing these spectacular monasteries on a misty morning; they float in the air just as they have floated down through the ages. It is thought that the first hermits started settling on these rocks around 1000 AD. The monastic community was not established until the 14th century. The construction was a feat of wonder, considered a miracle of the Byzantine world. At its peak, around the beginning of the 16th century, the community boasted 24 monasteries. The next 100 years saw a steady decline under Turkish rule until only eight monasteries remained at the beginning of the 17th century. The seven monasteries standing today are living testament to those wondrous days of the Byzantine age.

ABOVE Varlaam Monastery

Monasteries of Daphni, Hossios Lucas and Nea Moni Chiou

LOCATION

Daphni: N 38° 01', E 23° 38';
Chiou: Island of Chios, N 38° 00', E 26° 00';
Lucas: Beotia, N 38° 24', E 22° 45'.

DESCRIPTION

This listing comprises three Byzantine monasteries. All are similar in design, basically consisting of an octagonal church with a full width porch across the front and a domed roof. Mosaics and paintings decorate the interior walls.

SIGNIFICANCE

These monasteries are the best preserved of their type and represent the zenith of Byzantine civilization and culture. The mosaics and wall paintings are invaluable records of Byzantine art.

Mount Athos

LOCATION

On the peninsula of Athos, in the province of Macedonia.

DESCRIPTION

This fortified medieval monastic city comprises 20 monasteries, 12 skites (small retreats), 700 cells and numerous caves spread over an area of 360sqkm (144sqmi). The area is wooded and mountainous and is accessible only by boat. Karyes, a small village, is the capital of this Theocratic Republic and contains the oldest basilican church on the Mount, the Protaton, built in the 10th century AD.

SIGNIFICANCE

Monastic life started in the 10th century AD when the first monastery was built in 963. Of the 40 monasteries built over the centuries, only 20 have survived. They date from the 13th century to the 19th century. Mount Athos is a veritable museum of treasures. The Library of Vatopedi has over 13,000 manuscripts and is probably the richest manuscript library in the world. There are over 100,000sqm (1,111,000sqft) of murals and frescoes and countless icons, mosaics, sculptures and paintings.

TOP Hossios Lucas Monastery
ABOVE A view of Mt. Athos, perched on the Aegean

Paleochristian and Byzantine Monuments of Thessaloniki

LOCATION

Macedonia, N 40° 40', E 23° 00'.

DESCRIPTION

There are four main elements to this site: 1. the old city walls, 4km (2.5mi) long, 10m (33ft) high, over 2m (7ft) thick with 46 towers; 2. the Byzantine bath which dates from the 13th century; 3. Church of St. Catherine, built around 1320, a Byzantine church which was converted to a mosque in 1430; 4. Church of St. Panteleimon, built in the late 13th century.

SIGNIFICANCE

A fascinating and diverse collection of remains, all in good repair, which preserve the varied and often turbulent history of this important city.

Olympia

LOCATION

On the Peloponnese in the Province Elis, between the confluence of the Alpheics and Kladeos Rivers, N 37° 40', E 21° 36'.

DESCRIPTION

The Panhellenic Sanctuary of Olympia was famous throughout the ancient world. Site of the quadrennial Olympic Games, it has the ruins of the ancient stadium, training buildings for the athletes , and hotels for the visitors. There is also the Bouleuterion where the Olympic Senate met, various temples and monuments to games victors and patrons. The temple which held the world famous Statue of Zeus from sculptor Pheidias was also here. Earlier tomb remains are to be found along the river banks.

SIGNIFICANCE

The Olympic Games were the greatest celebration in antiquity. Their fame was such that wars were halted to allow athletes to compete. For 1,000 years the Olympic ideal inspired the youth of Greece and its colonies to feats of athletic and artistic prowess. These ruins and the ideals of the original games inspired the modern Olympics.

ABOVE Part of the mosaic-covered dome of Santa Sophia

The Acropolis, Athens

LOCATION

Center of Athens, N 37° 58', E 23° 43'.

DESCRIPTION

This famous complex consists of four main buildings: 1. the Parthenon - a pitched roof building of brick construction, surrounded by a colonnaded verandah; 2. the Propylaea - the gate house to the Acropolis complex, it is constructed of marble and shows both Ionic and Doric styles; 3. the Erechtheion - an Ionic style building with projecting porticoes and sculptured figures used instead of columns; 4. the Temple of Athena Nike —a perfect miniature square temple.

SIGNIFICANCE

'Acropolis' meaning 'city at the top' was the name used by the ancient Greeks for citadels built on elevated sites. The one at Athens is by far the most famous. It shows every phase of Greek architecture right up to the fall of Athens. The Parthenon is the best known of all Greek temples and is considered the apogee of Hellenistic architecture. Extensive renovations have been going on for many years.

Temple of Apollo Epicurius at Bassae

LOCATION

On the Peloponnese in the limits of three departments; Messenia, Arcadia and Elis.

DESCRIPTION

The temple is a colonnaded rectangle with a gabled roof. Externally, a classic temple in Doric style, it is 39.87m (131ft) by 16.13m (53ft) and is constructed of light grey limestone. A number of features are of marble. A magnificent Ionic frieze in 23 slabs depicts both the battle of the Centaurs and the Amazons. The temple stands isolated on a natural plateau on Mount Kotilion and is in a fine state of preservation.

SIGNIFICANCE

Of tremendous natural beauty in the harsh and lonely mountains of the Peloponnese, the temple's 'rediscovery' in 1765 by French archeologist Joachim Blocher caused a sensation in Europe. The frieze went to the British Museum, and many scholars flocked to study the well preserved temple.

ABOVE A view of St. Peter's Square from the cupola
ABOVE LEFT St. Peter's Basilica

The Vatican City

LOCATION

Within the City of Rome, E 12° 39', N 41° 53'.

DESCRIPTION

The territory of the Vatican City covers an area of 44ha (106ac). St. Peter's Basilica, built on the foundations of Constantine's Basilica, has a dome which is 132m (430ft) high and dominates the Vatican skyline. St. Peter's Square which is 320m (1,050ft) long and 240m (800ft) wide has a large colonnade which is supported by 240 columns and is adorned with 140 statues. Other important buildings include the Pope's palace, a complex of buildings dating mainly from the 15th and 16th centuries, the Sistine Chapel which was built in 1473 and is the Pope's personal chapel, 11 museums, famous for their antiquities, collections, sculptures and paintings. There are also three 'extraterritorial' churches included as part of the Vatican's inventory: San Giovanni in Laterano (the actual Cathedral of Rome); Santa Maria Maggiore; San Paolo Fuori.

SIGNIFICANCE

The Vatican City State was established by the Lateran Treaty, signed between the Holy See and Italy in 1929. It is the center of the Roman Catholic Church, and a place of pilgrimage. St. Peter's Basilica is the biggest funeral building in the world with the tombs of more than 240 Popes. The painting on the ceiling of the Sistine Chapel by Michelangelo, entitled 'Creation of the World' along with the fresco 'The Last Judgement' on the wall above the altar are the most famous of a multitude of art treasures held within the Vatican.

HUNGARY

Budapest, Banks of the Danube with the District of Buda Castle

LOCATION

Budapest.

DESCRIPTION

The city of Budapest is divided by the Danube. On the flat left bank is Pest, with the Parliament House as its most striking feature. On the right bank rises Buda, with its medieval fortifications on Castle Hill, its massive baroque royal palaces, the Neo-Roman fishermen's bastion, the staircase leading to the river, Matthias church, famous for its colored tiles on the roof and the Gothic tower of Mary Magdelena. In the center of the old quarter of the castle is St. Trinity Square with the Coronation Church distinguished by its graceful spire. There are also numerous medieval houses with 18th century facades.

SIGNIFICANCE

The fortress of Buda was built by King Bella IV in the second half of the 13th century to protect the city from the Tartars invasions. One hundred and fifty years of Turkish occupation left the castle in ruins. Buda was extensively restored in the 19th and 20th centuries. One of the features of the castle quarter of Buda are all the Gothic niches at the entrances to the houses.

A Village in the Hills

The road wound its way through wooden hills or between copses, with now and then a glimpse of a few sleepy cows. I was driving in northern Hungary, looking for a village. Tucked away at the end of a road, it rarely appears on maps and the signposts along the road are somewhat erratic. At each fork I hesitated: left or right?

Yet Hollókö is no ordinary place. Since 1987 it has been the only village in the world inscribed on UNESCO's World Heritage List. Situated in the Cserhát mountains, some hundred kilometers north west of Budapest, it is still a backwater as far as large-scale tourism is concerned.

Suddenly, through the foliage of the trees lining the road, I caught sight of a green sign and on it, in white lettering, there at long last was the name of the village. A few hundred meters further on, at the crest of a slope, I came across the first houses and was beset by doubt. These were sturdy modern buildings, surrounded by gardens, of the kind which has been springing up in the Hungarian countryside over the past few years. Could Hollókö be a tourist trap, with a pile of stones passed off as a historic ruin?

Before long I came across a sign bearing the World Heritage emblem. Then, all at once, the look of the place changed. The real village sprang into view. As though in a fairy tale, cottages as white as wedding gowns, each with a wooden balcony, appeared along the main street. This street of uneven cobblestones is named after Sándor Pétöfi, the great Hungarian revolutionary poet who died in 1849. With rare exceptions, cars are not permitted here.

Unlike other Hungarian villages, which are centered on a church, this ancient village in the Cserhát mountains leads to a tiny and charming whitewashed chapel dating from the 15th century. With its pointed, slate-covered steeple, it is the last vestige of the Middle Ages. Inside, there is no baroque ornamentation, just plain whitewashed walls and a wooden ceiling. To the right of the entrance hangs a crucifix by Ferenc Kelemen, a local sculptor. On feast days, old villagers still attend mass in traditional costume.

Hollókö

LOCATION
Northeastern part of Hungary, 100km (62mi) from Budapest in the Paloc region.

DESCRIPTION
This listing includes 141ha (340ac) of vales, pastures and forests. The village of Hollókö is nestled on the slope of a hill. The ruins of a fortified castle sit on the top of the hill. The historical center of the town includes 126 houses and a small Roman Catholic church.

SIGNIFICANCE
One of the most authentic reminders of traditional Paloc rural architecture, Hollókö is a complete and lasting testimony to a now vanished rural European lifestyle. The adjoining essay by Edouard Bailby gives a fascinating insight into this fairytale town.

No more than a hundred people live in the old village. Dressed in typical Hungarian peasant fashion, black trousers or gaily colored skirts, they go about their business, some bearing pitchforks, others carrying baskets of vegetables. On the nearby hills are a few vines, vegetable gardens, fields of maize and sunflowers. Sheep graze in the meadows. The farmland is divided into small plots. I did not see a tractor. The bucolic landscape adds to the charm of the village.

The neat rows of immaculate houses, facades embellished with finely carved wooden balustrades, surmounted by tiled roofs with tiny square windows set in them, are built in a uniform style characteristic of the architecture of northern Hungary. Their patches of garden, filled with summer flowers, are enclosed by low fences. Often, above the front door, there hangs a horseshoe, a garland of red paprikas, a cob of maize or a holy picture.

The village museum, situated in an old house converted for the purpose, is a perfect reconstruction of a traditional interior. The front door leads straight into the main living room, furnished with a dining table and benches decked out in embroidered covers. The kitchen is at the back and to the left is the bedroom in which parents and children all slept. To the right of the living room is a more spacious room, reserved for the grandparents, where farm implements, firewood and provisions for the harsh winter months are stacked up in a corner. Porcelain or pewter plates, generally hanging from the walls, gaily colored blankets, red and green cushions, and hand-decorated earthenware vases brighten the place up.

All the houses in Hollókö date from the beginning of the century. Unfortunately, nothing remains from earlier periods. Mongol hordes laid waste this area in the mid-13th century, and in the 16th century the village was sacked by Turkish troops, who left a garrison of sixty men in a fortress which towers over the neighborhood. The ruins, accessible by a steep path, are in such a state of disrepair that they have been closed to visitors for the past 17 years. But the fortress, which is indissociable from the history of Hollókö, is now being restored and will soon regain its former splendor.

'Now that we are part of the UNESCO heritage', a village woman told me, 'we are no longer anxious about our future'. The entire village is the focus of attention from both local and regional authorities. Since last year it has even had its own post office, and it also boasts a grocery store, a primary school, an old people's home and three small cafe restaurants, which are open until late in the evening.

To lovers of the past, the local tourist office rents out at a modest price a few charming cottages equipped with modern amenities. The number of these dwellings is limited so as not to alter the life of the village. In the summer season, romantics can hold weddings and country dances here, for which the village women will deck themselves out in all their finery.

EDOUARD BAILBY, French journalist and former correspondent with the Paris weekly magazine L'Express , served for a number of years as press officer with UNESCO's Office of Public Information.

IRELAND

TOP Iron Age tumulus, or burial mound
BOTTOM Eastern chamber recess within the main mound

Archeological Ensemble of the Bend of the Boyne

LOCATION

County Meath, approximately N 53° 40', W 06° 40'.

DESCRIPTION

This area of 780ha (1,880ac) which is situated in a hairpin bend of the River Boyne, consists of a ridge with three enormous burial mounds (Dowth, Knowth and Newgrange) surrounded by numerous passage-graves. The site also contains many monuments. The two main periods of settlement were the Late Western Neolithic and the Late Iron Age, though evidence of human inhabitation dates from the 4th millennium BC. The agricultural nature of the area began in the earlier period with the destruction of woodland and the introduction of a field system. Developments in this period include the transition from circular houses to rectangular ones. Later buildings and fortifications exist from the Early Christian and the Anglo-Norman/Cistercian periods.

SIGNIFICANCE

The collection of megalithic art found at this site is unrivalled in Europe. The various monuments scattered around the area are of great antiquity, stretching back into prehistory. One of the most remarkable aspects of this site is the evidence of continued occupation, displaying important cultural, social, artistic and scientific developments over a considerable period of time. Remains at Knowth from the later period of settlement show that the settlement was involved in extensive trade, and from the Early Christian period to the Norman invasion, Knowth was the capital of a great kingdom of the same name. The amazing passage graves and the evidence of the intricate social and ideological systems of the area's prehistoric inhabitants, represent the survival of ancient belief systems which are of inestimable value.

Historic Center of Florence

LOCATION

Florence, Tuscany,
E 11°15', N 43° 46'.

DESCRIPTION

Overlooked by the graceful dome of its cathedral, Florence lies in a natural setting which rivals the architectural beauty of the town renowned as the birthplace of the Renaissance. Originally a Roman town, it was not until the 13th century that it rose to real prominence, with the building of religious and civic monuments reflecting its new position of economic, cultural and political power. After the period of Ducal Florence, few important changes were made to the squares and public buildings, and the artistic activity of the whole region became concentrated within the city itself.

SIGNIFICANCE

Florence was a Roman colony conquered in the 1st century BC and laid out as a garrison town. The town flourished under Hadrian until the 4th century AD. It was during the rise of the Medici family (1418-34) that new scientific and artistic visions came into prominence. The court of the Medicis became the center of the Renaissance and this was expressed through brilliant new architecture and an intense concentration of artistic activity within the city.

ITALY

TOP *Ponto Vecchio*
BOTTOM *Il Duomo and la campanile*

Historic Center of San Gimignano

LOCATION

40km (24mi) northwest of Siena, Tuscany,
N 43° 28' to E 11° 24'.

DESCRIPTION

San Gimignano is a remarkably well preserved medieval town. The center is protected by ramparts that extend for 2,177m (7,250ft) and incorporate five cylindrical towers. There are five gateways, two facing north, two facing south and one facing east. There is also an outer rampart, much of it in ruins. The circuit between the ramparts holds the town's famous towers, which were built by the families of nobility of the day. Fourteen of these towers remain standing of the 72 originally built. There are also numerous civil buildings, a cathedral, many palaces and several town squares.

SIGNIFICANCE

This town is a living museum of regional medieval architecture and planning. Each of the Sienese, Pisan and Florentine styles are represented in very well preserved and original forms. Several notable frescoes are housed in the buildings of this town, including works by Benozzo Gozzoli on the life of Saint Augustine and by Lippo Memmi on the Madonna.

Venice and its Lagoon

LOCATION

On the Adriatic coast, N 45° 26', E 12° 33'.

DESCRIPTION

Occupying one of the most remarkable sites in the world, the city of Venice is situated in the estuaries of the rivers Brenta and Sile. It is exposed to the tides of the Adriatic and is annually threatened by floods. The center of the 'sinking city' is well defined by the Piazza San Marco with the Basilica of St. Mark, the Palazzo ducale (Palace of the doges) and the Procuratie - two parallel buildings on the sides of the palace. The main avenue is the Grand Canal adorned with innumerable Renaissance palaces and crossed by the world famous Rialto Bridge. The Gallery dell' Academia as well as the campanile (bell tower) are some of the other notable landmarks. The lagoon of Venice is composed of several islands, each with an historical center. The main ones are Venice itself, Chioggia, Murano, Burano, and Torcello.

SIGNIFICANCE

Venice has a long and colorful history. From its humble beginnings as a fishing community, through its fiercely fought independence and growth into a major trading power throughout the rule of the Byzantium Empire; thence on to its rapid expansion after claiming the spoils from the 4th Crusade; through the bitterly fought Genoese Wars, on to decline through the Turkish Wars and the final blow to the Empire, struck by Napoleon in 1797. The legacy of such a rich history lies in the wealth of architectural and artistic heritage which is now being preserved 'en masse'.

ABOVE Torcello Cathedral
RIGHT High water in Piazza San Marco
INSET RIGHT Grand Canal

Piazza del Duomo, Pisa

LOCATION
In the north of Tuscany,
N 43° 42' to E 10° 25'.

DESCRIPTION
Piazza del Duomo includes the complex of the Cathedral of Santa Maria Assunta, which is in the Latin cruciform pattern, a large baptistery with an octagonal front and the famous campanile, or 'leaning tower'. Construction of this belltower began in 1173 and was not completed until two centuries later. It stands 60m (200ft) tall and is inclined 5m (17ft) from the perpendicular. This inclination began almost as soon as work started and has shown no signs of diminishing, prompting many studies aimed at stabilisation.

SIGNIFICANCE
These remaining buildings in the Piazza del Duomo bear witness to the former supremacy of the maritime republic which centered around Pisa. The leaning tower is famous worldwide as the symbol of the town.

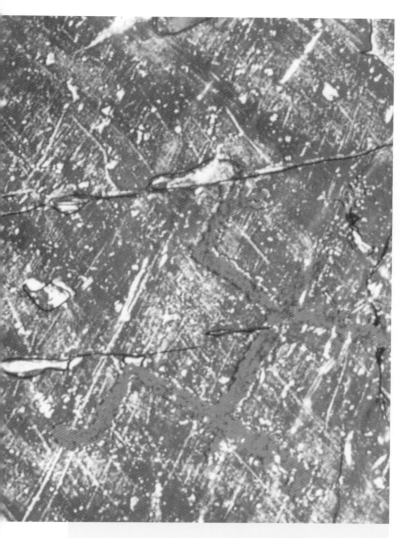

Santa Maria delle Grazie with 'The Last Supper' by Leonardo da Vinci

LOCATION

Milan, Lombardy, E 09° 12', N 45° 28'.

DESCRIPTION

The Church of Santa Maria delle Grazie was built in the second half of the 15th century. The magnificent Renaissance architecture is overshadowed by Leonardo da Vinci's 'Last Supper' painted on the end wall of the refectory. The work is rectangular in shape, 8.85m (29ft) long and 4.97m (16.3ft) high.

SIGNIFICANCE

The complex of Santa Maria delle Grazie represents a milestone in the history of Italian architecture. Built originally by the famous architect Solari, the gallery was added by the great architect Bramante before he left for his period of activity in Rome. A masterpiece of perspective and compassion, 'The Last Supper' is considered a pivotal painting in the development of western art. It is currently undergoing restoration.

Rock Drawings of Valcamonica

LOCATION

Lombardy region, E 10° 10' to 10° 20', N 45° 30' to 46° 30'.

DESCRIPTION

There are more than 130,000 individual carvings to be found on approximately 2,400 different rock surfaces in this area. The area itself stretches over 70sqkm (28sqmi), is lightly timbered, and includes many fields of long grass and shrubs.

SIGNIFICANCE

These carvings were created over an 8,000 year period, beginning in the Camunian era. Due to the overgrown nature of the local vegetation, these carvings remained unstudied until 1929. It was not until 1956 that serious research commenced on the site. Studies over the following eight years brought the tremendous significance of these finds to light. Valcamonica is now considered to be the most important complex of prehistoric art in the world.

I Sassi di Matera

LOCATION
Basilicata Region, approximately N 40° 42', E 16° 39'.

DESCRIPTION
Matera is an old town with associated archeological sites which date back to the Palaeolithic period. The earliest settlement was based around the two boulders, Sassi Caveosa and Sassi Barisano. In-between these rocks, a fortified town was established which included a cathedral, workshops, granaries, and a complex water supply system.

Surrounding the area is a belt of soft tufa, which rises 400m (1,320ft) from the valley floor. Early dwellings were carved into the tufa and a closing wall built from excavated blocks. The roofs of some houses acted as streets for houses above. The center of the valley was built up with excavated stone and most of the dwellings form groups around water cisterns. The plateau above was reserved for agriculture and grazing.

SIGNIFICANCE
I Sassi di Matera is an astounding and extremely beautiful example of human skill and imagination. The rock-cut settlement was adapted perfectly to the surrounding environment and operated successfully for over two millennia. This ensemble is the most complete and best preserved example of this type of settlement which has maintained its harmonious relationship with its natural surroundings. It also clearly demonstrates successive stages of its cultural development, from prehistoric times, through Greek colonization and Byzantine occupation, up to its eventual desertion in the 1950's.

OPPOSITE PAGE TOP *The Colosseum*
OPPOSITE PAGE BOTTOM *The Forum, with Victor Emanuel II Monument in the background*

Historic Center of Rome

LOCATION

Central Rome, E 12° 29', N 41° 54'.

DESCRIPTION

This is an extensive listing that includes countless buildings, arches, aqueducts, statues, archeological sites and other monuments. The remains of the old town wall, built by Emperor Hadrian, define the limits of this site. Some of the well known features are the Roman Forum, the Colosseum, Hadrian's Temple, the Pantheon and the various Roman baths.

SIGNIFICANCE

Capital of the ancient Roman republic and of the entire Roman Empire, Rome has a longer record of continuous political and religious importance than any other city. The historic center is home to the finest urban antiquarian ensemble in the world. It has been the center of the Christian church for many centuries and is an important destination for pilgrims. The extensive remains of the old city continue to provide invaluable clues to the understanding of the greatest of all the ancient empires.

MALTA

Valletta

LOCATION

Valletta (capital city), island of Malta, E 14° 30', N 35° 54'.

DESCRIPTION

There are around 320 buildings in Valletta considered to be of architectural or historical significance. There is an old city wall which encloses an area of about 55ha (133ac). Some of the more notable monuments are: the Grandmaster's Palace; several 'auberges' - headquarters for the different divisions of the Knights; the National Library and also Manoel Theater.

SIGNIFICANCE

Valletta was established by the Order of St. John, the first foundation stone being laid by Grandmaster Jean de La Valette in 1566. The architectural style developed over the years - blending the Roman baroque style with indigenous forms to create a distinctive new style. Physically and aesthetically, the capital is still very much a city of the Knights, its outward appearance having changed little since the Order of St. John left in 1798.

Hal Saflieni Hypogeum

LOCATION

Near the center of the town of Paola, Island of Malta,
E 14° 30', N 35° 52'.

DESCRIPTION

The Hal Saflieni Hypogeum is an underground monument
comprising several series of man made chambers and passages on
three main levels, the deepest of which descends 10.6m (34.5ft)
below ground level. These days the hypogeum is accessible from a
modern spiral staircase. Its uppermost level may have been of
natural origin, a cave or caves used for cult purposes, but the lower
levels were hewn out and shaped as megalithic architectural features
with great precision and sophistication.

SIGNIFICANCE

The hypogeum is unique among the prehistoric temples of the
Maltese Cooper Age (c.3500-2200BC) in that it was excavated
below ground level. The monument, when discovered in 1902, was
found to contain the jumbled remains of some 7,000 individuals:
evidence that in prehistoric times it had been converted from a place
of worship to an ossuary.

Ggantija Temples

LOCATION

Island of Gozo, E 14°15', N 36° 02'.

DESCRIPTION

The prehistoric monument of Ggantija consists of a complex of two
separate temples enclosed within a continuously curving outside
wall and a common facade. There is an open space in front of the
monument which was the original terrace. It is supported by a
retaining wall of huge blocks.

SIGNIFICANCE

These prehistoric temples are some of the oldest free-standing stone
monuments in existence. The earliest construction dates back to
3000BC.

Glance at the sun. See the moon and stars. Gaze at the
beauty of earth's greenings. Now, think. What delight God
gives to us with all these things...All nature is at our
disposal. We are to work with it. For without it we cannot
survive.

HILDEGARD OF BINGEN

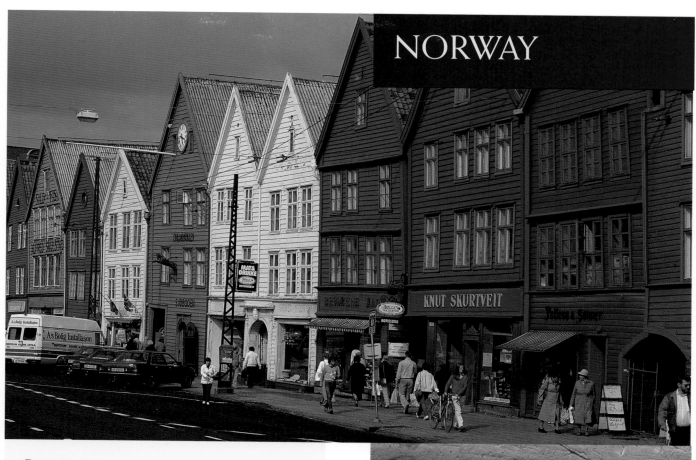

NORWAY

Bryggen

LOCATION

City of Bergen, E 05°19', N 60° 23'.

DESCRIPTION

The Bryggen area is found on the eastern shore of the old harbor of Bergen. The 58 remaining buildings represent only about a quarter of the original settlement. Most of them are three-storeyed timber houses which stand in slightly curved parallel rows, perpendicular to the harbor shore.

SIGNIFICANCE

Archeological evidence dates this site back to the 12th century. It is extremely likely, however that it dates back further to the foundation of Bergen by King Olar Kyrre - thought to be in 1070. Successive fires destroyed many buildings in 1198, 1248, 1476 and 1702. Each time the buildings were reconstructed, they increased in size a little but retained their traditional features.

Rock Drawings of Alta

LOCATION

Alta Municipality, E 23° 12', N 69° 55'.

DESCRIPTION

These rock drawings and carvings are located in five areas. The carvings, most of which are 20 to 40cm (8 to 16in) across, are of reindeer and moose, humans, other animals, birds, boats, pattern lines and dots. There are more than 3,000 carvings, and fifteen red-brown paintings between 2,700-2,400 years old.

SIGNIFICANCE

The oldest carvings date back to 6,000 years. Along with the paintings, they provide a crucial key to the understanding of ancient rock art. Excavations to prehistoric settlements adjacent to the sites have uncovered tools and materials which would have been used for the carvings and paintings.

Urnes Stave Church

LOCATION

Municipality of Luster, E 07° 02', N 61° 18'.

DESCRIPTION

An entirely wooden structure, much of the timber within the church is intricately carved. The portal, shaped like a keyhole, contains a carved decoration of interlaced fighting animals. The walls are covered with paintings, scrolls, architectural motifs and carved apostles all dating back to 1601.

SIGNIFICANCE

Urnes Staves Church was built in the second half of the 12th century and is the oldest and best preserved of Norway's 30 surviving stave churches. Much of the timber used to construct it came from a structure about 100 years older. Some of this reused material is adorned with exceptionally fine wood carving, giving rise to the term 'Urnes style'

Røros

LOCATION

Municipality of Røros, E 11° 23', N 62° 35'.

DESCRIPTION

This heavily populated town comprises three major streets and several interesting narrow side streets which cross the river over numerous bridges. The buildings resemble compact farmhouses and are constructed to face the street. Some 80 buildings are protected by law.

SIGNIFICANCE

Mining and smelting activity commenced in Røros in 1644 and continued uninterrupted for 333 years until 1977. The community evolved slowly and many of the early 17th century buildings have survived remarkably well. Residential and commercial structures from the 18th, 19th and early 20th centuries are also in an excellent state of preservation, presenting a representative cross section of changing architectural styles throughout the centuries.

The Old City of Zamosc

LOCATION

The province of Lublin, approximately N 50° 43', E 23° 17'.

DESCRIPTION

Zamosc was purpose built between 1582 and 1591 under instructions from the head of the Polish army (the 'hetman'), Jan Zamysky. Located on the trade route linking western and northern Europe, it was conceived as an economic center based on trade. There are fortifications surrounding the old town, and the modern town has grown mostly outside of these, endowing the old town a great deal of integrity, and allowing the original plan to be clearly seen. The space was organised into two distinct sections: on the west, the noble residences, and on the east the town proper, laid out around three squares.

SIGNIFICANCE

Zamysky was educated in Padua, Italy and commissioned an Italian architect, Bernardo Morando, to design the town as a trade center and as the home of the hetman. Unlike the fate of many Polish towns during the Second World War, Zamosc escaped the destructive effects of bombing, and is considered to be an outstanding example of a Renaissance planned town of the late 16th century, which retains its original layout and fortifications as well as a large number of buildings of particular interest, blending Italian and central European architectural traditions.

ABOVE 16th century town hall
RIGHT An altar of salt

Wieliczka Salt Mine

LOCATION

About 13km (8mi) southeast of Cracow, N 50° 00', E 20° 05'.

DESCRIPTION

The mining works are underneath the town of Wieliczka. There are nine levels of descent and the depth is 327m (1,073ft) at the lowest point. There are 16 extraction ponds inside the mine. The east-west axis is 5km (3mi) long and it is 1km (0.62mi) along the north-south axis. There is a museum with an historical exhibition attached to the mine.

SIGNIFICANCE

The richest salt mines in Poland, these works are also one of the oldest operational salt mines in Europe. Salt was being extracted here as early as the 11th century. It was opened as a royal mine in the 13th century. The most remarkable feature of the mine is the multitude of carvings found underground - throughout the long history of the mine, many 'mining artists' have left their unique stamp. There are various statues, and many altars, chapels and pulpits all painstakingly carved out of the rock salt.

Auschwitz Concentration Camp

LOCATION

N 50° 04', E 19° 21'.

DESCRIPTION

The camps of Auschwitz and Birkenau cover areas of 20ha (48ac) and 171ha (412ac) respectively. Auschwitz has 41 stone buildings, eight wooden barracks and eight watchtowers. Birkenau counts 47 stone buildings, 22 wooden barracks and 27 watchtowers. Within the camps are the remains of gas chambers and four crematoria. The camps are surrounded by a total length of 15km (9.3mi) of barbed wire.

SIGNIFICANCE

These camps were the scene of the largest scale mass murder in the history of humanity. Four million people of mixed race and religion were killed here between June 1940 and 27th January 1945 - the date of the liberation by the Soviet armies. A national museum, the camps have been declared a monument to the martyrdom of the Polish people and to the people of 29 other nations.

Historic Center of Cracow

LOCATION

Southern Poland, N 50° 03', W 20° 00'.

DESCRIPTION

The old city lies at the center of Cracow. Originally surrounded by walls and a moat, only two towers and two gates remain. Market Square (Ryneb) forms the nucleus of the town, three parallel streets running from each of its four sides. Draper's Hall (Sukiennice) and the Church of the Virgin Mary dominate the square. Wawel Hill holds ruins of the oldest buildings. Traces of two cathedrals, preceding the existing one, have been found. The Royal Castle dominates the hill. There is a multitude of other historic buildings including no less than 58 old churches.

SIGNIFICANCE

Cracow is the early capital of Poland and, like the rest of the country, has had an extremely turbulent history. No Polish city has more historical monuments than this one. Items like the silver coffin, which holds the alleged relics of Poland's patron saint, St. Stanislaw, are invaluable relics of this country's history. Its University is the second oldest in Europe and its library contains more than one million books.

ABOVE Wawel Hill

Historic Center of Warsaw

LOCATION

Warsaw, capital city, E 21° 00', N 52° 15'.

DESCRIPTION

Situated mainly on the left bank of the Vistula River, most of the buildings of Warsaw are reproductions constructed after the bombings of World War II. The old city was focused on the Royal Castle (Zamek), but this was not rebuilt after being destroyed. One of the main areas of interest is the market place as well as the 14th century Gothic Cathedral of St. John - faithfully reconstructed. Cracow Boulevard, which is lined with palaces and churches, dates to the 15th century and is most imposing.

SIGNIFICANCE

Founded as a city at the beginning of the 13th century, Warsaw originally had protective walls, towers and gates. Around 150 years later it became capital of the Duchy of Mazovia and then in 1596 King Sigismund III ordained it as the capital. Numerous palaces, churches, residences and new town walls were built. An extremely turbulent and violent history culminated in 1944 when the retreating Germans methodically destroyed this grand old city. The massive and detailed reconstruction that followed is one of the amazing building feats of this century.

Monastery of Hieronymites and Tower of Belém

LOCATION

In Belém, a suburb of Lisbon, N 38° 41', W 09° 12'.

DESCRIPTION

The Monastery of Santa Maria of Belém of the order of St. Jeromimo consists of a church and a cloister, both built of limestone. The church is remarkable for its southern and western portals, which are extensively decorated with statues. There are two commemorative tombs dedicated to Vasco da Gama, the explorer, and Camoes, the famous poet, to be found in the church. The hexagonal tower of Belém is built from limestone on a basalt foundation. Designed as a defensive tower, it has sentry boxes and a bastion that overlooks the Tagus River. There are extensive external decorations, including maritime and religious motifs. Entrance is gained by crossing a drawbridge.

SIGNIFICANCE

These 16th century buildings are some of the few remaining examples of Manoellian architecture - a style that is named after King Manoel I. It is also one of the few structures to survive the devastating earthquake that struck Lisbon in 1775.

PORTUGAL

ABOVE Tower of Belem
LEFT Monastery of Hieronymites

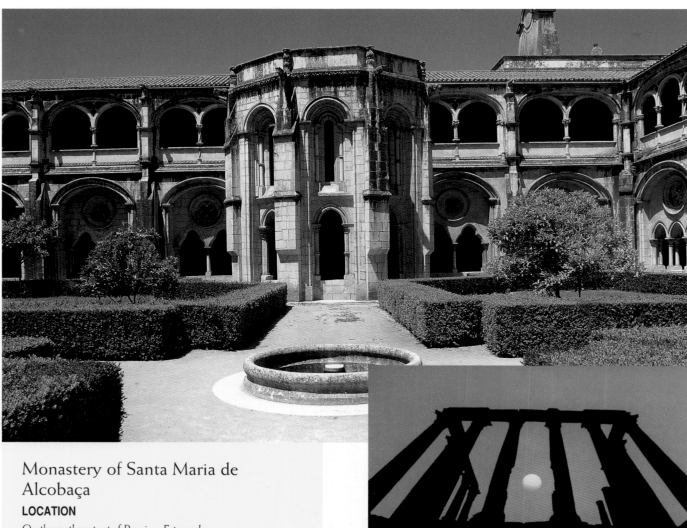

Monastery of Santa Maria de Alcobaça

LOCATION

*On the northern part of Province Estremadusa,
N 39° 33', W 08° 58'.*

DESCRIPTION

*This 12th century Cistercian monastery is dedicated to St. Bernard
and is situated in a marshy plain where the two rivers Alcoa and
Baça meet. The interior of the church is massive but simple in
design, with the chapel of St. Bernard standing opposite the Royal
Pantheon. The imposing 221m (725ft) facade is composed of three
parts; the northern aisle, the church and the southern aisle. The
facade was modified in 1702, conserving only seven portals in the
Gothic style. The Cloister of Dinis also known as the Cloister of
Silence, the dormitory, the refectory, the chapter house and the Hall
of the Kings which is richly decorated, are the other main
buildings.*

SIGNIFICANCE

*The monastery was founded in 1153 by King Afonso Henriques
after his victorious conquest over the Moorish town of Santarem.
This was the golden age of the Cistercians, or White Monks as
they were known. This monastery is well preserved and is one of the
most significant monuments of medieval Cistercian architecture in
Europe.*
ABOVE The Cloister of Silence
ABOVE RIGHT The Temple of Diana, Evora

Historic Center of Evora

LOCATION

In the province of Alentejo, N 38° 00', W 08° 00'.

DESCRIPTION

*The modern day capital of Alentejo Province, Evora is an old
fortified town. It is protected by walls, towers and two forts. There
is a richly decorated Romanesque cathedral which has been
restored in the Gothic style. The Church of São Francisco is in the
distinctive Manoellian style. There are several Roman ruins,
including the Temple of Diana.*

SIGNIFICANCE

*Originally known as Ebora, the town's origins predate 80BC
when it was an important Roman military station. A bishopric in
the 5th century AD, it was conquered by Moors around 712AD
and held by them for around 450 years. The Spanish ruled from
1663 to 1665. The town's long history of religious and political
importance has left a rich heritage of architectural and artistic
treasures, many of which are stored in the numerous museums.*

Convent of Christ in Tomar
LOCATION

In the province of Ribatejo, 143km (89mi) northeast of Lisbon, N 39° 36', W 08° 25'.

DESCRIPTION

This complex was founded when the small Oratory of the Templars was erected at the end of the 12th century. It has a Roman-Byzantine interior. Several cloisters were later added, including the main cloister and the hastately cloister. The window of the sacristy and the portal of the nave are both fine examples of the decorative art to be found within this convent.

SIGNIFICANCE

The origin of the complex dates from the mid 12th century when several members of the Knights Templar Order settled here. In 1320 this became known as the Order of Christ. The main cloister was built by Diego de Torralva in 1557. It is a fine example of Portuguese High Renaissance architecture and shows a marked Italian influence.

Angra do Heroismo in the Azores
LOCATION

The main town on the island of Terceira, part of the Azores group, N 38° 38', W 27° 12'.

DESCRIPTION

Angra is an old fortified port town. There are two imposing fortresses to defend the natural twin harbor. Religious buildings abound - São João Baptista do Castelo, San Francisco Convent, Colegio Church and São Gonçalo Convent are the most notable.

SIGNIFICANCE

These volcanic isles were discovered at the beginning of the 15th century by Diogo de Silves, a pilot of the Portuguese king. Settlement began around 1432. They were the scene of many a battle, especially between the English and the Spanish. The fortifications at Angra are a vestige of those turbulent times.

Monastery of Batalha

LOCATION

In the province of Estremaøura, south of the town of Leiria, N 39° 39', W 08° 49'.

DESCRIPTION

This monastic complex includes a royal cloister, built in Gothic and Manoellian styles by Alfonso Domingues as a place of prayer and meditation. The pantheon of King João I and his Queen, along with the Unfinished Chapels are the other notable buildings. The monumental portal, which is 15m (49ft) high and 7.5m (24.5ft) wide, was built by King Manoel.

SIGNIFICANCE

King João I built this complex in gratitude to his loyal subjects who fought fiercely for their independence against the Castillians in the Battle of Aljubarrota on the 15th August 1385. The Unfinished Chapels were started in 1433 by King Duarte but were left after his death in 1438. The portal was erected in 1509. The complex is well preserved and presents a broad segment of Portuguese architectural history.

Danube Delta

LOCATION

*Tulcea Country,
N 45° 00', E 29° 00'
(approximate mid-point).*

DESCRIPTION

*This 6,792sqkm (2,650sqmi)
reserve is vast in European terms. It
encompasses the delta of one of
Europe's most important rivers,
where it drains into the Black Sea,
and includes numerous freshwater
lakes and interconnecting channels,
large areas of aquatic vegetation,
floating islands of decaying
organic matter and extensive
marshlands. There are also several
brackish lagoons, separated from
the sea by sandbars. Areas of dry
land support stands of forest, with
oak, willow, poplar and alder
predominating. More than 300
species of birds have been recorded,
and it is an important breeding
ground, with over 176 species
regularly nesting. Fish numbers are
also significant, more than 45
freshwater varieties are known.
Otters, weasels and minks are also
present.*

SIGNIFICANCE

*This large alluvial delta is the
second largest delta in Europe (the
Volga is the largest) and provides
a crucial wetland habitat for
many migratory birds and other
fauna. It contains the largest
continuous marshland in Europe
and the greatest stretch of reed beds
in the world. The sheer scale and
immense diversity of this wetland
habitat is of critical value to the
species it protects as well as to our
body of human knowledge and
understanding.*

Inset Purple heron with her chicks

ROMANIA

The Fortified Church of Biertan

LOCATION

Department of Tirnava Mare, Transylvania.

DESCRIPTION

Biertan is a medieval town where the fortifications are centered around the church. The church sits on a low hill and is surrounded by a circuit of walls with four towers. Most of the structure is brick, with doors, window frames and parts of the vaulting made of stone. Despite some later modifications, the interior largely retains its original appearance. There is a second line of walls at the foot of the hill. The town itself retains its medieval layout and structure almost complete, and there is a group of important buildings, including a 16th century pharmacy, around the central square.

SIGNIFICANCE

This type of fortified medieval town, where the nucleus of the fortifications are the fortifications of the church, was once found widely around Europe. The Transylvanian Saxons, in particular, built many of these towns, as they didn't have the resources to fortify an entire town. These towns had a strong influence on the architectural styles of neighboring regions. Biertan is the best preserved and most complete of the surviving examples. It also has particular historical significance, as it was the see of the Transylvanian Lutheran Church for three centuries and so has links with several important historical figures such as Johan Michael Salzer.

Painted Churches of Northern Moldavia

LOCATION

Various locations within northern Moldavia.

DESCRIPTION

There are seven churches in this listing. All of them are within a 60km (36mi) radius of Suceava, residence of the Moldavian Princes. The Church of the Holy Rood at Patrauti was built in 1487 and is quite small. It has three apses and the interior walls display a series of important murals representing the Passion Cycle. The Church of St. George of the former Voronet Monastery is also a three-apse structure and also features murals of the Passion Cycle. There are also murals of the Calendar of Saints (the Menology) and exterior murals of traditional scenes. The Church of the Beheading of St. John the Baptist at Arbore was built in 1503 as the governor's residence and later became the village church. There are extensive high quality murals on interior and exterior walls. The Church of St. George at Suceava was originally the Metropolitan Church of Moldavia, but is now part of the Monastery of St. John. The interior and exterior murals are exceptional

by virtue of their colors, monumental composition, and perfect Cyrillic inscriptions. The Church of St. Nicholas and the Catholicon of the Monastery of Probota is another three-apsed building. It was built in 1531 and all the paintings are contemporary with it, except for those in the sanctuary. The Church of the Assumption of the former Monastery of Humor was built in 1530 on top of an earlier structure. It exhibits some variations from the traditional three-apsed monastery church, such as the lack of a drum over the narthex. The Church of the Annunciation of the Monastery of Moldovita was built in 1532 and painted five years later. It is very similar in form and decoration to the Humor church.

SIGNIFICANCE

This group of churches are unique in Europe, in that they are decorated with high quality murals not only on the inside walls, but also on the outside. They represent a relatively short lived cultural phenomenon in 16th century Moldavia which has no parallels. The murals are of exceptional aesthetic value, forming a perfect symbiosis between color and architecture, between the buildings and their surrounding environments.

ABOVE Church of St. Nicholas

The Monastery of Horezu

LOCATION

Little Wallachia, Department of Vilcea, approximately N 45° 10', E 24° 00'.

DESCRIPTION

This monastery is situated amongst a series of beautiful wooded hills. It is layed out symmetrically on an east-west axis, according to the precepts of the Athonite Order, around a large central structure known as the catholicon which is enclosed by a wall and surrounded by a series of skites. The catholicon has three aisles and a very large transverse vestibule (narthex) whose interior is highly decorated with carvings and paintings. On the south side, there is an elaborate two storey rectangular residence. There is a high standard of authenticity in the complex, and the restorations which have been carried out since 1960 have enhanced this by revealing previously hidden elements.

SIGNIFICANCE

This monastic complex is considered to be one of the finest expressions of the post Byzantine style of religious architecture and art known as Brancovan. This style is noted for its architectural purity and balance, the richness of its sculpted detail and its distinctive treatment of religious compositions and portraits. There was a flourishing school of mural and icon painting at this monastery during the early 18th century which had a profound influence on religious art and architecture in the Balkans. The monastery was founded in 1690 and was richly endowed by Prince Constantin Brancovan. It was the support of the Prince and his family which enabled the arts of icon and mural painting to flourish and which subsequently gave rise to the remarkable flowering of Brancovan art.

Kremlin Ensemble and Red Square, Moscow

LOCATION

Moscow, N 55° 45', E 37° 37'.

DESCRIPTION

This enormous ensemble of monuments contains numerous significant buildings and includes a vast wealth of important artwork. Some of the more notable buildings are: The Grand Kremlin Palace, Armoury Palace, the Cathedral of St Basil, the Assumption Cathedral, the Annunciation Cathedral, the Arsenal, the Senate, the Bell Tower of Ivan the Great, the Church of Deposition and the Cathedral of Archangel Michael.

SIGNIFICANCE

The Kremlin's origins date back to the 11th century when Slavs began settling on Borovitsky Hill. Its present day form was not established until the 14th century when its role as a defence fortress began in earnest. Around that time, the Great Prince took it as his principal residence and it became known as The Kremlin. Today, The Kremlin and the adjoining Red Square are seen as masterpieces of their time and present a unique testament to the architectural genius of their creators.

Khizi Pogost

LOCATION

Island of Khizi, N 62° 04', W 35° 13'.

DESCRIPTION

This is an ensemble of three buildings which are situated on the low, southern part of Khizi Island. They are: the Summer Church of the Transfiguration, the Winter Church of the Intercession and the Bell Tower. The entire ensemble is protected by a fence. In plan, they form the corners of a triangle. All are constructed of horizontally placed pine logs. The churches both have multi-domed roofs.

SIGNIFICANCE

This listing represents one of only five surviving such groupings which were typical of northern Russia in the Middles Ages and up to the 19th century. This particular ensemble is unique as both of its churches are multi-domed - a rare feature in Russian wooden architecture. The Church of the Transfiguration in particular, with its 22 cupolas, has no equal in the world of architecture. The state of preservation of these buildings is excellent and their originality has been unblemished.

Novgorod:
Church of the Nativity (LEFT), 17th century frescoes (BELOW)

Historic Monuments of Novgorod

LOCATION

Region of Novgorod, approximately N 58° 30', E 31° 20'.

DESCRIPTION

This ensemble incorporates numerous monuments in the town of Novgorod, as well as several in outlying districts. In the town itself, the monuments are found in two areas: the district of St. Sophia and the old commercial district. In St. Sophia, there is the Kremlin with its 15th century fortifications, as well as the 11th century Church of St. Sophia, and several other monuments from the 12th to 19th centuries. In the old commercial district are some of the oldest churches in the town, including the Church of the Transfiguration which features late 14th century frescoes by Theophanes the Greek. Outside the town, there are four religious monuments from the 12th and 13th century, including the famous church at Neredica.

SIGNIFICANCE

The town of Novgorod, dating from the 10th century, was situated on an important trade route linking central Asia with northern Europe. It was ruled by a Swedish prince who came to power through the invitation of the local People's Assembly. This unusual arrangement was similar to that of the Hanseatic cities with which Novgorod had close trading links. Culturally, Novgorod was one of the most important centers in Russia, it is the birthplace of Russian stone architecture and the site of the first national school of painting. It was the see of an archbishop, and some of Russia's oldest church manuscripts are to be found here - including the first complete translation (late 15th century) into Slavonic of the Old and New Testaments. With its broad range of well conserved monuments, Novgorod today shines a light onto the development of Russian architecture and art from the Middles Ages until last century.

Solovetskii Archipelago

LOCATION

Solovetskii Archipelago, western edge of the White Sea, Arkhangelskii Region, approximately N 65° 00', E 36° 00'.

DESCRIPTION

This is an extended monastic complex which stretches over the six main islands of the Solovetskii Archipelago and onto parts of the mainland as well. The heart of the complex is the monastery itself which is on Solovetskii Island. It is in three parts: the central square, which is flanked by several churches and cathedrals; the northern courtyard, which houses several craft buildings; and the southern courtyard, with its wash and bath houses. There is a fortress at the monastery which was built around 1582-94 from boulders. The monastery village includes chapels, a dry-dock, an early hydro-electric station and various other industrial installations. There are a number of other smaller monasteries, including four on Solovetskii Island, an early 17th century monastery on Anzer Island, a 16th century complex on Big Zayatskii Island and the St. Sergius Monastery on Big Muksalma Island.

SIGNIFICANCE

The Solovetskii Monastery was founded by three monks sometime during the 1430's. It expanded over the centuries to cover not only the main islands of the archipelago, but also large stretches of land on the neighboring mainland. A major re-organization was undertaken in the mid 16th century: roads were built, a dairy farm was started, a series of dams were created, and several small industries, including brick making and ceramics, were established. Between 1582 and 1594, a fortress was built, and into the 17th century Solovetskii became the economic, cultural, military and religious center of the whole region, attracting many pilgrims. Later that century, the monastery revolted against the reforms of Patriach Nikon; it successfully survived a siege by Government troops and went on to flourish further into the 18th and 19th centuries, with craft and trade activities expanding. The Revolution brought dramatic changes: the monastery was closed and a state farm was established in its place. In 1923, the islands became special prison camps, and later the Navy used the complex for training purposes. In 1967 a Museum Preserve was established and in 1990 the monastery was re-established. Today this complex survives in remarkably original condition, displaying all stages of its evolution, and represents an outstanding example of a successful monastic settlement in the harsh and inhospitable environment of northern Europe.

Trinity-Sergius Lavra in Sergiev Posad

LOCATION

Sergiev Posad, Moscow Region, approximately N 55° 53', E 37° 40'.

DESCRIPTION

This monastic complex comprises twelve main buildings. It is surrounded by 1.5km (1mi) of stone walls which form an irregular rectangle, with corner towers. The Trinity Cathedral is constructed of white limestone, with four pillars, three apses and a single gilded dome. The much smaller Nikon Annex, stands to the south of the Cathedral and is very similar stylistically. Adjacent to the Annex and placed symmetrically, is the small rectangular Tent of Serapion. Lying against the southern wall is the Palace of the Metropolitan, with its red facade and baroque interior. The Refectory and Church of St. Sergius adjoin and present richly painted facades. Sitting in the center of the complex is the Church of the Holy Spirit, one of the oldest buildings, featuring early glazed tiles on the interior walls. The magnificent Cathedral of the Assumption towers over the complex and boasts a light and spacious interior, embellished with magnificent blue and violet frescoes. On the northern side is the highest building, the Belfry, which reaches up 88m (290ft). The remaining buildings inside the complex are the Monk's Cells, the Palace of the Tsar and the Church of the Virgin of Smolensk. There are also a number of churches and chapels outside the walled complex.

SIGNIFICANCE

This monastery was founded around 1330 in the forest to the north of Moscow by the monk Sergius. The rules of monastic life which he instituted saw the construction of specialised buildings which resulted in the development of a defined layout. After being destroyed in 1408 by fire, it was rebuilt, again in wood, by Sergius's successor, Nikon. Sergius was canonised in 1422 and declared the Patron Saint of Russia. This coincided with the erection of the first stone building, the Trinity Cathedral, which still stands today. The strategically important location of the monastery saw it included in Moscow's defensive system and led to the construction of stone walls from around 1540 to 1560. This was an exciting period of growth for the monastery; it expanded considerably and many people came to work there. The early 17th century saw the monastery withstand a prolonged siege as a result of which it received many rich endowments. In 1744, Empress Petrovna awarded the highest title of Lavra to the complex. The Revolution saw the monastery close and the monks moved to a nearby cell. Today, the monks have returned to this remarkable complex, and continue their devotion amongst these ancient and influential buildings.

Above Palace of the Metropolitan

White Stone Monuments

LOCATION

Vladimir Region, approximately N 56° 10', E 40° 20'.

DESCRIPTION

This site is a collection of buildings in the Vladimir Region which are all constructed from white limestone. Within the ancient city of Vladimir, there are numerous important religious and secular buildings including the Cathedral of the Assumption and its Golden Gate, the Princely Castle at Bogolyubovo, the Church of the Intercession on the Neri River and the Cathedral of St. Demetrius. Some 25km (15mi) to the north is Suzdal, a town dating back to the 9th century. Dominating the town is the 13th century Cathedral of Nativity. Important buildings include the Kremlin, several 16th and 17th century cubic churches with tent roofs, a number of 18th century churches and several

monasteries. Just east of Suzdal, on the Neri River, is the Church of St. Boris and St. Gleb. This is the first church in Russia to be built in white limestone in the style that came to characterise the buildings in this listing.

SIGNIFICANCE

The architectural tradition established by these white limestone buildings was extremely influential across Russia. They now represent an important historical document relating to the development of architectural styles in the region. The quality of the structures is remarkable and the standard of restoration work carried out has been exemplary.

ABOVE Cathedral of the Assumption, Vladimir

Historic Center of Saint Petersburg

LOCATION

N 59° 57', E 30° 19'.

DESCRIPTION

This exceptionally broad listing comprises numerous monuments and some natural features. The historic center includes several islands, the entire central city space and numerous outlying areas. The balance of the listing is divided into 34 separate sub-listings and includes highways, palaces, parks, villas, cemeteries, forts, hospitals and river embankments.

SIGNIFICANCE

St Petersburg was one of the great cities of the 18th and 19th centuries. Its magnificence and splendor was world renowned. Peter the Great ordered a fort built on the site in 1703. A short ten years later, St Petersburg was thriving as the great and illustrious capital of the Russian Empire. This remarkable history is exceptionally well preserved today in the form of this most important World Heritage site.

ABOVE Samson Fountain, Czar's Summer Palace
RIGHT Catherine the Great Palace

SLOVAKIA

Historic Town of Banska Stiavnica

LOCATION

Central Slovakia, approximately N 48° 30', E 18° 54'.

DESCRIPTION

Banska Stiavnica is an old mining town and this listing also includes a wide tract of land surrounding the town. The historic center features many notable buildings, including two castles, a town hall, four churches, the buildings of the Mining Academy, and the baroque calvary complex. There are numerous burgher houses dating back to the 15th century. The surrounding area is rich with the remains of early mining operations. These include 30 water reservoirs, an elaborate series of dams, collecting channels, mine shafts, a silver-lead smelting plant, a wire cable factory and several drainage galleries.

SIGNIFICANCE

The town seal of Banska Stiavnica reads 1275, which makes it the oldest mining town in Slovakia. The tremendous wealth which was generated by mining activities is seen today in the rich and varied architecture of this well preserved and very original ensemble. The unique water management system which was developed in this area remained the most advanced in the world until last century. Many important technical advancements in the fields of mining and metallurgy were made here, and the town was a European center for mining education for several centuries.

Vlkolínec

LOCATION

Central Slovakia, approximately N 49° 05', E 19° 19'.

DESCRIPTION

Vlkolínec is a town of log-built dwellings which date mainly from the 19th century. The buildings have been unaltered and so retain many early constructional features. Characteristically, the houses are situated on the street frontages of narrow parcels of land, with stables, barns, and other outbuildings arranged behind. The houses are constructed of log walls on stone footings. The walls are coated with clay and whitewashed or painted blue. Most have three rooms, although some are smaller and a few have up to six rooms. The roofs are pitched and are covered with wooden shingles. There are 47 traditional houses of this type in the town, as well as a school house and the Church of the Blessed Mary. The main street is on a steep slope and forks in the village center. A canal runs through the center of town.

SIGNIFICANCE

It is thought that there was an early Slav settlement on this site from the 10th century, but the first documentary evidence of occupation is from 1376. It is known there were four homesteads and five other residences in 1675, but the present settlement consists almost entirely of buildings from the 19th century. These buildings, however, are essentially identical in style to buildings of a much earlier age. Vlkolínec is without doubt the most comprehensive and best preserved traditional village in the Slovak Republic.

'Tis not what man
Does that exhalts
him,
but what man
Would do!

ROBERT BROWNING

Spissky Castle

LOCATION
Spis Region, approximately N 49° 00′, E 20° 30′.

DESCRIPTION
Spissky Hrad (Castle) rises dramatically from the plains of western Slovakia. It began as a small fortified settlement in the 12th century and grew over the centuries to become one of the largest castles in eastern Europe. Much of the remains today are well preserved, although there has been considerable deterioration in some of the buildings. The castle consists of the upper keep and courtyard, two Romanesque inner baileys with internal fortified access gates, the outer bailey with the main entrance gate, and the large barbican area, now largely in ruins. The other elements of this site include the old town, Spisske Podhradie, which is focused around the Church of the Blessed Virgin Mary; the complex of buildings at Spisska Kapitula, which are based on the Cathedral of St. Martin; and the Church of the Holy Spirit at Zebra.

SIGNIFICANCE
Construction of the castle began in the early 12th century, but earth tremors saw most of the structure collapse - so the building wasn't completed until the first half of the 13th century. After terrible onslaughts from the armies of Matthias Cak in the early 14th century, the castle was rebuilt in the Gothic style and extended to include a settlement with its own walls. Additions and modifications continued to be made until 1780, when it was abandoned after a fire destroyed it. Spisske Podhradie was founded in the 12th century as a settlement at the base of the castle, but quickly became independent of the castle. It was granted town status in 1321 and thereafter became an important industrial center for its large Saxon community. Following a fire in the 16th century, most of the residences were rebuilt in the Renaissance style. Spisska Kapitula began as a small fortified settlement in the 12th century overlooking Spisske Podhradie, of which it now forms part. Zebra is one of the earliest Slovak settlements in the region; in the later feudal period it became part of the castle domain. The remains of these settlements constitute a remarkable ensemble of military, political, cultural and religious elements of a type that was common in medieval Europe, but of which so few have survived in such a complete and original state.

SLOVENIA

Skocjan Caves

LOCATION

In Slovenija, N 45° 39', E 14° 00'.

DESCRIPTION

Skocjan Caves are the beginning of a vast underground network which extends 40km (25mi) on to the springs of the Timaro River in the Gulf of Trieste. The protected zone covers 200ha (480ac) and includes the above ground canyon of the Reka River, with the spectacular natural bridge which spans it. The main caves are Mahorcic and Marinic with their underground lakes and waterfalls.

SIGNIFICANCE

These caves were inhabited in prehistoric times and were known in antiquity. Their unique and spectacular formations accord them a special place in the study of speleology. They also provide the habitat for several rare and endangered species of fauna, including five different bats and a salamander.

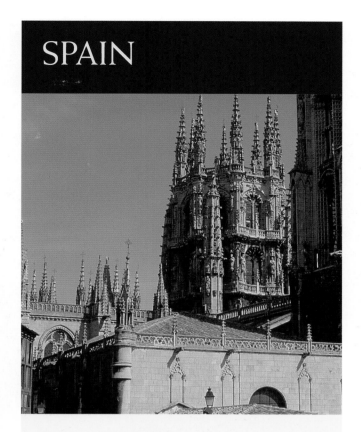

Burgos Cathedral

LOCATION

Burgos, 240km (150mi) north of Madrid, W 03° 40', N 42° 23'.

DESCRIPTION

This massive limestone cathedral dominates the entire town of Burgos. Its cruciform design is somewhat hidden by the wealth of additions that have been made since its initial construction. There are 15 chapels, a 14th century cloister and an archiepiscopal palace, joined to and surrounding the original structure. The western facade houses the three central doorways and is flanked by two lofty towers. It is also crowned by a dome, another late addition. The interior features a famous curiosity: a crucifix covered with buffalo hide to resemble human skin.

SIGNIFICANCE

Founded in 1221, this magnificent example of a floral Gothic cathedral was not completed until 1567. The bones of that most celebrated of medieval Spanish captains, 'El Cid' have rested here since 1919.

ABOVE LEFT San Miguel de Lillo

Churches of the Kingdom of the Asturias

LOCATION

Asturias Region, N 43° 09' to 43° 22', W 02° 11' to 02° 33'.

DESCRIPTION

There are three churches here: Santa Maria del Naranco, San Miguel de Lillo and Santa Cristina de Lena. The first two are situated on Naranco Hill which is a specially protected area.

SIGNIFICANCE

Asturias was formerly an independent Christian kingdom founded after the Moslem invasion of Spain. These churches are representative of the later stages of this kingdom. They are the first Asturian churches not built according to the 'Visigothic' style. Pillars instead of columns, round-headed arches, wider aisles and a larger sense of space are distinctive of this innovative style.

Toledo (Historic Town)

LOCATION

Region of Castille la Nueva, 70km (43mi) southwest of Madrid, N 39° 51', W 00° 20'.

DESCRIPTION

Surrounded on all sides except the north by the River Tagus, Toledo sits on a rugged outcrop of granite 720m (2,400ft) above sea level. A pair of Moorish bridges span the river, and numerous gateways allow entrance to the old town. The alcázar, a massive stone structure with four corner towers, sits on the highest point and dominates the setting. A large cathedral with Gothic, Renaissance and baroque features has an impressive spire which towers over the streets below. Numerous other churches, a Franciscan convent, several synagogues, Arabic baths and many significant residential mansions are also found in this magnificent town.

SIGNIFICANCE

Toledo was conquered in 193BC by the Romans and became a major regional center. Its history is strongly rooted in Catholicism, and it was one of the important early Christian centers until the Moorish invasion. Prospering under Moorish rule, it became an important trading center, especially in textiles. The large Jewish community thrived and the city's culture developed into a unique blend of Arab and Hebrew. When the Catholics recaptured the city in 1085, it was made Spain's capital and remained so for almost 500 turbulent years which saw, amongst other events, the infamous massacre of the Jews in 1392. Today, the old city is very well preserved and so remains an important relic of the vibrant history of this region.

ABOVE *The Alcazar at Toledo*
RIGHT *Courtyard of the old University, Salamanca*

Old City of Salamanca

LOCATION

In the region of Castille la Vieja, N 40° 58', W 05° 40'.

DESCRIPTION

The city of Salamanca is situated on the northern bank of the Tormes River and is entered by crossing a Roman bridge. Within the walls are the old quarter of the cathedral and the baroque square of Plaza Mayor. The city has two cathedrals which are joined; the old 12th century cathedral and the newer 17th century cathedral. The facade of the old university is in the Spanish Renaissance style called plateresque. There are numerous convents, churches and mansions.

SIGNIFICANCE

Conquered by Hannibal in 222BC, Salamanca not long after became an important Roman station. Gothic and Moorish control was followed by Alphonso VI at around 1100AD. Soon after, the town's university gained much acclaim and prosperity endured until the 16th century. The university is still renowned and is the oldest on the Iberian Peninsula. The Plaza Mayor is one of the finest squares in Europe. It could hold 20,000 people - notably for bullfights - and is surrounded by Corinthian columns surmounted by a series of 90 arches. As one of the more important cities during the Renaissance, Salamanca holds an invaluable heritage.

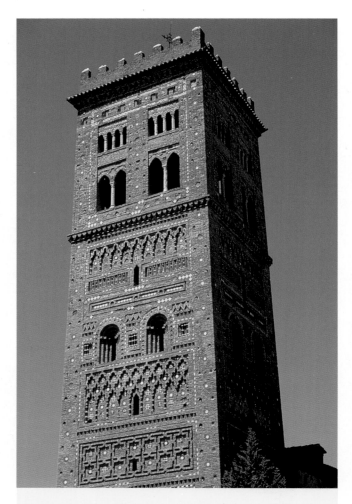

Mudejar Architecture of Teruel

LOCATION

Teruel, Aragon, N 40° 20', W 01° 06'.

DESCRIPTION

This is a group of four towers in the center of the old town, all built at the back of churches bearing the same name. They are; St. Peter, St. Salvador, St. Martin and the cathedral.

SIGNIFICANCE

These towers are the most important and best preserved examples of Mudejar architecture in Spain. This style was developed in Spain during the Middles Ages directly after the Christian re-conquest of Moorish-held territories, when Moslems were working under the supervision of Christians. It reached its apotheosis in the delicate brick and tile work that can be seen at Teruel.

Above Tower of St. Martin, Teruel

Santiago de Compostela

LOCATION

In the region of Galicia, northwest Spain, N 42° 52', W 08° 32'.

DESCRIPTION

Santiago has many buildings of historical and architectural significance, particularly its religious buildings. The main ones include the Romanesque cruciform cathedral with its Portico de la Gloria - a magnificent Gothic piece of art, the Palace Gelmirez, the Monastery of St. Martin Pinario, the Royal Hospital and the Place Rajoy.

SIGNIFICANCE

This town has a long and important history in Christendom. After the Moorish conquests of Spain, the northwest was the only area left unaffected. So the beginnings of the assault to reconquer Spain for Christianity began in Santiago. This created tremendous enthusiasm for the religion which was further inflamed with the reputed discovery of the remains of Saint James. A church was built over the spot and it rapidly gained acclaim as a pilgrimage destination. As a result, the town now has one of the richest legacies of Christian art and architecture to be found on the Iberian Peninsula.

Old Town of Ávila and its Extra Muros Churches

LOCATION

Ávila 100km (62mi) northwest of Madrid.
W 01° 00', N 40° 39'.

DESCRIPTION

The old town of Ávila is wholly enclosed by some 2.5km (1.5mi) of massive stone walls which are on average 12m (39ft) high and 3m (10ft) thick. These walls incorporate 82 forts and nine fortified gates. The historic center is characterised by narrow streets and small squares with low houses. There are several palaces and mansions and numerous religious buildings, the most significant are: the Cathedral of Salvador, the Church of Santo Tomé and the Convent of Saint Teresa. Outside the walls are four important 12th century Romanesque churches: San Vicente, San Pedro, San Andrés and San Segundo.

SIGNIFICANCE

This superb example of a medieval fortified town was built during the 12th century after Spain was reconquered from the Moors. Prior to that, it was the site of several ancient Roman, Celtic and Arab settlements. Its strong religious character stems largely from its being the birthplace of St. Teresa. Several notable works of art are kept in the town, particularly the paintings of Pedro de Berruguete and the work of goldsmith Juan de Arfe y Villafane.

The Escorial, Madrid

LOCATION

55km (34mi) north of Madrid, W 04° 10', N 40° 35'.

DESCRIPTION

This complex is of considerable size and is composed of five distinct areas; 'the College for the Sons of Noblemen', the seminary, the monastery, the palace and the church. The monastery, which is perfectly symmetrical, stands at the center of the complex which was built between 1563–1584.

SIGNIFICANCE

The ground plan of the monastery was based, according to scholars of the period, on that of the Temple of Jerusalem. This vast architectural ensemble is remarkable for its austerity and simplicity. The four solid towers which stand at the four corners of the monastery and the large dome are distinctly Spanish, but the slate-tiled roofs, virtually the first in Spain, are distinctly central European.

Old Town of Segovia and its Aqueduct

LOCATION

Segovia, Castilla la Vieja, around 80km (50mi) northwest of Madrid, N 40° 57', W 04° 26'.

DESCRIPTION

The old part of Segovia is placed high up on a narrow ridge and is encircled by stone walls. Plaza Mayor forms the center of the town and the main cathedral sits on one side of it. 'El Puente' is the Roman aqueduct which crosses the Plaza del Azoguejo. It is constructed of dark granite without the use of mortar and its highest point is 27m (90ft) above the ground. Consisting of two levels of arches, it is still in use. Numerous Romanesque churches are found within the walls, including those of San Lorenzo, Vera Cruz and San Esteban. The fortified castle, or alcázar, of the Castilian Kings is one of the best known monuments.

SIGNIFICANCE

A place of some importance in Roman times, Segovia was founded around 700BC. The first major upheaval was at the beginning of the 8th century AD when the Moors conquered the town. Almost 300 years later it was recaptured by Alfonso VI. Its position was then consolidated and the town grew and prospered, eventually becoming a major industrial center of the Middles Ages. The old town's state of preservation is excellent and the town now presents a storehouse of architectural wealth, particularly Romanesque and Gothic. The aqueduct is of particular significance, being easily the best preserved of its type.

Altamira Cave

LOCATION

Region of Vispieres in Cantabria Province, N 43° 22', W 00° 25'.

DESCRIPTION

Situated at the summit of a limestone cliff, this cave is almost 300m (1,000ft) in length and of varying width. There are numerous galleries branching off from the main chamber. Most of the paintings are found inside the 'Great Hall' which is 18m by 9m (60ft by 30ft) wide. Its ceiling is covered with paintings of bisons in bright shades of red, violet and black. There are also hand prints and outlines as well as some paintings of horses, boars and human figures. Other chambers have paintings of deer, cattle, goats, antelope and symbols. The total number of paintings is around 150.

SIGNIFICANCE

First discovered in 1868, the paintings in this cave were not recognised for their true value until some 40 years later. They are now considered one of the most valuable collections of prehistoric art in the world. It has been coined the 'Sistine Chapel of Quaternary art'.

ABOVE Right Casa Mila

Parque and Palacio Güell and Casa Milá in Barcelona

LOCATION

City of Barcelona, Cataluva, E 05° 50', N 44° 00'.

DESCRIPTION

Güell Park, which was originally proposed as a revolutionary residential center by Catalan architect Antonio Gaudi, was left unfinished after Gaudi was tragically struck by a trolley. It is now enjoyed as a public park. Palacio Güell was designed and built on the commission of Eugenio Güell, a Catalan philanthropist, as his main residence. Casa Milá stands on a plot of 1,600sqm (18,000sqft) and is privately owned.

SIGNIFICANCE

These three artistic architectural monuments celebrate the achievements of Antonio Gaudi Cornet (1852-1926), a brilliant architect of Catalian modernism. These three structures illuminate Gaudi's interest in medieval and Gothic tradition. Much of his work includes innovative and daring sculptural forms, and he is considered to have been one of the great architects of his time.

The Route of Santiago de Compostela

LOCATION

From the French border to Santiago de Compostela, through the provinces of Huesca, Zaragoza, Burgos, Palencia, León, Lugo and Coruña.

DESCRIPTION

This legendary pilgrim's route extends from two points on the French border, progressing through two passes, merging west of Pamplona, just before Puente la Reina, and continues on to Santiago. Many religious buildings line the route as well as buildings for the assistance of pilgrims such as hospitals and inns. Religious buildings of particular note include the cathedral at Santo Domingo de la Calzada, the cathedral at Astorga and the Romanesque church of Frómista. The town of Puenta la Reina is remarkable for its buildings and its 11th century bridge. In all there are more than 1,800 buildings of historical and architectural value. As well as the wealth of buildings, towns and villages which line the route, most of the ancient path itself also remains.

SIGNIFICANCE

Despite the individual value of these many buildings and numerous structures, it is their value as an entirety which is paramount. The route is astoundingly complete, retaining not only its original function for pilgrims but much of its original character also. Since its birth in the 10th century BC the route has flourished culturally and economically and displays many of the fruits of European development. It also displays the formative relationship of the culture of the Iberian Peninsular with that of the rest of Europe. The Route of Santiago de Compostela is the longest and most authentic of the pilgrimage routes which played such a vital role in the religious and spiritual lives of the people of Europe in the Middles Ages.

ABOVE One of the many churches along the route, San Miguel in Daroca

The Alhambra and the Generalife in Granada

LOCATION

Granada, Andalucia, W 03° 33', N 37° 10'.

DESCRIPTION

This magnificent complex of fortified palaces, the jewel of the final period of Moorish domination of Spain, was built on one of Granada's three hills. The quality and intricacy of the stucco work is unsurpassed. Ceramic tiles are used with verve and imagination. Amongst the many beautiful gardens and courtyards is the celebrated Court of Lions.

SIGNIFICANCE

The Alhambra and its extension, the Generalife, are the single most important pieces of architectural heritage from the Nasrides - the last of the Spanish Moslem dynasties. Nasrid art represents the zenith of Moslem art in the Iberian Peninsula.

Old Town of Cáceres

LOCATION

300km (186mi) west-southwest of Madrid, N 39° 28', W 06° 22'.

DESCRIPTION

The old part of Cáceres sits above the modern town and is protected by stone walls that are 1.2km (0.75mi) in length. There are three gates and only a few of the original 30 towers. The dominant feature is the tower of the Gothic church of San Mateo. There is a former Jesuit college and monastery which is now a hospital, as well as the Churches of Santa Maria and San Francisco Javier.

SIGNIFICANCE

Cáceres is of Roman origin and it is thought it occupies the site of the ancient Roman town of Norba Caesarina. It enjoyed considerable prosperity in the Middles Ages, mainly due to its proximity to the coast and the consequent trade with the New World of the Americas. Today, it is a fine example of an early fortified town with its extremely well preserved fortifications which are half Roman and half Arabic.

RIGHT Mosque of Cordoba with Roman bridge in the foreground

Mosque of Córdoba

LOCATION

Córdoba, W 04° 35′, N 37° 50′.

DESCRIPTION

The mosque, including successive additions to the original building, occupies a rectangular site 180m by 130m (600ft by 430ft). It is surrounded by a massive wall which is strengthened by square towers. Each tower has several doors which give access to the building. There is a courtyard on the northern side with orange trees which is surrounded by a high wall with archways on three sides. The interior is dark, with a low ceiling, and there is a forest of pillars and superb red and white arches.

SIGNIFICANCE

Probably modelled on the mosque in Damascus, this one nonetheless is more architecturally advanced. The series of double arches which supports the roof was a brilliant innovation for its time. Apart from being a major center of architectural experimentation and innovation, this mosque is also a storehouse for some fabulous artistic treasures.

Poblet Monastery

LOCATION

Cataluna, N 41° 30', E 01° 00' (approximately).

DESCRIPTION

This complex comprises numerous structures and buildings from various eras. The focus centers around the large Cistercian abbey. North of this is a group of monastic buildings, including a cloister, fountain, chapter room, monks' dormitory, parlor, library, calefactory, refectory and kitchens. To the west are the lay brothers' buildings (which were later partially converted to a royal residence), while to the north is the infirmary. Within the complex, there is an inner wall 608m (1,968ft) in length which is 2m (7ft) thick with crenelated battlements, walkways, towers and a gateway.

SIGNIFICANCE

Poblet has a fascinating history that is reflected in the diverse nature of its architectural forms. The blend of architectural styles is unusual in that the major functions of Cistercian monastery, military fortress and royal palace, residence and pantheon were all served within its boundaries. The monastery was founded in 1150 by the Cistercian monks of Fontfroide. It was fortified and transformed to serve these other functions during the 14th century by Peter IV the Ceremonious, King of Aragon. The entire complex is a unique artistic achievement and represents the zenith of the Cistercian style which endured throughout the 12th, 13th and 14th centuries.

Mérida

LOCATION

Autonomous Community of Extremadura, approximately N 38° 58', W 06° 18'.

DESCRIPTION

Mérida is an old Roman town dating back to 25BC. The excavated sites have been well conserved and the buildings have all been sympathetically restored. The Roman monuments include: Guadiana Bridge, one of the longest known Roman bridges, and still in use; the Amphitheater, with seating for 1,500; the Theater, inaugurated in 15BC, and seating 5,500; the Temple of Diana; the Arch of Trajan; the Circus, the largest in the Roman world; two Columbarii (family tombs); the water supply system, including dams, aqueducts and underground channels; and the Basilica de Casa Herrera, a Paleochristian basilica. There are also monuments from later periods, including the 18th century Martyr Church of Santa Eulalia, built on top of a Diocletian church; and the alcázabar, built during the 9th century.

SIGNIFICANCE

Mérida was founded by Augustus at the end of his Spanish campaign. Soon after it became the capital of the new Roman province of Lusitania, and assumed a major role in the Roman conquest of the north west of the Iberian peninsula. The town was built on a classically strategic site, where an important river (in this case the Guadiana) crosses a major road. It is this pivotal role that Mérida played in the expansion of the Roman Empire, which makes it now one of the most important old Roman towns in existence - the remains today provide outstanding examples of the public buildings of a major Roman provincial capital.

ABOVE Roman theater at Merida

Garajonay National Park

LOCATION

Island of Gomera, Canary Islands,
N 28° 05' to 28° 12', W 17° 10' to l7 °18'.

DESCRIPTION

Situated right in the center of the island, Garajonay has an area of 3,984ha (9,605ac), just over 10% of the island's landmass. Its highest point is 1,492m (4,895ft) above sea level and vegetation is largely subtropical rainforest.

SIGNIFICANCE

The majestic forests of this mountainous island park are remnants of the subtropical vegetation which once flourished in southern Europe until sudden climatic changes led to their disappearance. The flora is particularly rich here, with over 450 different species, 34 of them endemic to the region and eight endemic to the park.

Cathedral, Alcázar and Archivo de Indias in Sevilla

LOCATION

In the region of Andalucia, southern Spain E 05° 05', N 37° 25'.

DESCRIPTION

An inland city on the left bank of the Guadalquivir River, the old part of Seville is a maze of small streets and squares, although the district of the alcázar and the cathedral is more spacious. The alcázar is a fortified Moorish palace with ten sides and is of brick construction. The Cathedral of Santa Maria de la Sede is mainly in the Gothic style and is of immense proportions - 90m (300ft) wide and 30m (l00ft) high. Casa Lonja is a superb Renaissance building and houses the Archivo de Indias - a collection of documents, books, manuscripts, maps and plans all relating to Spain's administration of its empire in the Americas.

SIGNIFICANCE

The Cathedral was erected to commemorate the reconquest of Spain by Christianity - it is the second largest in area of all Gothic churches and the largest in Europe. The alcázar, begun in 1181, is a superb example of Moorish architecture. The Archivo de Indias is the definitive documentation of the Spanish Empire in the New World and, as such, is of absolutely crucial historical importance.

ABOVE *The Archivo de Indias*

Royal Monastery of Santa Maria de Guadalupe

LOCATION

Autonomous Community of Extremadura, Province of Cáceres, approximately N 39° 26', W 05° 26'.

DESCRIPTION

This monastery ensemble is large and diverse, covering an area of over 20,000sqm (218,000sqft) with many buildings from different historical periods. The main Church is in the Gothic style and is highly ornamented both inside and out. The Camarín de la Virgin is a small baroque octagonal building possessing magnificent art works including murals by Luca Giordano, as well as this complex's most famous statue - the Virgin of Guadalupe. The Chapel of Santa Catalina is a square building from the 15th century, with a magnificent octagonal cupola which is lit by a lantern; it contains magnificent 17th century tombs. The oldest building in the complex is the Mudéjar cloister, a small white and red brick building built between 1389 and 1405. There is also a Gothic cloister with tiers of galleries and arches, and a 'new' church in the baroque style.

SIGNIFICANCE

The construction of this complex commenced in the 13th century with the building of a chapel to house the statue of the Virgin of Guadalupe, after a shepherd unearthed her near the Guadalupe River. A few years later it became a church, and after invoking the Virgin in his victory at Salado in 1340, Alfonso XI declared it a Royal Sanctuary. For 447 years under the Hieronymite Order, the monastery was the most important in Spain and one of the most important in all of Christendom. The cult of the Virgin of Guadalupe became associated with the discovery of the 'New World' in 1492 and became an important symbol in the colonization and conversion of South America. In the same year the Moslem forces were expelled from the Iberian Peninsular, an event also associated with the monastery. The buildings themselves are of high artistic value and show architectural developments over several centuries. The natural setting of the site adds to its beauty, creating a superb backdrop for these magnificent artistic achievements.

Historic Areas of Istanbul

LOCATION

Within the Province of Istanbul,
N 45° 25', E 29° 00'.

DESCRIPTION

This historic area is 17.2sqkm (7sqmi) of
densely populated urban development,
bounded by the Golden Horn to the north,
the Bosphorus to the east, the Marmara Sea
to the south and land walls to the west. The
following four areas have been particularly
singled out for conservation; 1. archeo-
logical park with the hippodrome, Agia
Sophia (Byzantine Church), Agia Irene,
numerous cisterns, various Byzantine
remains and the Blue Mosque and Sokollu
Mehmet Pasa complexes; 2. Süleymaniye
conservation site with numerous small
mosques and houses clustered around two
major Ottoman religious complexes - the
Sehzade and Süleymaniye Mosques. These
are complete with Koran schools, kitchens,
mausoleums, etc; 3. Zeyrek conservation
site, another traditional area centered on the
church of the monastery of Pantocrator,
now known as Zeyrek Mosque; 4. Land
walls conservation area which aims at
maintaining the old fortified walls with 96
towers, 13 gates and 11 combined
tower/gates. Near the walls and included in
the conservation site are several religious
complexes, a number of mosques and former
churches, plus the mighty Kara Ahmet
Pasa complex at Topkapi.

SIGNIFICANCE

Taken together, these complexes and sites
chart an unbroken record of one of the
greatest empires of the Christian and
Moslem world. From St. Sophia, the
greatest church in antiquity, through the
city's role as Byzantium, then
Constantinople, then as Istanbul, capital of
all the middle and near east as well as most
of eastern Europe, it is impossible to overes-
timate the importance of 'Old Stamboul'.

RIGHT The Blue Mosque seen from the top of the
Aya Sophia Mosque

TURKEY

Istanbul, the Capital of Two Empires

Istanbul is the largest and most significant city in Turkey. Standing on two continents and situated at the mouth of the Bosphorus, it owes much of its beauty and glorious history to its topographical character. Throughout history it has controlled the sea traffic between the Black Sea and the Mediterranean and the land routes between Asia and Europe. As the capital of the Byzantine and Ottoman Empires it has been an urban center for centuries, hosting different peoples and cultures. All these have led to its unique cultural heritage.

Although there are traces of settlements dating back to the end of the 4th millennium, archeological evidence shows that the city itself goes back to the 7th century BC when it was colonized by the Greeks; its name Byzantium derived from its legendary founder, Byzas the Megarian. In 196AD Byzantium fell to the Roman Emperor Septimus Severus who destroyed it. Soon enough he realized the strategic signifi-

St. Sophia

cance of the city and restored it in the manner of a Roman town, building a hippodrome, now the Sultanahmet Square, and a colonnaded road leading to the main gate in the walls.

In 324 the city was taken by Constantine the Great, who decided to declare Byzantium the new capital of the Roman Empire, the Nova Roma. In 330 Constantine enlarged the city to five times its original size, completed the hippodrome and added the Forum Constantine midway along the colonnaded road. He built several churches including the first Haghia

Sophia and the great imperial palace overlooking the Marmara Sea. His successors followed the same path. Valens built the monumental aqueduct, one of the landmarks of the city, which served the city well for centuries. In a short time Byzantium had grown into a metropolis of 14 districts over seven hills and came to be known as Constantinopolis named after Constantine.

A new epoch began for the city when Justinian came to power in 527. The city was then reconstructed on an even grander scale, making the city the largest capital of the medieval period. The Church of Haghia Sophia, which crowned the glory of this medieval capital, was built on the ruins of the original basilica erected by Constantius, successor of Constantine. In 537 Justinian resurrected it, appointing two renowned architects, Anthemius of Tralles and Isidorus of Miletus. The Haghia Sophia is a basilica with a dome of grandiose size buttressed by half domes and barrel vaults, a great achievement for its period. Although this church underwent several restorations during the Byzantine and Ottoman times, it still adorns the city as a symbol of traditional Roman monumentality and Christian spirituality.

Although in the following centuries of Byzantine reign the city went through states of unrest with assaults of Slavs, Russians, Arabs and Turks, the city was guarded by its walls. The Latin armies of the fourth Crusade in 1204 sacked Constantinople, ruining the city. The last Byzantine rulers, the Paleologus family, recaptured the city in 1261 restoring the monuments and adding smaller churches and imperial residences. Among the late Byzantine monuments, the Monastery Church of Chora (Kariye) is noted for its mosaics and frescoes, which in style and inconographical content, rival the painted churches of the Early Renaissance .

By the end of the 14th century, the Byzantine Empire had narrowed down to a small state around the city of Constantinople. The Byzantine capital was totally surrounded by the Ottomans and subjected to their continued attacks. In 1451 Sultan Mehmed II built the fortress of Rumeli Hisar on the Bosphorus, cutting the city from the north: he proceeded to conquer the city in 1453. This victory earned him the title 'conqueror', or 'Fathi' in Turkish.

A new phase started for this imperial city when Mehmed II declared it the capital of the Ottoman Empire. The city came to be called 'Kostantiniyye' by the Turks and through the years its name was transformed to 'Stimbol' then to 'Istanbul'. Mehmed II had Turks and Christians brought from

Sultan Ahmet Mosque

all parts of the empire to settle in Istanbul with Venetians and Genoese already living in the town. Conscious of both Islamic and Mediterranean heritage, the Sultan was equally tolerant to all his subjects regardless of belief or provenance. He was also a great patron of the arts. He converted the largest Byzantine church, the Haghia Sophia, into a mosque and on the site of the ruined church of the Holy Apostles, he built a complex of buildings in his name, the Fatih Kulliye.

During the following century the Ottoman Empire reached its furthest boundaries, spreading across three continents, and Istanbul lived through a golden age of prosperity and artistic production. It had become the center of the Islamic world, the seat of the caliphate, acquired by Selim I after his conquests of Mesopotamia and Egypt. His son, Suleyman the Magnificent, reigned for 46 years marking the peak of Ottoman power. Suleyman had inherited a sound administrative system and was conscious of his cultural heritage. He commissioned great many buildings in the capital giving the city its Ottoman skyline. It was during his reign (1520-1566) that Ottoman art and architecture achieved perfection in function and aesthetics. Sinan, the renowned architect of this period and one of the greatest figures in world architecture built several hundred buildings establishing the classical style in Ottoman architecture. Sinan's many works in

Istanbul range from mosques to schools, bridges to waterworks marking Istanbul's architectural glory in the 16th century.

The classical expression stayed with Ottoman architects in the 17th century up until the end, when after continued loss of land in the Balkans, Ottoman history took a new course. Ottoman sultans of the 18th century, realizing that Ottoman supremacy was beginning to wane, established diplomatic and cultural relations with the European countries to acquire technical knowledge and a European way of life. The new relations were influential in the cultural sphere. European travellers and artists frequented Istanbul and exchanges with Europeans brought a new style to the capital. The westernizing elite built houses on the Bosphorous for pleasure, so did the sultans. The 19th century sultans now preferred to live on the Bosphorus in the palaces of Dolmabahoe, Ciragan, Beylerbeyi or Yildiz instead of the Topkapi.

In the 19th century, with the reorganization of the administrative system and social structure, the city grew in the direction of the Galata region and the banks of the Bosphorus, with new government buildings, schools, military barracks and apartment buildings. Today, Istanbul is no longer the capital of the country, but is still the largest city in modern Turkey.

PROF. DR. GÜNSEL RENDA
Hacettepe University, Ankara

Nemrut Dag

LOCATION

In the Province of Adiyaman, 65km (40mi) from Kähta,
N 38° 00', E 39° 00'.

DESCRIPTION

Nemrut Dag is a mountain 2,150m (7,054ft) above sea level
crowned by the tumulus (burial mound) of Antiochos I. The
tumulus is 50m (164ft) high and 150m (492ft) in diameter. It is
piled with fist-sized stones and surrounded on three sides by
terraces, of which the eastern and western are symmetrical and
adorned with colossal statues of kings and deities. The eastern
terrace has two podiums with five statues of various deities flanked
by double eagle and lion statues. A pyramidal stepped fire altar
stands opposite the statues. The western terrace is similar but
lacking the fire altar. A lion relief has astronomical symbols and is
called the horoscope of Antiochos. The northern terrace has no
statues and may have been a processional way while the tomb is
believed to lie under the tumulus.

SIGNIFICANCE

Antiochos was the richest of the petty kings following the decline of
the kingdoms which succeeded Alexander the Great. An inscription
suggests that Antiochos intended the sanctuary for his own tomb
but this has never been found. It is postulated that if it could be
found it would contain fabulous wealth. The above ground statues
similarly suggest this and are themselves of great religious and
eclectic interest. The site itself, which commands vast vistas over a
desolate, mountainous landscape, engenders an air of mystery
which is unique.

Göreme National Park and the Rock Sites of Cappadocia

LOCATION

Nevsehir Province (Cappadocia) in Central Anatolia between the
cities of Urgup and Avanos, N 38° 26', E 34° 54'.

DESCRIPTION

The area is an erosion basin, and forms an open air museum. Due
to severe weathering of the soft rock and soil, a large number of
conical or dome shaped features have evolved, creating a fantastic
landscape of so-called 'fairy chimneys', and these have been
hollowed out to form churches, chapels and houses. There are seven
churches within the valley, dating from the 10th to 13th centuries.
These religious structures are noted for their wall-paintings.

SIGNIFICANCE

In the dispute over representation of human form, particularly with
regard to holy personages, that shook the Catholic Church during
the 8th and 9th centuries, many monks retreated to Cappadocia to
continue their artistic devotion, safe from iconoclasts. Later, under
the persecution of the invading Moslems many more men of religion
took to finding a refuge in the rocks of Göreme. As time went by the
various murals became increasingly sophisticated, until the
expulsion of the monks in the Middles Ages. Geologically, the area
is one of the most unusual on earth, being similar to places such as
the Badlands of Dakota (United States), but having far more
bizarre formations in a much smaller area.

ABOVE 'Fairy chimneys', Cappadocia

Hacettepe University, Ankara
Hattusha

LOCATION

In the Province of Corum, district of Sungurlu,
N 40° 01′, E 33° 39′.

DESCRIPTION

The ruins of the ancient city of Hattusha cover an area of 3sqkm
(1.2sqmi). They consist of several mounds, rocky peaks and
plateaus which rise in a gentle slope approximately 300m
(1,000ft) above the surrounding plain. A pair of gorges determine
the natural boundaries of the site, which is split into an upper and
lower city. A great wall 8km (5mi) long surrounds the whole site
with several ruined towers. The individual monuments within the
city are in varying states of excavation but include a royal citadel
(Büyük kale), the Sphinx gate, the New Castle and the Yellow
Castle. Near the main area are several temple sites and the remains
of the Hittite living quarters, plus a hieroglyphic inscription carved
into a cliff-face detailing numerous exploits of the ancient kings
and warriors. A tremendous series of rock reliefs is also to be seen at
Yazilikuya nearby.

SIGNIFICANCE

This was the capital of the mighty Hittite Empire which ruled over
a great part of Asia Minor and Syria between 2000 and 1200BC.
The three archives of clay tablets which form the main body of
knowledge on the Hittites were found here. It is interesting to note
that it is thought that perhaps the Hittite language was a precursor
to modern European languages.

ABOVE The Sphinx Gate, Hattusha

Great Mosque and Hospital of
Divrigi

LOCATION

In the Sivas Province of Eastern Anatolia, N 39° 45′, E 37° 00′.

DESCRIPTION

This site is a large rectangular area which contains the mosque,
hospital and some tombs. It is on a hillside where the castle of
Divrigi was sited. The mosque has five aisles leading to the mihrab
(niche indicating the direction of Mecca) and 25 multi-colored
vaults. The main dome is the outstanding characteristic of the
mosque, with 16 supporting columns and some intricate ornamental
details. The hospital has various unique plant-like and geometric
stone decorations.

SIGNIFICANCE

The mosque dates from 1228AD, the time of the first appearance of
the Ottoman Turks. It is considered to be one of the finest examples
of early Turkish architectural work. The decorative stone sculp-
turing of the northern portal arcade is particularly renowned.

Hierapolis—Pamukkale

LOCATION

East of Denizli on the northern side of the valley of the Curuksu River, N 37° 57', E 28° 50'.

DESCRIPTION

Pamukkale is a collection of terraces running down the foothills of the Cokelez Mountains. A series of hot thermal springs bubble up from the rock and flow down the terraces forming pools. The water from the springs is heavily laden with calcium carbonate and this has caused white stalactite configurations to form over the rims of the basins, suggesting a fanciful picture of melting pools. These white pools extend 2.5km (1.6mi) and are up to 500m (1,640ft) wide. Above the terraces, on a plateau, sits Hierapolis, the ruins of an ancient Roman spa town. It has a necropolis, baths, tombs and a theater, all in a good state of preservation.

SIGNIFICANCE

One of the most striking visual experiences in Turkey, if not the world, Pamukkale has outstanding aesthetic value. The ruins of Hierapolis and its monuments give insight into a Roman spa town, more a holiday resort than a residential city. The hot waters which formed Pamukkale were the basis of the city's wealth.

Above Terraced pools of Pamukkale

Xanthos - Letoon

LOCATION

Province of Mugla and Antalya, District of Fethiye and Kas, E 29° 16', N 36° 22'.

DESCRIPTION

These ruins are of the ancient Lycian city of Xanthos and its sanctuary, Letoon, 3km (1.9mi) distant. The city is on a hill overlooking the ancient Xanthos River and has impressive remains of rock-cut tombs, temple and pillar tombs, stone mounted sarcophaguses, 7th century BC houses, a Roman theater and early Christian and Byzantine churches. A bishop's palace remains unexcavated. At Letoon are several Greek temples and theaters, as well as many later Roman public buildings.

SIGNIFICANCE

The Lycian Kingdom controlled much of southern and southeastern Turkey and the Mediterranean until being conquered by Alexander the Great. It was at Xanthos, the capital, and in Letoon that royal decisions were made. The remains of the various monuments attest to the wealth, power and artistic skills of these early peoples.

Above The Roman theater at Xanthos

Saint Sophia and Kiévo-Pechersk Lavra, Kiev

LOCATION

Kiev, N 50° 27', E 30° 29'.

DESCRIPTION

Located in the city of Kiev, this is a collection of historically important architectural sites dating from the 11th century to the 19th century. The area known as the 'Laure of Kiévo-Petchersk' includes two catacombs, a collection of religious monuments incorporating the College of Dormiton, the Trinity and the Saviour of Berestovo churches, ramparts, St Nicholas and the All Saints churches, a refectory and a 17th century convent and its walls and the Saint Sophia Cathedral. This Byzantine style cathedral was built in the 11th century and houses a variety of mosaics and frescoes. The pyramid style of the two galleries and the interior stairway make the cathedral one of the most majestic structures of its type.

SIGNIFICANCE

Kiévo-Petchersk was the birth place of Kiev's Christian movement and is linked to the development of Christianity in Russia. The architecture of the 'Laure' reflects the major stages in the historical development of the area. Apart from its religious significance, Kiévo-Petchersk was the cultural center of the Ukraine. The first known Russian artist, Alipi, lived and worked in the Laure, as did the writer Nestor and the first Russian doctor Agapit. Since the Academy of Art was established in Kiev in the 17th century, the center has attracted many people of different artistic backgrounds.

ABOVE Saint Sophia Cathedral

UNITED KINGDOM

Britain has fourteen World Heritage sites including one in a British dependency. Some sites, like the 'Giant's Causeway', a series of perfect hexagonal columns rising vertically out of the Irish Sea, are the product of geological activity, which in this case took place some 55 million years ago. Others, landscapes and buildings of beauty and grandeur, are the result of nature and resources harnessed to human needs.

Fourteen may seem a high number, but it is important to remember that they represent only a minute fraction of the British heritage. We also have 900 miles of unspoilt coastline in England and Wales alone, the Scottish coast and islands, open spaces of outstanding landscape beauty, a rich variety of natural habitats, and, from the peculiarly British tradition of country house building, a world-famous abundance of stately homes and gardens.

The World Heritage sites are valuable both as individual achievements and as symbols of particular periods or collective achievements. Thus Durham and Canterbury Cathedrals, Westminster, Bath, and Fountains Abbey represent the finest periods of English ecclesiastical architecture, Ironbridge represents the beginning of the industrial revolution and a breakthrough in civil engineering, and the Houses of Parliament, another World Heritage site, symbolise a system of government whose influence has been felt throughout the world.

As objects of beauty, they have assisted our worship, kindled popular myths and legends, and inspired some of the greatest works of Turner and Constable, Shakespeare and Wordsworth, Jane Austen, Elgar and Vaughan Williams. Without the visible evidence of the land, stones and walls to which these works refer, or in which important historic events have taken place, the understanding of our culture and our history would be infinitely poorer.

Until the 20th century, the survival of these monuments in the face of Viking invasions, civil war, enemy bombardment, periods of rapid industrial development and profound demographic change, has been largely a matter of chance. Since the end of the last century, however, the UK has been more aware of the need for conservation and so more organised in its approach. This has been due to the efforts of private individuals like Octavia Hill, founder of the National Trust, to stop the disappearance of the natural and built heritage, and growing public concern. Voluntary bodies continue to play a key role in preserving open spaces and historic buildings today, through ownership and fundraising. The National Trust, the largest of these charities, owns 231,000 hectares (554,400ac) of land, 840km (525mi) of coastline and 190 historic houses in England, Wales and Northern Ireland, and has over two million members.

At government level, conservation policies are incorporated in planning law and protect country side, archeological sites and buildings, according to a hierarchy of designations. The existence of a hierarchy of designations is particularly important in the case of some 20,000 archeological sites covering a high proportion of land available for development. The designations provide a distinction between sites, like a river bed, which can be excavated prior to development, and others, like the stone circles of Stonehenge and Avebury, which must be preserved as well as recorded.

World Heritage site status enables us to take a wider, global, view of our monuments and refine our priorities. Such recognition has important consequences, bringing, as it does, responsibility and visitors. Property-owning bodies have learnt that the wider the recognition, the greater number of visitors, and the more onerous the burden of preservation. Without proper visitor management and reinforcement of the historic fabric, the effect of the tramp of thousands of pairs of feet on fragile and ancient sites is as devastating as neglect.

Amongst the more familiar pressures which lead to conflict with conservation in Britain are a high population density, economic development and a widespread desire to live in the countryside. The demand for more roads and houses, for example, the abandonment of agriculture in areas which have been farmed since the earliest recorded settlements, the exploitation of natural resources, and the desire for access to fragile landscapes and ancient buildings, have made the balancing of social, commercial and conservation interests a difficult process.

Whilst it is necessary to accommodate change, it is also vital to preserve what is most precious in our environment for future generations. Within this changing environment, we welcome World Heritage as a protector of those sites whose integrity should never be breached.

LORD CHORLEY

Chairman, The National Trust for Places of Historic Interest or National Beauty